FACULTY TRAINING FOR WEB ENHANCED LEARNING

EDUCATION IN A COMPETITIVE AND GLOBALIZING WORLD

FACULTY TRAINING FOR WEB ENHANCED LEARNING

MANUELA REPETTO
AND
GUGLIELMO TRENTIN
EDITORS

Nova Science Publishers, Inc.
New York

NOTICE TO THE READER

LIBRARY OF CONGRESS CATALOGING-IN-PUBLICATION DATA
Faculty training for web enhanced learning / editors, Manuela Repetto and
Guglielmo Trentin.
p. cm.
 Includes index.
 ISBN 978-1-61209-335-2 (hardcover)
 1. Education, Higher--Computer-assisted instruction. 2. College
teachers--In-service training. 3. College teaching--Web-based instruction.
I. Repetto, Manuela. II. Trentin, Guglielmo.
 LB2395.7.F325 2011
 378.1'7344678--dc22
2010054398

Published by Nova Science Publishers, Inc. † New York

CONTENTS

PREFACE

The pedagogy of faculty members is usually characterized by spontaneity, developed first as a student and later as a teacher. Teachers, especially those at higher education level, hardly ever have the opportunity to approach instructional design methodologies. While in the case of traditional classroom activities this limit can be ignored, it cannot when a teacher chooses to adopt Web-Enhanced Learning (WEL) strategies.

WEL provides students with access to electronic resources and learning activities that would not be available to them in traditional classroom-based study. Simple forms of WEL envisage access to the Web from within the classroom, using the Web as a platform for real-time demonstration or as a digital library. More sophisticated forms of WEL blend activities in the classroom with Web-enabled learning activities that promote collaborative learning among students, even when they are distant from the classroom.

In putting together important contributions from leading international experts in the field, this book will seek to provide a valuable tool and source of knowledge for all those involved in the enhancement of learning through network technology in higher education: faculty members, researchers in the educational field, academic managers.

The main topics dealt with are:

- university teacher training on the use of WEL Design methodologies;
- models to support the acquisition of knowledge and the development of WEL competencies;
- technology-enhanced learning approaches, methods and taxonomies;
- analyses and comparative studies of teachers' attitudes towards WEL strategies;
- case studies on the adoption of WEL approaches;
- experiences in and considerations on how to embed TEL in higher education.

The underlying assumption shared by the prominent authors of this book is that faculty members' training in WEL is one of the keys to improving the quality and pedagogical sustainability of ICT use in higher education.

The book is divided into two parts. The first part consists of Chapters 1-5 which through various theoretical frameworks explore WEL sustainability and deal with critical issues that in some cases hinder WEL diffusion. The second part, consisting of the next eight chapters (Chapters 6-13), describes a series of experiences and good practices in the use of WEL approaches.

Chapter 1 - What are the conditions which favour web enhanced learning (WEL) sustainability in the academic environment? How is it possible to act so that these conditions are fulfilled? To what extent does the pedagogical training of teachers affect WEL sustainability? How is it possible to train teachers to use WEL effectively?

These are the main questions which this chapter aims to answer.

To this end, the authors will begin by describing a possible multidimensional model for WEL sustainability.

Then the authors will focus on the two dimensions which are retained to be fundamental for high-quality WEL: the pedagogical dimension and the dimension of professional growth of faculty members as concerns WEL design methods. In this regard, an example will be given of a specific faculty training approach centered on progressive construction by the teacher him/herself of a personal instructional design (ID) mental model.

Chapter 2 – This chapter examines why technology innovation at the institutional level is insufficient to transform universities and higher education institutions and presents a framework for explaining the key role of teacher preparation in achieving transformation. Starting from the claims of leading scholars that universities will need to embrace computer-supported collaborative learning (CSCL), the chapter explains the difference between organizational (university) level and individual (teacher) level innovation and shows how they are related to one another. While adoption of Web enhanced learning (WEL) technologies such as learning management systems (LMS) are organizational level innovations, teaching models such as CSCL are adopted by individual teachers. In order to explain why some teachers adopt CSCL as a strategy for teaching within the LMS environment, it is insufficient to focus on use or non-use of the LMS or its features. The focus needs to be on teaching with CSCL as a behavior, i.e., not just the features that a teacher uses but how they use these features to design social learning experiences into their courses. This view of what teachers do with technology innovations adopted by universities is similar to information systems scholars' recent focus on post-adoption behavior and how users choose, adopt and adapt technology in their own ways. Once teaching model adoption is characterized as a behavior, it is possible to explain that behavior using theories drawn from psychology. The theory of planned behavior (TPB) is used in this chapter to differentiate teachers who adopt CSCL within an LMS environment from teachers who use non-interactive or less interactive teaching models. Teachers who adopt CSCL have more positive attitudes to online social interaction and to the value of online social learning, report fewer overt influences on their adoption of CSCL or of the LMS, and have a stronger sense of their ability to control aspects of online teaching including ability to resolve problems or shortcomings with an LMS. The complexity of teaching with online collaborative learning, which requires strong understanding of the pedagogy of social learning combined with skills in adapting technologies to support teaching and learning appropriately, demands high level pedagogical understanding and technology skills. This chapter challenges university teachers, teacher-trainers and administrators to find ways to develop the attitudes, social norms and perceived control necessary to transform teaching among teachers who do not have a background in pedagogy.

Chapter 3 - Many far-reaching expectations have been echoed in the last decade as to the huge impact that the information and communication technologies might have on the academy and on the conventional ways in which professors teach and students learn. There has been a widespread belief that the new technologies will transform teaching and learning processes from being highly teacher-dominated to student-centered. However, many studies point to the fact that the applications of the advanced technologies in higher education settings worldwide are currently quite limited in the teaching domain. This chapter analyzes five major reasons for the reluctance of academic faculty to utilize the wide spectrum of possibilities embedded in a web-enhanced teaching: (1) Unbundling of the professional responsibility; (2) Work overload and burnout; (3) Lack of ongoing support systems; (4) Add-on functions rather than substitution; (5) Intellectual property concerns. It is of tremendous importance to comprehend the reasons underlying the reluctance of academic faculty to adopt a web-enhanced teaching in order to tackle the existing obstacles and pave the way for harnessing the immense possibilities offered by the advanced technologies for the benefit of both students and teachers in higher education institutions. The chapter concludes with some recommendations for respective higher education mangers of how to enhance the effective use of the digital technologies in academia.

Chapter 4 - This chapter will address the question of how a transformation in teachers' use of information and communication technology can be achieved. There is evidence to suggest that the use of information and communication technology (ICT) in higher education can enhance and extend the learning experience. There is also evidence that although many teachers recognize this, many resist using ICT in formal education contexts, resulting in a shortfall in the adoption of technologies. An analysis of the barriers and constraints, and how they might be managed and overcome will feature during the discussion. A particular emphasis on Web Enhanced Learning (WEL) approaches will be made and strategies for university-wide adoption of social software (Web 2.0) tools and services will be presented.

Chapter 5 - Encouraging faculty's adoption of and innovation in teaching and learning with technologies continues to be a critical challenge for those responsible for faculty development in today's higher education institutions. This chapter examines current practice in Web-enhanced faculty development to promote Web-enhanced learning in university teaching. It begins by locating faculty development within the context of workplace learning and professional learning. Faculty development is seen as a continuum of formal and informal learning experiences offering a range of options. Critical questions are offered to assist the planning and implementation of faculty development to address the need for new learning models and pedagogy for the 21st century, followed by an overview of learning perspectives which dominate the design of faculty development to support adoption and widespread use of new technologies. Specific frameworks used to design faculty development to support Web-enhanced learning are explained and illustrated–technology adoption, skills acquisition, scholarly engagement, and the use of resources to support faculty learning. This chapter concludes with a summary of implications for faculty development practice.

Chapter 6 - This chapter is geared toward faculty members new to Web Enhanced Learning (WEL), as well as the seasoned faculty seeking to incorporate WEL into their traditional classroom settings. The chapter begins with the importance of community within the WEL, especially for the students that are far away from the institute of Higher Education. We discuss current research on the importance of social presence in regards to student learning, feelings of acceptance, and the retention of students at a distance as well as including tips creating a community of learners and sustain this community through the course. Essential elements of Universal Design for Learning are presented with examples provided for each of the three tenets of this approach to instruction (Multiple Means of Expression, Multiple Means of Engagement, and Multiple Means of Presentation). With one of the daunting facets of teaching through web enhanced activities and learning environments is the amount of time needed to effectively teach, respond, and interact with students, this chapter suggests tips and strategies to assist with the time demands needed for course management. Some of these tips will include how to effectively manage emails, posting announcements for maximal effect, using tools within the system such as time and conditional releases, and methods for creating student independence within the WEL environment. Additionally, suggestions for maintaining academic integrity within course activities and work submissions are given. With the increase of students with varying abilities (e.g., visual impairments, hearing impairments, physical impairments, learning disabilities) enrolling in institutions of Higher Education, WEL environments must be accessible to all learners. The chapter closes with preplanning and course design ideas which meet the needs of a variety of learners.

Chapter 7 - This chapter describes a project that researched the use of Web Enhanced Learning (WEL) with postgraduate students from rural and remote communities who were studying through two Australian universities. We examine, in detail, the experiences of a university teacher using WEL in an off-campus course for the first time. As with many academic teachers, she was willing to use new technologies and integrate these into her teaching but required time, technical support and professional development to achieve this. Using a design-based methodological approach, the experiences and frustrations in introducing WEL are described from the teacher's perspective through her progressive reflections at stages throughout the course. The findings and their implications for university policy and leadership are detailed with conclusions about how teachers and students are best supported in their engagement with WEL.

Chapter 8 - Based on a theoretical framework for the concept of eCompetence of academic staff, this chapter develops explores principles for the design of faculty development measures. It carries out a literature review that identifies key components and combines them into a model of action competence, which serves as point of departure to develop an concept for eCompetence. We define eCompetence in higher education context as the motivation and capability of faculty members to use information and communication technologies (ICT) in the classroom. This general view on eCompetence is specified by contextual factors that teachers face in eLearning scenarios. A discussion of portfolio models, which aim to increase the motivation of faculty to use learning technologies for their teaching and learning activities, is concluding this study. Main conclusion of this work is that universities have to create holistic portfolios for faculty development which extend considerably both the scope and the breadth of traditional training measures, and they have to offer institutional incentives to increase the motivation of faculty to sustainably use learning technologies for their courses.

Chapter 9 - This chapter synthesizes three data streams relating to web enhanced learning: literature on the time it takes to teach online as compared with classroom teaching, the author's original research on faculty methods teaching online and in classrooms, and science emerging from neurobiology describing the features of face-to-face communication that bear on social intelligence. Principle findings are that it takes more time to teach online, that faculty are less satisfied with and less enthusiastic about teaching online as compared to classroom teaching, and that evolutionary biology has conditioned us to make decisions based on trustworthiness in the physical world. Relating these findings develops an argument for distinguishing between asynchronous online and synchronous communications, whether online or face-to-face. A conclusion is reached that learning about and practicing synchronous online communications should be a priority in faculty training to improve web-enhanced learning.

Chapter 10 - This chapter describes an approach to faculty training and course redesign in the area of Technology Enhanced Learning (TEL) which tried to build bridges between the TEL research expertise of a research intensive university in the UK and its pedagogic practice. It describes the origins of the PREEL project (From Pedagogic Research to Embedded E-Learning) within the context of UK national initiatives of which this specific project was a part. The issues around the research-teaching divide in universities are described through a review of the literature, and the design approaches to faculty training and course redesign adopted in the PREEL project are described in relation to ways of tackling this divide suggested in the literature. An account is given of evaluations of the project at the end of the first year and then again two years later. The chapter concludes by reaffirming the value of connecting research to teaching practice as a method of faculty training and course redesign and reflecting on the limitations of the specific approach adopted and suggesting how it might be improved.

Chapter 11 - The purpose of this chapter is - at a first level - to analyze the concept of "Web-Enhanced Learning" in online education within the European Online Academic Education's context, how this concept takes shape, and how it becomes part of teaching practices within the instruction of a specific course. Subsequently, the chapter will present tools and strategies to help teachers develop self-awareness about the way they teach online and about how the cultures they belong to also have an impact on their teaching. Not only is there an increasing need of teaching methodologies able to address individuals and groups while reckoning with cultural differences, there is also a need to learn about culture itself in order to identify its rich and multi-faceted variability.

The theory discussed hereof is part of the results of a research aimed at exploring the impact of cultural differences on the design of online courses offered by several universities throughout Europe.

Chapter 12 - This chapter discusses a model for faculty development for the integration of web-enhanced learning tools to increase student engagement and active learning. Web-enhanced learning environments allow students opportunities to increase critical and creative thinking, problem solving, and inquiry and analysis. A challenge before modern colleges and universities is to facilitate widespread pedagogical shifts away from simple lecture/examination models of teaching and toward learning environments that motivate students to become actively involved in the learning process. This chapter presents an emerging case study on the use of a faculty learning community (FLC) as an impetus for pedagogical change. The FLC provides opportunities for faculty groups to address web-enhanced active learning strategies for large enrollment courses. The discussion focuses on a rationale and implementation process for facilitating adoption of technology- and web-enhanced active learning across disciplines to increase student engagement and fluency with information technology (FITness) in ways that allow undergraduates to succeed as 21st-century professionals and citizens. Further, the authors examine best practices for faculty learning communities, institutional support for creating effective faculty learning communities, and provide a brief overview of several web-based tools that faculty may use.

Chapter 13 – The purpose of this chapter is analyzing the results of an innovative initiative of faculty member training in Web-Enhanced Learning (WEL). After an overview of the context, a brief review of the literature and a description of the methodology and structure of the initiative, this chapter reports qualitative findings from a survey which investigated academic staff perceptions of the use of WEL approaches at different phases of the training process.

The study explores which organizational, contextual and subjective factors affected faculty members in the choice of the WEL approaches at three key phases: at the beginning of the training, during the design process and close to delivery of their academic course.

Furthermore, focusing on the question as to whether this action has affected lecturers' teaching and learning practices and enhanced students' learning processes, the chapter reports the problems, potentialities, and benefits of the courses delivered at the end of the WEL intervention.

LIST OF RECURRENT ACRONYMS

CSCL	Computer Supported Collaborative / Cooperative Learning
CSCW	Computer Supported Collaborative / Cooperative Work
FLC	Faculty Learning Communities
HE	Higher Education
ICT	Information and Communication Technology
ID	Instructional Design
LMS	Learning Management System
NCL	Networked Collaborative Learning
TEL	Technology Enhanced Learning
WEL	Web-Enhanced Learning

In: Faculty Training for Web Enhanced Learning   ISBN: 978-1-61209-335-2
Editors: Manuela Repetto and Guglielmo Trentin   © 2011 Nova Science Publishers, Inc.

Chapter 1

FACULTY TRAINING AS A KEY FACTOR FOR WEB ENHANCED LEARNING SUSTAINABILITY

Guglielmo Trentin and Serena Alvino

Institute for Educational Technology, National Research Council, Italy

ABSTRACT

What are the conditions which favour web enhanced learning (WEL) sustainability in the academic environment? How is it possible to act so that these conditions are fulfilled? To what extent does the pedagogical training of teachers affect WEL sustainability? How is it possible to train teachers to use WEL effectively?

These are the main questions which this chapter aims to answer.

To this end, we will begin by describing a possible multidimensional model for WEL sustainability.

Then we will focus on the two dimensions which are retained to be fundamental for high-quality WEL: the pedagogical dimension and the dimension of professional growth of faculty members as concerns WEL design methods. In this regard, examples will be given of a specific faculty training approach centered on progressive construction by the teacher him/herself of a personal instructional design (ID) mental model.

INTRODUCTION

One of the parameters used to measure the sustainability of an innovation is the number of those who adopt it permanently and can therefore contribute to guaranteeing a sort of self-maintenance (Bass, 1969). What can be said in this respect with regard to the educational use of ICT?

After the initial hype, fostered also by the technological boost induced by the new economy, there is now a growing awareness of the exaggerated expectations that were placed, for instance, on e-learning in the past (Trentin, 2007a). Furthermore, the main financiers (often public) have gradually become increasingly wary of distributing resources and have dwindled and, sometimes, even withdrawn their support to initiatives centered on e-learning.

In many cases this has led to a sort of backlash, a trend reversal in attitudes of those who potentially could have benefited and could benefit from it (each individual and/or institution).

In other words, instead of following the classical S-curve (dotted line in Figure 1), typical of the trend of every successful innovative process over time (Bass, 1969),the path of those who use e-learning would seem destined to follow a similar trend to the one indicated by the continuous line in Figure 1 (Rogers, 1995).

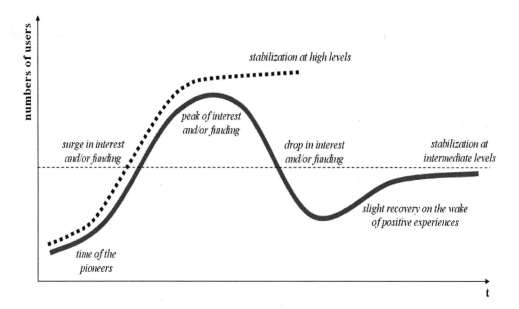

Figure 1. Trend of innovation processes over time.

This is a trend that has already been observed in the past for other processes related to the introduction of new methods in education, for example distance education (DE). High expectations and large investments resulted in a boom in the use of corresponding technologies. However, once the initial hype had subsided and the funds, particularly, had come to an end, there was then ultimately the decline. This may be attributed to cultural aspects (the potential user is not ready to adopt these methods) and organizational aspects (the contexts are not ready to be able to provide the necessary structure for a systematic use of DE) as well as disarming experiences often due to a lack of professionalism and sloppiness on the part of who, when proposing new teaching strategies, aimed above all at cutting the training costs.

In some cases actually, there was a slight recovery (shown by a sort of rebound in the diagram of Figure 1), especially corresponding to specific projects aimed at the introduction of DE methods, projects based on investment in human, cultural, organizational and technological resources i.e. an investment towards systemic quality.

Nevertheless there are and have been too few successful initiatives of this kind and even less diffusion towards new potential users. Consequently there is a sort of asymptotic convergence towards median values shown in Figure 1 (Trentin, 2007a).

The same trend may be observed in e-learning even though the pervasiveness of ICT at various times of our daily life (work, home, etc.) could play a decisive role in accustoming people to consider its use also in the educational and/or continuous training processes. It would therefore be reasonable to assume that the educational use of network technology still has enormous penetration margins on both an individual and institutional level, although one cannot disregard engaging in a deep reflection on the conditions required to fully use its potential in order to enhance the teaching/learning processes (Bates, 2002).

At this point it is fair to ask ourselves: What actions should be undertaken to ensure that such practices take permanent root and become diffused? Can WEL establish itself as an integral part of educational practices or will it keep its connotation of being extraneous to the system, with the risk of sooner or later ending up in the very same dusty storage area with other educational technologies which had promised so much in the past in terms of teaching innovation? Besides the quality and professionalism of the staff, what other elements come into play to achieve real WEL sustainability especially in view of the increasing lack of ad hoc funding?

THE KEY ISSUES

In the WEL field two problematic situations still need to be addressed:

- the various experiences of using the web in education have not led to significant changes in the management of educational activities at the institutional level, and it has so far been mainly anchored to funded projects and/or on pilot or even personal actions;
- many WEL projects which have been started with great enthusiasm and on a solid qualitative basis have been abandoned as soon as their funding has run out.

Fundamentally, rarely are the right conditions created for the full incorporation of WEL approaches into teaching practice, in terms of teaching methodology innovation and positive feedback based on sustained costs and tangible and intangible returns on investment.

This would seem to imply that, without public or private sponsors, those same methods and technologies are unable to achieve self-sustainability, despite the fact that they have often demonstrated their validity from the point of view of educational effectiveness.

Hence the fundamental question: is WEL just a flash in the pan that will be replaced by the next trends in technology, teaching and pedagogy which are related to the educational use of ICT? Or does it actually have the potential to become a springboard for learning/teaching processes?

If we analyse the current situation according to the criteria indicated by Rogers (1995) for the diffusion of innovation (advantages, compatibility, complexity, trialability and observability), the resulting outlook is far from encouraging. From surveys conducted on significant samples of the potential user, it would in fact seem that (Seufert, 2003; Seufert and Euler, 2003):

- the advantages of adopting WEL are relative and the benefits deriving from it are still not clear (apart from the hope of cutting costs);
- there is great difficulty in integrating WEL approaches into the higher education structure (organizational, technological, cultural, etc.);

- WEL is still perceived as a complex methodology to manage and its experi-mentations have provided little reassurance in this regard;
- WEL is not considered as providing the same educational quality as traditional methods;
- it is hard for an institution to completely understand what WEL is, what this new way of perceiving educational processes entails, and what possible benefits can derive from its use.

That is why in recent years experts in the area have initiated a lively, complex debate on what factors may be for and what factors against WEL sustainability.

One of the most controversial points is to understand on what basis a WEL-centered educational project can be considered a success from the sustainability point of view.

A POSSIBLE REFERENCE MODEL FOR WEL SUSTAINABILITY

So far though the use of WEL techniques has found fertile ground mainly among those who, after careful reflection on precisely how to innovate and improve teaching, have acquired them, beyond any formal commitment, as a standard educational approach or at least as one of the possible approaches.

The key is therefore to identify the most effective way to spread this attitude, in order to encourage the change from occasional use of WEL to its formal integration into the practices of higher education.

Discussing the stabilization stage of an innovative process, Euler and Wilbers (2002) write:

> "... if a foreign body is getting implemented in a system, either it adapts and will not be regarded as alien or it will continuously be identified as a foreign body and be eventually rejected from the system."

In fact, the more sustainable an innovation process is, the more it has those features for integrating itself effectively and efficiently into the reference institutional context. Thus, sustainability may be considered the measurement of the success of an innovation process.

From these considerations, and drawing on some specific sector studies (Seufert and Euler, 2003; Attwell, 2005; Trentin, 2007b), we have derived and herewith describe a possible reference paradigm for WEL sustainability, as an aid to understanding the problems connected to it.

The Model Overview

If we analyse the elements which can potentially affect WEL sustainability, they can be placed in a space of at least 8 closely-interrelated dimensions (Figure 2), each referring to a specific disciplinary domain.

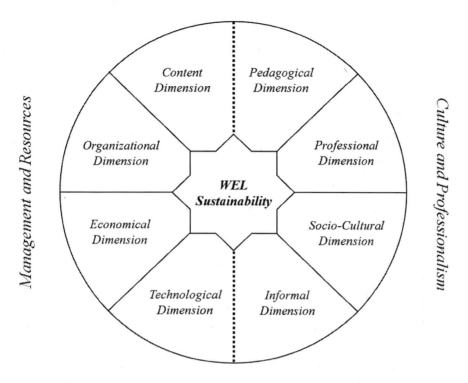

Figure 2. The eight-dimensional model for WEL sustainability.

The following is a detailed examination of each of the eight dimensions of the model proposed in this chapter (Trentin, 2007a).

The Economical Dimension – This comprises all the aspects related to the optimization of the resources at hand, ranging from the costs of development and practice to those for subsequent reinvestment. The economic aspects have always been considered one of the key elements in favour of WEL sustainability. However, it is known that to guarantee appreciable quality in WEL, the economic elements should not be put before those more specifically related to its pedagogical dimension. It has now been shown that whenever this happens, the choice of pedagogical approach is generally conditioned and channelled towards a WEL based primarily on the individual (and passive) study of educational materials. Despite usually being considered cheaper, content-driven approaches almost always curb the quality of the learning process, since they deprive it of its other important key dimension: social interaction (Trentin, 2010).

The Pedagogical Dimension – It concerns the added value and the pedagogical potentialities introduced by media use in order to promote WEL sustainability with regard to the quality of the teaching/learning processes. Moreover this includes the possibility of using specific functionalities of the technological platforms to improve the monitoring process of the learner's state of progression during most of the learning course, so as to achieve a summative and formative assessment (William and Black, 1996; Trentin, 2009).

The Professional Dimension – This regards identifying the key figures needed for the design, development, delivery and management of WEL, as well as training methods for them. The professional dimension also includes issues concerned with the formal recognition and appreciation of these figures, as well as strategies for a generalized cultural growth of faculty members in WEL use.

The Informal Dimension –This concerns those processes that help individuals to meet their cognitive demands through the autonomous use of e-content and, above all, participation in networked interaction within online communities, aimed at sharing knowledge and good practices. This dimension therefore implies a WEL that is not so much based on a specific 'formal' educational event, such as a course, than on the individual ability to find, through a sound use of ICT, what may be required to resolve a problematic situation, to meet a specific info-cognitive demand, and so on.

The Organizational Dimension – This refers to creating the organizational conditions (adaptation and development of structures and processes) for actually integrating WEL methodologies into the standard practices of higher education, in order to 'institutionalize' them. A WEL initiative conceived as an isolated project – i.e. not integrated into the institution and where maintenance cannot be guaranteed – has the remotest chance of surviving in the long run. Hence the need for an adequate organizational development within the reference context.

The Content Dimension – This regards both the quality of the transmitted content and its implementation into e-content; also the aspects related to its transportability, reusability and adaptability to contexts which may even be different from the original one for which they were created. This dimension is strongly correlated to at least three other dimensions of the model: the pedagogical, technological and economical dimensions.

The Technological Dimension – This is concerned with aspects related to the functionality and stability of a technological infrastructure which should be capable of adapting to the requirements of both the context and the individual user. This dimension very often meets with difficulties regarding WEL sustainability, in particular when investments in hardware/software resources are over-estimated. In these cases, the result is that technology over-absorbs those resources intended for other purposes such as human resource development (especially hiring of faculty members). It is not unusual even nowadays to note how the technological aspects are over-emphasized, at both the organizational/institutional and the individual project levels, often to the detriment of the pedagogical dimension.

The Socio-Cultural Dimension – This refers to the socio-cultural changes required for a wide diffusion of WEL approaches. From this point of view, the key idea seems to be that of sensitizing individuals to self-management of the learning process, also as an effect brought about both by a culture that considers WEL as an integral part of working practice, and an ever-greater need for life-long learning.

While all these dimensions are important, two of them in particular play a key role for quality WEL sustainability: a) the pedagogical dimension and b) the professional dimension with specific reference to the faculty training processes. These are two closely-related dimensions, since the former aims at defining the theoretical/methodological principles underlying quality WEL and the latter at defining the operational principles for diffusing the knowledge and skills necessary for the effective application of said theories and methodologies.

THE PEDAGOGICAL DIMENSION

It has been mentioned that the pedagogical sustainability of WEL is closely related to the added value and to the new possibilities that the educational use of ICT can offer teaching/learning processes. One imagines, for example, using more stimulating and interactive study resources (simulation environments, adaptive computer-based tests, intelligent tutoring systems, pedagogical agents, etc.); new forms of interaction and cooperation (also at a distance) among the participants to the same course; different ways of relating to teachers/tutors during individual and/or collaborative study; the use of integrated multimedia learning environments; and so on.

In view of these possibilities, it is therefore worth reflecting on how sustainable the extensive use of teaching/learning processes is pedagogically, fully knowing how it sometimes even implies radical changes in teaching, be it pedagogical or organizational, especially if compared with more traditional approaches.

Hence, the pedagogical sustainability of WEL is developed through a clear understanding of the various ways of intending and proposing the educational use of the Web and on how these can bring about important changes and/or improvements in the teaching/learning process. In other words: how can WEL really make the difference?

It recurrently emerges from international debate on this issue (Attwell, 2005) which predominant characteristics are considered necessary for a pedagogical sustainability of WEL. In short, the use of web-technology should face some critical educational issues (Rusten, 2003) and foster:

- learner-centered processes – implying that teachers take on a new role, namely that of facilitating the students in playing an active part in their own learning process, by formulating questions, experimenting, collaborating and developing new knowledge and understanding;
- Individualized instruction – differences in individual knowledge and in styles and pace of learning are not usually catered for in a traditional classroom. As a result, students often demonstrate low retention rates of what is said and done in the classroom. Besides having a negative influence on their performance, this produces a habit of mechanical rote learning and consequently a lack of enthusiasm towards studying. Current learning models show that individualized, project-based instruction can reverse these negative effects and contribute to greater student and teacher satisfaction and motivation;
- higher-order cognitive skills – new curricula and new teaching practices are needed to enable students to develop and refine critical thinking skills;
- learning processes based on reflection and creativity – in education there is the need to create learning environments which enable students to acquire and use information that helps them understand their world, so that they can in turn generate/acquire new knowledge;
- active inquiry, research, and analysis - students must learn to formulate critical questions, to identify, acquire, and organize information from different sources, and to analyze and make judgments about collected information;

- learning processes based on social interaction and collaborative, artifact/project-based development - students must be enabled to study and work cooperatively in groups, on projects and across the different disciplines, constructing new knowledge by means of a variety of both electronic and printing resources, working just as we do when tackling real-world and work problems;

- lifelong learning processes - learning takes place before, during, and after any formal education, beyond the classroom and through a variety of means (Cross, 2006). Thus, the sustainability of WEL will also be evaluated in terms of (a) the learner's education in the individual use of these resources and services and (b) in his/her capacity to become autonomous in providing for his/her own continuous training, once the 'formal' learning process has been completed, or if the scaffolding provided by the professional community he/she belongs to were to disappear;

- learning relevant to the professional/real world – education must provide information, knowledge, experiences and skills that are relevant to the everyday world in which students live and work;

- technological literacy - digital technologies have now penetrated most work environments. So the lack of technical literacy and skills, already at the learning process stage, is a serious handicap for the modern economy.

After this preamble, we shall now seek to outline a framework for analyzing the pedagogical sustainability of WEL. The basis of this framework is the three key elements introduced in Figure 3 below; in other words, the ability of the teacher to know how to:

- choose the most effective WEL approach for the declared learning goal and the learning activities for achieving said goal;
- apply the key elements common to the various instructional design (ID) approaches;
- apply the most suitable assessment strategies for the declared learning goals and for the chosen WEL approach and technologies.

Figure 3. The three key elements of the proposed framework for WEL pedagogical sustainability.

Educational approaches – This element focuses on the added value and pedagogical potential deriving from the vast range of available WEL approaches.

In this sense it is fundamental for teachers to be familiar with the particular features of each approach so as to be able to choose them in compliance with the specific learning goals they wish students to achieve through WEL.

These approaches can be placed on a continuum that stretches from learning processes based on *individual study* to those centered on group interaction (*collaborative learning*) (Figure 4) (Trentin, 2010).

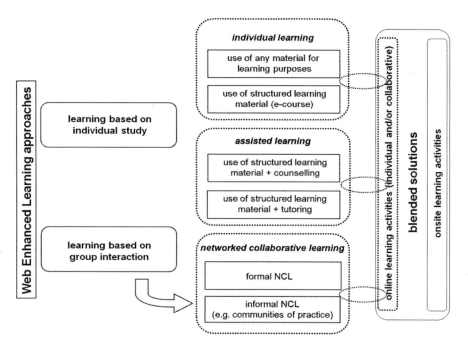

Figure 4. A possible taxonomy of WEL approaches.

Individual learning – this refers to individual use of material not necessarily produced for learning and of educational contents explicitly designed for individual study, such as standalone and networked educational software, as well as material produced for Open and Distance Learning (ODL).

Assisted learning – this covers individual study conducted by means of structured learning paths that can be implemented in two different ways:

- with some degree of support (even minimal) from the course provider, such as guidance from a tutor in using the material;
- assistance in subject material use from teachers/tutors who may also act as moderators in online workshops/seminars.

Networked collaborative learning (NCL) – The previous two cases largely concern content-driven learning, in that it is the materials that guide learners towards the stated educational objectives. By contrast, NCL regards educational processes based on the integration of individual study and collaborative learning (Trentin, 2010).

Blended solution(or mixed approach) – Although 'blended solution' actually regards the integration of different educational methods and tools, it is commonly seen as alternation between onsite and online teaching/learning activities, where the latter are not merely optional but an integral part of a course (MacDonald, 2008; Stacey and Gerbic, 2009).

Although knowledge of the various WEL approaches is the first fundamental step towards WEL diffusion in higher education, we must not neglect another important condition that influences pedagogical sustainability: the adoption of effective approaches to the design, running and evaluation of WEL, which by extension includes suitable training of those involved in these processes.

The instructional design approaches– Clearly, the design of WEL activities cannot draw on the same criteria as adopted for face-to-face courses. There is an evident need for methods that take into account and exploit the dynamics that make computer-mediated communication (CMC) unique. So, specific approaches to instructional design are required which support those intending to adopt WEL approaches in their courses.

In this sense it is interesting to note that some authors (Hense et al., 2001; Trentin, 2010), in discussing the question of teacher training in the basic elements of instructional design, suggest that this could provide the opportunity for a broader analysis of the general problems related to education and learning. The same authors rather aptly compare the adoption of WEL approaches to a sort of 'Trojan horse' that, while stimulating research into how to use ICT effectively to benefit teaching/learning processes, also leads to a more general reflection on those same processes, and on the way to innovate and improve them. Thus, WEL may have the potential to play a role in establishing a new culture which favours and supports the learning processes.

The evaluation and assessment approaches– One of the most critical aspects in WEL is the difficulty of evaluating (a) individual learning and (b) the learner's participation in and contribution to group activities when a collaborative learning strategy is adopted. Consequently, there is a clear need to understand what approaches can be used for formative and summative evaluation. This includes making use of the specific functions that online platforms offer for more accurate monitoring of learners' progress through the course (MacDonald, 2004).

This is a particularly delicate aspect, and it is thus important that the assessment activity be well-planned, clearly defining key elements such as (a) the purpose of the assessment, (b) the methods and means for performing it, and (c) the method for analyzing the results obtained. These criteria must already be considered at the planning stage of the educational intervention (Rowntree, 1994), in order to guarantee that in the carrying out of the educational activity, the above-mentioned platform functions can be used to achieve the specific goals which have been stated for assessment.

THE PROFESSIONAL DIMENSION AND THE ENHANCEMENT OF TEACHER'S COMPETENCES IN E-PEDAGOGY

One of the keys to WEL sustainability is the investment of human resources in design, development, delivery and management. The introduction of Web-technology in teaching/learning processes entails adopting specific educational approaches that differ from those normally adopted in "chalk and talk" teaching.

In addition, WEL incorporates elements from both the educational/pedagogical and the technological domains and thus calls for special professional competencies. These concern design and implementation not only of e-content, but also collaborative learning activities (Paulson, 2002; Williams, 2003), such as the so called "e-tivities" (Salmon, 2002). In this sense, WEL sustainability in higher education also relies on the professionalism of faculty members and on access to suitable ongoing methodological training (Fullan, 2005).

But if it is true that WEL sustainability is underpinned by the professionalism of teaching staff, then that professionalism needs not only to be developed but also to be formally recognized at institutional level. This means redefining and negotiating new faculty roles introduced by the adoption of WEL.

Both teacher training and professional recognition fall within the broader area of the ongoing cultural development of everyone involved in the educational fields, from those at management level to those playing a technical role.

WEL involves a myriad of different roles, but in this chapter we will concentrate specifically on that of the teacher, whose involvement in online interaction is central, especially in the case of networked collaborative learning.

From Teacher to E-Teacher

We have seen that the faculty continues to play a key role in WEL, albeit one that differs significantly from that played in the classroom or lecture hall. Instead of simply lecturing, the teacher becomes a facilitator who fosters learning of the domain contents in which he/she is an expert by contributing to the development of e-contents and supervising online e-tivities.

Hereafter, the term "e-teaching" will be used to identify the function the teacher performs when managing network-based learning activities. This function can be performed for the duration of an online course (pure online learning) or as part of online activities integrated into a course run face-to-face (blended learning).

Although this function is of strategic importance, the knowledge and competencies required for performing it do not appear to be so widespread at the academic level (Robinson and Latchem, 2003). So, given the broad range of strategies that the teacher can adopt to support learning processes, WEL sustainability clearly relies on adequate professional training of faculty members. In this way, the conditions can be established for more widespread, high-quality online learning.

This training also needs to respond to the emergence of the so-called "digital native" generation (Culligan, 2003) and their new ways of using communication technologies (Web 2.0, mobile technology), something which is also bound to influence their demands/ expectations regarding the way they are taught.

The Teacher's Changing Role

WEL calls on teachers and learners alike to assume different roles from the ones they are accustomed to playing in classroom learning. It is in this sense that Elliot (2008) proposes the development of an e-pedagogy that requires a radical rethink of traditional teaching practices.

Teachers who intend to adopt network-based learning in their practice therefore need to understand fully the philosophy underpinning WEL and the paradigm shift it involves. Traditional teaching/learning practices are focused on the teacher, whose objective is to transfer a given body of knowledge directly to learners. By contrast, WEL concentrates on the relationships among learners, and on that between the learners and the knowledge to be acquired. Students are helped to be more autonomous, proactive and responsible towards their own learning processes.

Reiterating then, systematic uptake of e-pedagogy is conditional on faculty having access to suitable professional training so that they become capable of making autonomous and informed decisions about what WEL strategies will prove most effective for meeting the needs at hand. Moreover, teachers need to learn how to select the most appropriate interaction/communication strategies for the medium they have adopted. This is a particularly critical competency for teachers; acquiring it should help dispel any impression they may have that WEL simply means transferring onto the web the contents and teaching approaches that have proved effective in the classroom. In short, the special characteristics of a given medium mean that it is never neutral in terms of communication dynamics and strategies (Trentin, 2010).

FACULTY TRAINING ON INSTRUCTIONAL DESIGN

From the above considerations it appears clear that one of the most critical aspects linked to the diffusion of WEL approaches is teachers' acquisition of at least the basic skills of instructional design (ID).

In fact, university teachers are essentially experts in a given disciplinary/content domain and they often lack pedagogical skills and know-how. What can be realistically asked of them is to (Zemsky and Massy, 2004):

1. make available their knowledge on a specific content domain, together with the methods to teach them;
2. invest a reasonable amount of time in acquiring elementary instructional design skills;
3. acquire familiarity with the typical dynamics of an educational process based on online interaction, and with the methods for conducting it.

In this perspective, a number of faculty training projects on the basic ID concepts have been set up in Italy since the '90s, to foster the effective integration of WEL methods into university teaching.

Some of these projects, particularly those organized by the universities of Turin (Trentin, 2006), Milan (Klobas and Renzi, 2003) and Genoa (see the WEL project described in Chapter 13) have led to the working out of specifically-targeted approaches for helping teachers build a personal instructional design (ID) mental model.

HOW SUPPORT FACULTY TO BUILD A PERSONAL ID MENTAL MODEL

Providing novices and unskilled faculty with examples of best practices, reusable learning materials and lesson plans is a fundamental step towards enriching their expertise. Unfortunately, this step is often not sufficient to foster the integration of these heuristics into everyday practice. In fact, teachers often do not know for instance how to integrate Learning Objects (LOs) and reusable lesson plans into the learning experiences they are designing. Whereas expert designers tackle educational design problems on the basis of a well-known and shared set of principles and heuristics that form their mental model (Silber, 2007), novices or unskilled teachers who have not yet developed the same mental structure cannot act likewise, unless supported by a scaffold. Thus, initially they need to refer to a simplified and structured model in order to approach the design problem.

Teacher training in the field of ID should take these premises into account. Teachers should be fostered to build a personal ID mental model by providing them with a scaffolding that progressively fades out once the mental model is more structured. This should be a "multidimensional" scaffolding characterized by:

- *basic general ID models*, which provide a clear structure for the main steps and decisions of an ID process, especially in the field of networked collaborative learning (NCL);
- *reusable educational resources and models*, such as LOs and CSCL scripts, that teachers can retrieve on the Web and reuse to design individual or collaborative activities or entire courses;
- *heuristics and best practices* concerning (a) how to progressively introduce recursivity into the basic general ID models and (b) how to integrate reusable resources into an ID process.

According to this approach, teachers should primarily build their own ID mental model on *a clear structure of the main steps of an ID process*. To this end, traditional models such as ADDIE[1] (Clark, 1995) turn out to be very useful, since they can be considered as phase models of problem-solving, which try to represent what an expert designer knows schematically, procedurally, and in an outlined form (Jonassen, 2008). Although we could identify at least 13 versions of the ADDIE model, each of them is characterized by a "cascade" sequence of design steps and by the fact that the output of each design phase is the input of the following one. Using these models as a reference in ID teacher training could help to clearly outline the main elements, constraints and decisions which characterize each phase and which are necessary to develop the subsequent steps. In addition, the teacher or the designer has to take some decisions on a number of fundamental topics, such as (Alvino et al., 2009):

---

[1]ADDIE is an acronym deriving from the main phases of the model itself: Analysis, Design, Development, Implementation, Evaluation.

- definition of the aims of the learning process and structuring of the learning objectives;
- definition and structuring of the learning content;
- definition of the learning strategies and techniques (and possible reuse of schema-level CSCL[2] scripts, such as pedagogical design patterns[3]);
- definition of the learning activities (and possible reuse of instance-level CSCL scripts, such as lesson plans) and of the learning groups (in terms of number, dimension and composition).
- definition of the required learning resources: identification of already-available resources, development of new ones, reuse of LOs retrieved on the Web;
- definition of monitoring and evaluation aims, criteria and indicators;
- definition of course schedule and other detailed design elements;
- identification of the communication needs and of the interaction channels and rules;
- definition and structuring of tools and areas characterizing the systems and tools supporting WEL processes.

When an expert designer tackles ID as a problem-solving process, he/she normally does not analyse these topics exactly in this order; firstly he/she focuses on some decisions and then refines the design through an iterative and recursive process. This can be done because expert designers are well aware of the reciprocal conditioning of the different design elements. Thus the "cascade" structure could provide a first fundamental scaffold for novices, since it acts as an "ordinate checklist" which reminds them of the fundamental steps they should not neglect.

Once this basic structure has been embedded in unskilled teachers' mental ID model, they could be provided with heuristics and best practices about how to introduce recursivity into the linear-cascade model, progressively approaching a problem-solving perspective.

A first step could be to identify a *two-layered design process* characterized by a *macro-design phase* and a *micro-design phase* (Trentin, 2010). The linear-cascade model is split into two main partially-overlapping ID phases (see Figure 5). In the "macro" phase, aims, objectives, contents, learning strategies and evaluation criteria are generally defined and outlined. In the following "micro" phase there is an iterative process of revision and/or integration of what has been defined in the macro-design; each decisional topic being reviewed and defined in greater detail; subsequently, learning techniques, activities, groups and resources are defined, together with the characteristics of the monitoring process, the schedule, etc. Parallel to the two-layered process, interaction and communication issues are tackled and technological decisions taken.

This model has revealed its effectiveness in a number of faculty courses and teacher training curricula (Klobas and Renzi, 2003; Trentin, 2006; Repetto, Chapter 13).

Once they are skilled in managing this two-layered ID process, teachers could try to carry out more iterative processes of revision. To this end, they should be provided with further rules and heuristics to effectively manage the constraints which characterize the ID, especially when a collaborative learning is adopted.

---

[2] Computer Supported Collaborative Learning.
[3] See http://www.pedagogicalpattern.org.

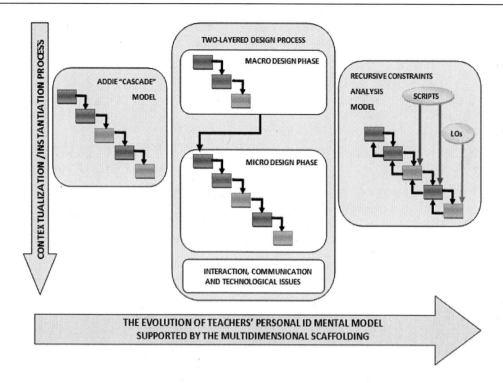

Figure 5. A comparison of three ID models: the ADDIE model, the two-layered design model and the *Recursive Constraints Analysis* model.

In fact, in a collaborative learning process we can identify three main types of constraint (Alvino et al., 2009): 1) *initial*, i.e. technical, financial and contextual constraints characterizing the specific learning context; 2) *structural*, i.e. constraints deriving from choices and decisions taken during the design process which condition posterior choices (i.e. objectives, contents, etc.); 3) *heuristic*, i.e. constraints related to the application of the heuristics and good practices for effectively structuring the learning community, organizing collaborative activities and modeling the learning environment. According to the *Recursive Constraints Analysis model* (Alvino, 2008), each decision taken during the ID process and concerning the above mentioned topics: (a) should take into account the initial, structural and heuristic constraints introduced before that step and (b) might introduce new structural and heuristic constraints which will condition subsequent choices. If previous structural and heuristic constraints conflict with the new decisions, some changes could be introduced into the design without modifying the general framework. In this way, to obtain a coherent instructional design, *teachers need to assume a permanent attitude of iterative review* (see Figure 5). These rules are especially true when teachers want to integrate LOs and CSCL scripts into the ID process. In fact, these resources are normally characterized by structural and heuristic constraints which have to be taken into account when integrating them into a specific ID process. As stressed before, LOs and CSCL scripts can be integrated at different steps of the ID process, when defining learning strategies, techniques, activities and materials. For instance teachers should be aware that specific collaborative activities require specific tools (such as forum, wiki, etc.) and specific group configurations, or *social structures*, in terms of number, dimension, composition and participants' tasks (Alvino et al., 2009).

All the heuristics and good practices characterizing the scaffolding described above should be supplied to teachers gradually, so they can be integrated step-by-step into their mental ID model.

This approach requires the faculty trainer to manage direct and indirect support and to propose theory and practice in a flexible way, gradually introducing elements of complexity and variability and progressively fading out the scaffolding. To provide the described multidimensional scaffolding, faculty trainers should be expert instructional designers who master the main heuristics and best practices for the design of WEL processes, as well as the know-how to use the main resources, models and tools which could support unskilled teachers in the design process. In addition, WEL approaches should be learnt firsthand, so faculty training should include active and collaborative online activities, such as case study, problem-solving, learning-by-designing, etc. Setting up effective faculty training courses therefore requires particular attention both in choosing the teaching staff, and in defining the learning and communication management tools.

CONCLUSION

Although in the last fifteen years there has been a gradual increase in WEL projects, there are actually very few cases where they have brought about significant changes in terms of stability and quality. This is rather puzzling given that expectations about educational use of the Web were being hyped on the wave of the more general diffusion of state-of-the-art technology.

It is a common opinion that one of the most obvious reasons for this "lull" (especially in the Mediterranean area) is the persistent lack of culture in the use of Web technology as a routine educational practice which would meet the need not only for reduced training costs, but also for new improved processes in teaching. This inadequate culture is reflected (particularly within the university) in the current lack of adequate regulations which could enhance innovation, attributing equal dignity to network-based and traditional face-to-face education.

Consequently, to date the sustainable implementation of Web-supported teaching /learning processes still remains an open question. This is why experts in the area have begun a lively, complex debate as to what factors may be for and what factors against WEL sustainability.

However there appear to be a certain points of agreement among these experts; in order to be sustainable, WEL should:

- first of all offer real added value to education by introducing interactivity and simulated environments;
- by organizing students into learning communities, foster collaborative study and mutual support, which can act as a backing for a new culture of WEL use in informal learning processes (based precisely on active participation in online professional communities) (Cross, 2006);

- propose a use of the technology which is able to effectively support specific teaching methodologies for specific disciplinary contexts; considering case studies in the medical field, role-plays in the managerial sector and so on;
- foster development of teaching materials so that they are easily reusable in different situations, thus cutting the time and costs required for creating them;
- take initiatives aimed specifically at WEL sustainability, i.e. initiatives for creating (on both institutional and individual user levels) the necessary cultural, professional and infrastructural conditions for the frequent use of WEL approaches in managing entire courses, as well as for integrating it into the more traditional classroom teaching.

In an attempt to contribute usefully to the ongoing debate, this chapter has outlined a possible model for WEL sustainability. The model highlights the complex relations among the dimensions characterizing it, which mean that in analyzing one of these dimensions it is unthinkable to ignore the influence it may have on the others. Nevertheless, in the light of what has been said above, the possibility of analyzing each of these dimensions separately may indeed be useful for the critical evaluation of WEL sustainability.

In the chapter the two dimensions retained to be most crucial for quality WEL sustainability are particularly analyzed: a) the pedagogical dimension and b) the professional dimension, with specific reference to the faculty training in WEL approaches and their design.

Regarding the latter aspect, the experiences gained in specific Italian projects on faculty training have led to the working out of an approach which is specifically targeted at supporting teachers in the construction of a personal ID mental model.

As has been emphasized at several points in this chapter, this passage is retained to be essential for the effective integration of WEL practices into university teaching.

REFERENCES

Alvino, S. (2008). CSCL and reusability: an approach to the integration of reusable resources in collaborative learning processes. *Unpublished doctoral thesis*, University of Genoa, Genoa, Italy.

Alvino, S., Asensio-Perez, J.I, Dimitriadis, Y., and Hernandez-Leo, D. (2009). Supporting the reuse of effective CSCL learning designs through social structures representations. *Distance Education - Special Issue on Learning Design, 30*(2), 239-258.

Attwell, G. (2005). E-learning and sustainability. *EdTechPost: Technology for Learning, Thinking and Collaborating.* http://www.ossite.org/Members/GrahamAttwell/ sustaini bility/attach/sustainibility4.doc.

Bass, F.M. (1969). A new product growth model for consumer durables. *Management Science, 15,* 215-227.

Bates, A. (2002). *Managing technological change.* San Francisco: Jossey-Bass Publishers.

Clark, D. (1995). *Introduction to Instructional System Design. Performance, Learning, Leadership, and Knowledge.* http://www.nwlink.com/~donclark/hrd/sat1.html.

Cross, J. (2006). *Informal Learning.* Hoboken, NJ: Wiley Publications.

Culligan, M. (2003). Digital natives in the classroom. In B. Hoffman (Ed.), *Encyclopedia of Educational Technology*. http://coe.sdsu.edu/eet/articles/digitalnatives/start.htm.

Elliot, B. (2008). *E-pedagogy: does e-learning require a new approach to teaching and learning?* http://d.scribd.com/docs/22rc8wz72z067xrb1fpk.pdf.

Euler, D., and Wilbers, K. (2002). Selbstlernen mit neuen Medien didaktisch gestalten. In D. Euler, C. Metzger (Eds.), *Hochschuldidaktische Schriften*, chapter 1, St.Gallen: Institut für Wirtschaftspädagogik (quoted in Seufert and Euler, 2003).

Fullan, M. (2005). *Leadership and Sustainability*. California: Corwin Press.

Hense J., Mandl, H., Kruppa K., and Gräsel, C. (2001). Concept, realisation, and evaluation of SEMIK. *Proceedings of WCCE'01*, 777-786.

Jonassen, D.H. (2008). Instructional Design as Design Problem Solving: An Iterative Process. *Educational Technology*, 48(3), 21-26.

Klobas, J.E., and Renzi, S. (2003). Integrating online educational activities in traditional courses: University-wide lessons after three years. In A. K. Aggarwal (Ed.), *Web-Based Education: Learning from Experience* (pp. 415-439). Hershey, PA: Information Science Publishing.

MacDonald, J. (2004). Developing competent e-learners: the role of assessment. *Assessment and Evaluation in Higher Education*, 29(2), 34-41.

MacDonald, J. (2008). *Blended Learning and Online Tutoring*. Aldershot, UK: Gower.

Paulson, K. (2002). Reconfiguring faculty roles for virtual settings. *The Journal of Higher Education*, 73, 123-140.

Robinson, B., and Latchem, C. (Eds.) (2003). *Teacher education through open and distance learning*. New York: Routledge Falmer.

Rogers, E.M. (1995). *Diffusion of innovations*. 4th Edition. NY: Free Press.

Rowntree, D. (1994). *Preparing material for open distance and flexible learning*. London, UK: Kogan Page.

Rusten, E. (2003). *Using computer in schools. Digital opportunities for development.* http://learnlink.aed.org/Publications/Sourcebook/chapter4/Computers_in_Schools_modelofuse.pdf.

Salmon, G. (2002). *E-tivities: the key to active online learning*. London, UK: Kogan Page.

Seufert, S. (2003). *Shaping Innovations: eLearning as a catalyst for a new culture in learning and teaching?* ICNEE 2003. http://www.scil.ch/docs/2003-05-icnee-seufert-shaping innovations.pdf.

Seufert, S., and Euler, D. (2003). *Sustainability of eLearning innovations: findings of expert interviews.* http://www.scil.ch/publications/docs/2003-06-seufert-euler-sustainability-elearning.pdf.

Silber, K.H. (2007). A Principle-based Model of Instructional Design: A New Way of Thinking About and Teaching ID. *Educational Technology*, 47 (5), 5-19.

Stacey, E, and Gerbic, P. (Eds.) (2009). *Effective blended learning practices: Evidence-based perspectives in ICT-facilitated education*. Hershey, PA: IGI - Idea Group, Inc.

Trentin, G. (2006). The Xanadu project: training faculty in the use of ICT for university teaching. *Journal of Computer Aided Learning, 22*, 182-196.

Trentin, G. (2007a). A multidimensional approach to e-learning sustainability. *Educational Technology*, 47(5), 36-40.

Trentin, G. (2007b). Pedagogical sustainability of network-based distance education in university teaching. In E.P. Bailey (Ed.) *Focus on Distance Education Developments* (pp. 79-106). New York: Nova Science Publishers, Inc.

Trentin, G. (2009b). Using a Wiki to Evaluate Individual Contribution to a Collaborative Learning Project. *International Journal of Computer Assisted Learning*, *25*(1), 43-55.

Trentin, G. (2010). *Networked Collaborative Learning: Social Interaction and Active Learning*. Chandos Publishing Limited, Oxford, UK.

Williams, P.E. (2003). Roles and competencies for Distance Education programs in higher education institutions. T*he American Journal of Distance Education*, *17*(1), 45-57.

Zemsky, R., and Massy, W.F. (2004). Thwarted innovation: what happened to e-learning and why. *Final Report for The Weatherstation Project of the Learning Alliance at University of Pennsylvania*. http://www.csudh.edu/dearhabermas/ WeatherStation_Report.pdf.

In: Faculty Training for Web Enhanced Learning ISBN: 978-1-61209-335-2
Editors: Manuela Repetto and Guglielmo Trentin © 2011 Nova Science Publishers, Inc.

Chapter 2

ADOPTION OF COMPUTER SUPPORTED COLLABORATIVE LEARNING BY TEACHERS AT UNIVERSITY: A FRAMEWORK FOR INVESTIGATION

Stefano Renzi[1] and Jane E. Klobas[2]

[1]Bocconi University, Italy
[2]Bocconi University and University of Western Australia, Australia

ABSTRACT

This chapter examines why technology innovation at the institutional level is insufficient to transform universities and higher education institutions and presents a framework for explaining the key role of teacher preparation in achieving transformation. Starting from the claims of leading scholars that universities will need to embrace computer-supported collaborative learning (CSCL), the chapter explains the difference between organizational (university) level and individual (teacher) level innovation and shows how they are related to one another. While adoption of Web enhanced learning (WEL) technologies such as learning management systems (LMS) are organizational level innovations, teaching models such as CSCL are adopted by individual teachers. In order to explain why some teachers adopt CSCL as a strategy for teaching within the LMS environment, it is insufficient to focus on use or non-use of the LMS or its features. The focus needs to be on teaching with CSCL as a behavior, i.e., not just the features that a teacher uses but how they use these features to design social learning experiences into their courses. This view of what teachers do with technology innovations adopted by universities is similar to information systems scholars' recent focus on post-adoption behavior and how users choose, adopt and adapt technology in their own ways. Once teaching model adoption is characterized as a behavior, it is possible to explain that behavior using theories drawn from psychology. The theory of planned behavior (TPB) is used in this chapter to differentiate teachers who adopt CSCL within an LMS environment from teachers who use non-interactive or less interactive teaching models. Teachers who adopt CSCL have more positive attitudes to online social interaction and to the value of online social learning, report fewer overt influences on their adoption of CSCL or of the LMS, and have a stronger sense of their ability to control aspects of online teaching including ability to resolve problems or shortcomings with an LMS. The complexity of teaching with online collaborative learning, which requires strong understanding of the pedagogy of social learning combined with skills in adapting technologies to support teaching and learning appropriately, demands high level pedagogical understanding and technology skills. This chapter challenges university teachers, teacher-trainers and administrators to find ways to develop the attitudes, social norms and perceived control necessary to transform teaching among teachers who do not have a background in pedagogy.

INTRODUCTION

Online teaching in higher education is in need of transformation. Leading scholars call for a significant change in pedagogy and information and communications technology (ICT) use, moving away from simply delivering educational material toward social and collaborative learning. Educational technology used in this interactive way is expected to support a productive and engaging learning environment (Biggs, 2003; Kimball, 2002; Rudestam and Schoenholtz-Read, 2002), to encourage reflective learning (Palloff and Pratt, 1999), and to support effective learning through discourse (Kirschner et al., 2004; Laurillard, 2002, 2007).

Several international surveys of ICT strategies in higher education institutions highlight the widespread use of ICT (mostly learning management systems, LMS) to support classroom delivery. Yet, this strategy has brought with it little impact on teaching and learning methods, and face-to-face teaching remains the core instructional form (Becker and Jokivirta, 2007; Caruso and Salaway, 2007; Collis and van der Wende, 2002; Garrett and Jokivirta, 2004; OECD, 2005).

Among these surveys, those carried out by the Observatory on Borderless Higher Education (OBHE) have included specific questions to monitor the number of programs or courses available online. Data collected in 2006 from 67 institutions (mostly members of the Association of Commonwealth Universities and Universities UK) showed that use of e-learning (in terms of the proportion of a course made available online) is increasing over time. In 2002, an average of 81% of the courses of the respondent institutions had low online presence while this percentage fell to about 75% in 2004 and 63% in 2006 (Becker and Jokivirta, 2007). Thus, the number of courses offering higher proportions of online presence is increasing over time.

The OBHE survey further distinguishes between two levels of online presence. A *significant* online presence is described as "key 'active' elements of the program are online BUT no significant reduction in face-to-face classroom time" while *Web dependent* is similar to significant but "face-to-face classroom time is significantly reduced" (Becker and Jokivirta, 2007, p. 15). While the number of universities reporting a significant online presence increased from 14% to 20% between 2004 and 2006, the increase in Web dependent presence was much lower and from a lower base, from 8% to 9% (Becker and Jokivirta, 2007).

The difference between significant online presence and Web dependent presence is relevant because the latter implies not only a change in the proportion of face-to-face and online activities, but also a change in teaching. Following Leidner and Jarvenpaa (1995), a change toward Web-dependent teaching could be interpreted as transforming teaching, rather than automating classroom-based teaching practices.

Of course, it is the teachers who adopt teaching methods and implement them in their courses. Teachers, even in the absence of higher level policy or incentives, can develop pedagogical strategies and visions that differ from those currently in use in their educational institution (Wingard, 2004; Woods, Baker and Hopper, 2004). Thus, while the dominant situation in universities and other higher education institutions which continue to offer classroom-based courses is characterized by widespread use of ICT (and mostly LMS) to support classroom delivery, some teachers are using ICT in transformative ways.

In this chapter, we develop a framework for analysis of reasons why some teachers adopt CSCL rather than other approaches in their online teaching, with a view to establishing institutional teaching and learning policies that encourage transformation of teaching. We begin by introducing CSCL in more depth and highlighting the role played by social interaction. We then focus on the framework and its elements, before presenting a brief case report of its application and drawing conclusions. We focus on universities that have adopted LMS without abandoning classroom teaching, i.e., universities that offer WEL.

COMPUTER SUPPORTED COLLABORATIVE LEARNING

While CSCL has been a central concept in the instructional technology field for around 20 years, it has been difficult to define. In 1996, the crucial question about CSCL was to define what it really is; while it was easy to recognize examples of collaborative learning, it is was difficult to provide a precise definition (Koschmann, 1996). In 2004, research about CSCL was still looking for a specific theoretical framework (Strijbos, 2004). Nevertheless CSCL is claimed to be one of the most promising ways to promote and achieve changes in teaching and learning practices (Lipponen, Hakkarainen and Paavola, 2004).

In this chapter we define CSCL as learning that occurs primarily among peers, on the basis of designed activities, in an online environment. This definition covers a wide range of activities within a broad theoretical framework, a reflection of both the promise of CSCL and the difficulty of producing a precise definition and theory.

A critical aspect of peer learning is social interaction among learners (Gilbert and Moore, 1998; Gunawardena, Lowe, Constance and Anderson, 1997; Hiltz, 1994; Hooper and Hannafin, 1991; Northrup, 2001; Wagner, 1994) and many researchers have focused their attention on the effects of social interaction (and psycho-social processes in general) on learning (Jehng, 1997; Harasim, 1993; Kreijns and Kirschner, 2004; Kreijns et al., 2003; Liaw and Huang, 2000; Northrup, 2001; Zhang and Fulford, 1994). Social interaction therefore plays a key role in collaborative learning, and we consider the presence of online social interaction in WEL teaching activities as a necessary element (among others) to identify CSCL adoption by university teachers.

A FRAMEWORK FOR STUDYING TEACHING MODEL ADOPTION

CSCL is a particular approach to teaching which can also be described as a teaching strategy. Teaching strategies that are adopted by a sufficiently large number of teachers can be characterized as model strategies or teaching models which may be adopted to a greater or lesser extent by any individual teacher. In this section, we describe the components of a framework for studying teaching model adoption by individual teachers in higher education institutions. The framework draws together six main interconnecting issues: (a) LMS adoption by higher education institutions as innovation, (b) the features of LMS and how they might be used in learning and teaching, (c) LMS feature adoption by university teachers as innovation, (d) post-adoption behavior, (e) a taxonomy of online teaching models, (f) the theory of planned behavior (TPB) as a behavioral model to explain factors influencing online teaching model adoption.

LMS Adoption as Innovation

In this chapter we define an innovation as "an idea, practice, or object that is perceived as new by an individual or other unit of adoption" and adoption as "the decision to make use of an innovation" (Rogers, 1995, p. 21). In building this framework, we first note that two layers of innovation are involved in adoption of CSCL in universities that use LMS to enhance learning. The LMS is an ICT (an *object*) adopted, in this case, by a higher education institution (*other* unit of adoption). University teachers (*individuals*) may adopt CSCL as a teaching model within the LMS, i.e., they are adopting the *practice* of teaching with CSCL as an innovation. Since online teaching models (e.g., CSCL) are used in an LMS environment (i.e., within the LMS adopted by the university), the two innovations are strictly related to one another.

To find a framework that unites both innovations, we start by considering LMS adoption by a higher education institution as organizational innovation adoption within Rogers' (1995) model. Later, we will build on this to introduce a model that unites both levels of innovation.

Stages of LMS adoption and use by higher education institutions can be considered in relation to the stages described in Rogers' (1995) model of the innovation process in organizations. Rogers' model consists of five stages grouped into two higher-level activities. The stages are: (1) agenda-setting, (2) matching, (3) redefining/restructuring, (4) clarifying, and (5) routinizing. The first of the two high-level activities, *initiation*, includes agenda-setting and matching of an innovation with the organization's agenda. At the end of the initiation activity, a *decision* is made to adopt (or reject) an innovation in a particular form. After the decision, the *implementation* activities start. During this period, in a first stage, the innovation is re-defined and the organization re-structured in a mutual adaptation process while, in the subsequent stages, the innovation's role is clarified, and its use finally becomes so much a part of the organization's activities that it is no longer an innovation. Figure 1 shows the stages described above.

Table 1 describes how stages of LMS adoption and use by higher education (HE) institutions match with the stages of Rogers' model. *Agenda-setting* occurs when the higher education institution establishes its strategic goal for teaching and learning. The institution's identification and assessment of suitable LMSs based on technical and business criteria constitute the *matching* stage. The initiation period ends with the decision to adopt a specific LMS.

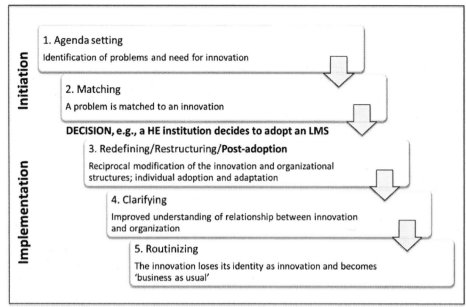

(adapted from Rogers (1995) and Klobas and Renzi (2003).

Figure 1. Post-adoption behavior in Rogers' model.

Table 1. LMS adoption in higher education institutions mapped to Rogers' model

Stage	Activities	Organizational innovations, generally	A new technology to be used for educational purposes
I. INITIATION			
	Agenda-setting	The organization becomes aware of problems that are perceived to require resolution through some form of innovation	The HE institution becomes aware of teaching and learning issues that could be addressed through some form of technology.
	Matching	A fit is found between a problem from the organization's agenda and a specific innovation	A fit is found between the HE institution's agenda and a specific new ICT, LMS
	DECISION	*The organization decides to implement the innovation (or not to go ahead)*	*The institution decides to implement an LMS*
II. IMPLEMENTATION			
	Re-defining/ Re-structuring	The innovation is re-defined and the organization re-structured in a mutual process of reinvention and restructuration as a fit is sought between the innovation and the organization	The teachers adapt their teaching to the LMS. There is a mutual and recursive influence between the new technology adopted and the innovation in pedagogy at the HE institution.
	Clarification	The relationship between the organization and the innovation is clarified	The relationship between the HE institution and the LMS is clarified. This clarification process will also impact also on the pedagogy of the university.
	Routinizing	The innovation becomes routine	Use of WEL becomes routine.

(adapted from Klobas and Renzi (2003).

The implementation process begins with definition of the technical and human requirements for implementation (e.g., teacher training). *Redefinition* of the teaching and learning process begins when teachers re-define their teaching models in the LMS environment. During the *Clarification* stage, the relationship between the institution and the new technology (LMS) is clarified. At the *Routinizing* stage, WEL becomes routine.

The Features of LMS

Before considering the second layer of innovation in teaching model adoption, we need to examine the nature of LMS software in more detail. An LMS is "software designed to provide a range of administrative and pedagogic services (related to formal education settings e.g. enrolment data, access to electronic course materials, faculty/student interaction, assessment, etc.)" (OECD, 2005).

Table 2. Typical features available in an LMS environment

LMS feature	Description
Course management	Teachers can define the LMS tools available within the course and other details, manage students' enrolment and registration, etc.
Course summary	Gives to students a course overview, e.g., pre-requisites, syllabus, objectives, grading criteria, course calendar and critical dates.
Announcements/ Notice-board	Teachers can publish relevant announcements for students, recent changes, and information about events.
E-mail	Teacher and students can exchange personal messages with each other through the LMS interface.
Student home pages	Enable students to know each other. Students can upload their photo and supply information about their educational background, interests, and other details.
Course outline	This is the roadmap for the course. Teachers, for each lesson/unit/module, can outline the objectives, present the content, list the educational material to be used, and describe the planned activities or assignments.
Course material	Teachers can upload different kinds of teaching material, e.g., slides presented in the classroom, teaching notes, various documents, and multimedia material. The course material can be associated with a specific lesson/unit/module.
Resources	Enable teachers and, often, students to contribute additional resources for the course, e.g., Web sites, papers, or document produced during the course.
Discussion forum	This is the place where discussions take place. Usually messages can be read in different ways, e.g., by date, person, threads/topics. Additional capabilities of this feature might permit creation of more than one discussion forum, a discussion forum shared only by members of a group, teacher rating and peer rating of each posting.
Chat	This feature allows students, or teacher and students, to have synchronous discussions. In some cases the chat session can be saved online as a text file to allow other students to be aware of what was discussed. Some LMSs make available other synchronous collaboration tools such as audio and video conferencing.
Assignment management	Students can submit assignments as individuals or groups. Various tools allow teachers to grade material submitted online or offline (e.g., face-to-face presentations).
Assessment	Teachers can prepare quiz tests, consisting of multiple choice, true-false, open answer questions and more. Questions can be submitted to the student randomly from pools or each student can have a different set of questions. Quizzes can be used for self-assessment (e.g., exam simulation) and can be automatically graded. Teachers can have the option to give feedback or to show correct answers. Other options might allow teachers to set up peer assessment so students can assess assignments each other.
Surveys	Teachers can use this feature in different ways, e.g., to set-up a quick poll to stimulate thinking or to have quick feedback from the class. Further options might include anonymous results or limits on the number of responses allowed.
Group collaboration features	Teachers can set up groups of students and each group can have a set of features reserved to the group, e.g., discussion forum, chat, file exchange area, resource area, etc.

The kind of services provided by LMSs, also named LMS features, once played a key role as universities selected the system to be adopted. Many Web sites listing and comparing

LMS features were available. LMS feature comparison is a less critical process today because the market is dominated by a small number of products. The most common proprietary LMSs worldwide are WebCT and Blackboard (the two companies merged in 2005) while Moodle is the emerging open source system. Furthermore, the features available in proprietary and open source LMSs are converging. In Table 2, typical features available in an LMS environment are summarized and described.

LMS features to be used in a course are selected by teachers. The design of any given course will include a number of teaching methods. A teaching method is a way of teaching used for a specific teaching task. Table 3 lists common teaching methods and describes their characteristics. It describes how the teaching method is implemented in a generic Web environment and identifies LMS features that support it. Note that the table does not list all LMS features. LMS also offer course management features, e.g., the announcements or notice-board feature, which can be used by a teacher to publish announcements and news.

Table 3. LMS features matched to teaching methods

Teaching method	Characteristics of teaching method	Implementation of teaching method in Web environment	LMS feature
Lecture or presentation	Teacher presents material to a class	Readings or presentations prepared or converted in HTML format; Web pages as index of downloadable material (text, tables, presentations); audio video material live or recorded distributed via streaming technology.	Course outline, course material, resources
Workshop or laboratory	Students complete set tasks designed to develop their skills; often live or recorded demonstrations presented or prepared by a teacher are included	Activities prepared using Web or other technology (including multimedia technologies), made available to students from a Web page	Assignment management, course material associated with discussion forum
Self-guided instruction	Students work individually (often in geographical isolation), to complete assigned readings and exercises	Readings, references, and activities, prepared using Web technology or distributed from a Web page	Course material, resources
Seminar or tutorial	Students, working in relatively small groups, discuss set topics, cases, or readings, with the teacher's guidance	Discussion or conferencing software	Assignment management, course material, resources associated with discussion forum
Consultation	Students (individually or in small groups) meet with the teacher to obtain answers or guidance on topics	Electronic mail, chat, audio and video conferencing	E-mail, discussion forum, chat
Collaborative learning	Students work together; the students learn through collaboration with one another rather than from material delivered by the teacher	Discussion or conferencing software, e-mail, chat, audio/video conferencing, specific tools for community building and collaborative work	Student home pages, group collaboration features, discussion forum, chat, e-mail

(adapted from Klobas and Renzi (2000)).

ICT Innovation by Individuals in Organizations

Thus, LMSs offer a wide range of features, which can be adopted or not by teachers and which, if adopted, may be used to support one or more teaching methods. Rogers', and other classic models of innovation based on stages (pre-adoption activities, the adoption decision, and post-adoption activities), do not readily reflect the complexity of selective adoption and adaptation of the features of a multi-faceted innovation (Jasperson, Carter, and Zmud, 2005). Information systems scholars have developed approaches to feature conceptualization (DeSanctis and Poole, 1994; Griffith, 1999; Orlikowski, 2000) which introduce a new perspective to the analysis of ICT innovations. The perspective focuses on post-adoption behavior, the adoption and use of the features of a software application by an individual user following the adoption of the software at an institutional level. Figure 1 shows where post-adoption behavior fits in Rogers' model.

It would be useful to have an integrated model able to explain ICT adoption and use at organizational level (looking at the ICT system as a whole) and at the individual level (looking at ICT system feature adoption and use). A prominent information systems scholar, Robert Zmud, has studied this aspect of ICT adoption for many years (Lucas, Swanson and Zmud, 2007). He has developed a model that integrates organizational and individual views, IT application adoption and feature level use, and post-adoption behaviors (Jasperson et al., 2005). Figure 2 shows the main characteristics of this model. At the top level is the organizational ICT application adoption decision followed by ICT application adoption at the individual level. Individual adoption is followed by post-adoption behavior which includes three different activities which can occur in any order: individual feature adoption decision, individual feature use, and individual feature extension. Individual feature extension occurs when individuals discover new ways to use a feature which were not included in the original ICT system design (Jasperson et al., 2005).

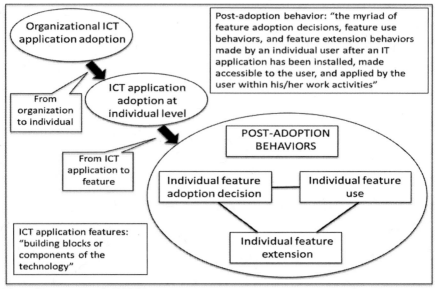

(adapted from Jasperson et al. (2005)).

Figure 2. Main characteristics of Jasperson, Carter, and Zmud's model.

Post-Adoption Behavior and LMS

Post-adoption behavior is defined by Jasperson, Carter, and Zmud as "the myriad feature adoption decisions, feature use behaviors, and feature extension behaviors made by an individual user after an IT application has been installed, made accessible to the user, and applied by the user within his/her work activities" (Jasperson et al., 2005, p. 531). Returning to the last column of Table 3 (LMS features), we can see that some features can be used to support more than one teaching method, e.g., the discussion forum feature supports workshop or laboratory, seminar or tutorial, consultation, and CSCL. So, another issue related to LMS feature use is how the teacher uses any given feature. A teacher may decide, for example, to use a more familiar feature rather than the feature designed for that purpose. In this way, the discussion forum might be used to publish announcements and news instead of using a task-specific announcements or notice-board feature.

It follows that explanations of ICT adoption that are based on explaining use rather than non-use or the frequency of overall use, or even of individual features, are adequate only for relatively simple systems such as transactional systems which offer the user little choice of which features to adopt and how to use them. When we consider more complex and flexible systems and technologies such as LMS we need to take the nature of the use made of a system and its features more fully into account. Several researchers have suggested adoption of a broader approach toward analysis of systems, looking more closely at elements such as: processes, dynamics, different forms of usage, and learning (Barki, Titah, and Boffo, 2007; Chin and Marcolin, 2001; Lucas et al., 2007; Schwarz and Chin, 2007).

In essence, if we monitor only the LMS features used by a teacher, we cannot accurately explain how the LMS is used to teach online. We need to monitor not just the LMS features used but also the combination of features and teaching methods selected by the teacher. This "deep usage" perspective enables us to study why, after a university has adopted an LMS, some teachers transform their online teaching and adopt CSCL, while others use the LMS only to support their classroom-based activities. The LMS features used by the teacher need to be examined in conjunction with the pedagogical choices the teacher makes. The teacher's LMS post-adoption behavior is, thus, the online teaching model they adopt in the LMS environment.

A Taxonomy of Online Teaching Models

To this point, we have identified social interaction as a fundamental building block for CSCL, drawn attention to the need to focus on the behavior of individual teachers following institutional adoption of LMS in order to explain why some teachers adopt CSCL in the LMS environment while others do not, and defined the post-adoption behavior of interest as the online teaching model adopted by a teacher in an LMS environment. Here we propose a taxonomy of teaching models adopted by teachers in an LMS environment.

We identify online teaching models from the set of teaching methods used by a teacher in one or more WEL courses. While there is, theoretically, a wide variety of teaching models, for the framework we first distinguish between teaching models on the basis of the dominant teaching method used. For example, a lecture-based teaching model means that most of the teaching methods adopted by a teacher are based on the lecture or try to reproduce, in an online environment, the lecture teaching method adopted face-to-face in the classroom.

At a first level, the online teaching models adopted by university teachers in LMS environments can be classified in a dichotomous way, i.e., manage information or manage relations (Rudestam and Schoenholtz-Read, 2002). In teaching models oriented toward managing information, the dominant teaching methods – like the lecture – aim to transmit knowledge efficiently from the expert to the learner. On the other hand, teaching models oriented toward managing relations are based on social learning where knowledge is built through interactions among peers. Table 4 distinguishes between the two types of teaching model and provides examples of their implementation in an LMS environment.

Table 4. Teaching models used with Learning Management Systems

Teaching model dichotomy	Goal of teaching	Examples of teaching models used with LMS
Manage information	Efficiently transmit knowledge from the expert to the learner	Traditional Web (static course information and educational material, no/little communication) Advanced Web (dynamic educational resource upload, communications about organizational aspects of the course)
Manage relations	Build knowledge through interactions of peers	Interactive (as in the advanced model plus student-student interactions based on course forums, resource contributions, etc.) CSCL-Computer Supported Collaborative Learning (as in the interactive model plus teaching and learning activities mainly based on learning among peers)

(adapted from Klobas and Renzi (2003; 2005), Leidner and Jarvenpaa (1995), and Rudestam and Schoenholtz-Read (2002)).

Approaches to social learning can be further broken down on the basis of the approach taken by the teacher to social learning, and in particular to social interaction among learners, online. Drawing on the work of Kreijns et al. (2003), we define online social interaction (OSI) as two-way communication among learners that includes socio-emotional and affective exchanges inside and outside the educational task context. Our taxonomy distinguishes between two online teaching models which reflect different approaches to (a) the level of OSI adopted by the teacher, (b) the presence of course activities based on online social learning, and (c) the presence of CSCL and its integration in course design. Teachers who adopt the first of these teaching models based on managing relations do so in a somewhat passive way, enabling OSI but not designing it into their courses while those who adopt the second social relationships-based model actively integrate OSI, social learning and CSCL into course design.

Our taxonomy therefore distinguishes between three teaching models that may be adopted by teachers in an LMS environment: (i) *Teaching material upload*, a model that summarizes the behavior of teachers who mainly use the LMS to upload teaching material; (ii) *Online discussion*, the model adopted by teachers who make a discussion forum or similar feature available to foster learning through OSI-based activities but do not incorporate its use in the formal course design; and (iii) *CSCL*, the model adopted by teachers who integrate collaborative learning activities based on OSI in their course design. Table 5 presents the characteristics of each teaching model in detail.

Table 5. Online teaching model taxonomy adopted for this study

LMS teaching model	LMS teaching model description
Teaching material upload (TMU)	The LMS is primarily used to store records of what happened in the classroom (audio-video recorded lectures, slides, and handouts) and to publish course schedule information (announcements and deadlines). Some course management activities such as assignments and quizzes may be automated. Either the discussion forum feature is not activated or it has been activated as part of the default configuration provided by the School or University and is used by the teacher as a kind of public e-mail to answer students' questions.
Online discussion (OD)	The LMS is used to store classroom related material, to publish course schedule information, and to automate some course management activities as in TMU. The discussion forum is included among LMS features by decision of the teacher either taken or alone as a participant in a project which included the discussion forum use. The discussion forum plays a key role in OSI. It is a place where teachers stimulate and encourage students to continue outside the classroom, on a voluntary basis, discussions about issues raised during classroom sessions. Teachers also use the discussion forum to answer specific questions raised by students and to clarify assignment or exam details.
CSCL	Nearly all the LMS features are used, especially the ones available to support OSI, in addition to the features used in TMU for course material upload and for course management, and in OD for student-student interaction. A key role is played by planned CSCL activities which are based on peer to peer learning through OSI that takes place in the discussion forum or using other suitable LMS features. CSCL activities are an integral part of the course structure, designed with their own learning goals and usually assessed (as distinct from the use of the discussion forum simply to extend classroom discussions as in OD).

A Behavioral Explanation of Online Teaching Model Adoption

To complete the framework, we need to be able to explain why a teacher might adopt CSCL rather than another online teaching model. Here, we turn to the theory of planned behavior (TPB; Ajzen, 1991), a well known social psychological theory of human behavior. The TPB proposes that a person's behavior in a given context reflects three motivational influences: attitudes, subjective norms, and perceived behavioral control (Fishbein and Ajzen, 2010). In addition, non-motivational factors that can condition the behavior (the actual availability of time, facilitating conditions, etc.) are represented by actual control over the behavior, or actual behavioral control. Relevant attitudes represent "the degree to which a person has a favorable or unfavorable evaluation or appraisal of the behavior in question", *subjective norms* represent "the perceived social pressure to perform or not to perform the behavior" and *perceived behavioral control* is "the perceived ease or difficulty of performing the behavior ... assumed to reflect past experience as well as anticipated impediments and obstacles" (Ajzen, 1991, p.188). Underlying each of these concepts, respectively, are the person's beliefs about the outcome of performing the behavior, about what other people want them to do, and about their abilities and the availability of resources that will permit them to go ahead. The TPB is widely used in many fields to explain behaviors that range from dieting to speeding to adopting new agricultural techniques to reproductive behavior. (An extensive bibliography can be found online at http://people.umass.edu/aizen/tpbrefs.html.)

Our model is presented in Figure 3. In the line with the TPB, we expect that a teacher's adoption of an LMS teaching model is influenced by one, or all, of attitudes, subjective norms, perceived behavioral control, and actual behavioral control. In addition to considering the relative influences of each of these higher level factors, it should be possible to identify how specific attitudes, subjective norms, perceived behavioral control factors, and actual behavioral control factors might explain adoption of each of the models. Furthermore, also in line with the TPB, we expect individual characteristics of teachers, such as the subject taught, their years of teaching experience and their general ICT capacity to act as "external factors" and be entirely mediated by the elements of the TPB.

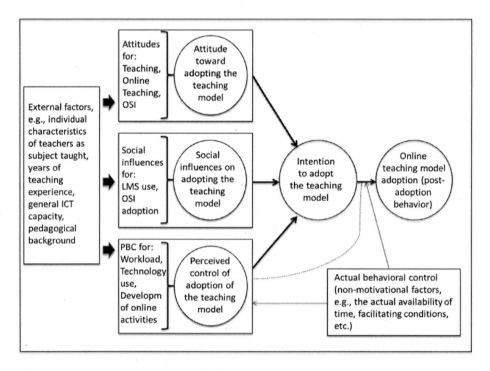

Figure 3. TPB model to explain adoption of different teaching models.

APPLYING THE FRAMEWORK IN PRACTICE

The framework described in this chapter was successfully applied in a cross-national study of factors influencing the strategies adopted by teachers at universities that use LMS to complement undergraduate classroom teaching (Renzi, 2008). Substantial differences were observed between teachers who adopted each of the three different online teaching models in attitudes to OSI, perceived norms for adoption of WEL, and perceived control for online teaching and social learning. Unlike teachers who adopted the other models, the teachers who adopted CSCL believed that online and classroom learning teaching were integrated, that online learning and teaching necessarily incorporated social interaction among students, and that students learn more through OSI. They were much less influenced by others to adopt their teaching model. Their perceived control of OSI was also high compared to teachers who adopt other online teaching models: all felt able to work around any problems they encountered with their university's LMS, and half of them reported that their decision to adopt CSCL was not influenced by workload considerations.

The differences in attitudes, subjective norms and perceived control between the teachers who adopted CSCL and the others could not be explained by differences in environmental conditions such as access to teaching and learning support; the courses taught or class sizes; teachers' attitudes to teaching in general; or demographic factors such as age, sex, position, country, years of experience in teaching and in LMS use. Instead, the teachers with the most positive attitudes to online social learning and the strongest sense of control were mostly trained teachers or teachers with high school experience. The complexity of teaching with CSCL, which requires strong understanding of the pedagogy of social learning combined with skills in adapting technologies to support teaching and learning appropriately, demands high level pedagogical understanding and technology skills.

CONCLUSION

Amid calls for use of ICT to transform universities, and acknowledgement that little transformation has been observed to date, our framework enhances understanding of what might be required to transform learning and teaching, a necessary outcome if institutional adoption of ICT is to lead to transformation rather than automation. WEL is the most common use of e-learning in higher education, so our framework focuses on change in WEL teaching models, away from teaching models designed primarily to automate processes and manage information toward adoption of the social learning and CSCL-based teaching models believed to be necessary strategies for higher education institutions that want to start the transformation process. The framework shows how a teacher's pedagogical choices about not only which features of e-learning systems they use but about how they fit into course design determine whether online teaching models will focus on managing information or social learning. Explanations of online teaching model adoption therefore need to consider this level of deep usage or post adoption behavior, and explanations are likely to be better sought from theories that explain human behavior, such as the TPB, rather than simple models of use or non-use of new ICT or the exhortations of senior institutional figures to use the ICT in a transformative way.

To transform universities, it is not enough simply to introduce system-wide ICT such as LMS and train teachers in use of their features. Universities need to focus on policies addressing the pedagogical preparation of university teachers and to improve their ability to integrate technology into teaching. The framework, and the results of its application described in this chapter, challenge university teachers, teacher-trainers and administrators to find ways to develop the attitudes, social norms and perceived control necessary to transform their teaching among teachers who do not have a background in pedagogy.

REFERENCES

Ajzen, I. (1991). The theory of planned behavior. *Organizational Behavior and Human Decision Processes, 50,* 179-211.

Barki, H., Titah, R., and Boffo, C. (2007). Information system use-related activity: an expanded behavioral conceptualization of information system use. *Information System Research, 18,* 173-192.

Becker, R., and Jokivirta, L. (2007). *Online learning in universities: selected data from the 2006 Observatory survey - November 2007* (Online report). The Observatory on Borderless Higher Education (OBHE). http://www.obhe.ac.uk.

Biggs, J. (2003). *Teaching for quality learning at university: what the student does* (2nd ed.). Buckingham: Society for Research into Higher Education and Open University Press.

Caruso, J. B., and Salaway, G. (2007). *The ECAR Study of undergraduate students and information technology, 2007 (September 2007)* (Research study). EDUCAUSE Center for Applied Research, Boulder, Colorado. http://connect.educause.edu/Library/ECAR/TheECARStudyofUndergradua/45075

Chin, W. W., and Marcolin, B. L. (2001). The future of diffusion research. *SIGMIS Database, 32*(3), 7-12.

Collis, B., and van der Wende, M. (Eds.). (2002). *Models of technology and change in higher education: an international comparative survey on the current and future use of ICT in higher education* (PDF). Twente: CHEPS, Centre for Higher Education Policy Studies. http://www.utwente.nl/cheps/documenten/ictrapport.pdf

De Sanctis, G., and Poole, M. S. (1994). Capturing the complexity in advanced technology use: Adaptive Structuration Theory. *Organization Science, 5*(2), 121-147.

Fishbein, M., and Ajzen, I. (2010). *Predicting and changing behavior: The reasoned action approach.* New York: Psychology Press.

Garrett, R., and Jokivirta, L. (2004). *Online learning in Commonwealth universities: selected data from the 2004 Observatory survey, Part 1 - October 2004* (Briefing Note). The Observatory on Borderless Higher Education (OBHE). http://www.obhe.ac.uk

Gilbert, L., and Moore, D. R. (1998). Building interactivity into Web courses: tools for social and instructional interaction. *Educational Technology, 38*(3), 29-35.

Griffith, T. L. (1999). Technology features as triggers for sensemaking. *Academy of Management Review, 24*(3), 472-488.

Gunawardena, C. N., Lowe, X., Constance, A., and Anderson, T. (1997). Analysis of a global debate and the development of an interaction analysis model for examining social construction of knowledge in computer conferencing. *Journal of Educational Computing Research., 17*(4), 397-431.

Harasim, L. (1993). *Global networks: computers and international communication.* Cambridge, MA: MIT Press.

Hiltz, S. R. (1994). *The virtual classroom: learning without limits via computer networks.* Norwood, NJ: Ablex Publishing Corporation.

Hooper, S., and Hannafin, M. J. (1991). The effects of group composition on achievement, interaction, and learning efficiency during computer-based cooperative instruction. *Educational Technology Research and Development, 39*(3), 27-40.

Jasperson, J., Carter, P., E., and Zmud, R., W. (2005). A comprehensive conceptualization of post-adoptive behaviors associated with information technology enabled work systems. *MIS Quarterly, 29*(3), 525-557.

Jehng, J. J. (1997). The psycho-social processes and cognitive effects of peer-based collaborative interactions with computers. *Journal of Educational Computing Research, 17*(1), 19-46.

Kimball, L. (2002). Managing distance learning: New challenges for faculty. In R. Hazemi and S. Hailes (Eds.), *The Digital University - Building a Learning Community* (pp. 27-40). London: Springer-Verlag.

Kirschner, P. A., Martens, R. and Strijbos, J.W. (2004). CSCL in higher education? In J.W. Strijbos, P. A. Kirschner and P. A. R. Martens (Eds.), *What we know about CSCL and implementing it in higher education* (pp. 3-30). Norwell, MA: Kluwer.

Klobas, J. E., and Renzi, S. (2000). Selecting software and services for Web-based teaching and learning. In A. K. Aggarwal (Ed.), *Web-based learning and teaching technologies: opportunities and challenges* (pp. 43-59). Hershey, PA: Idea Group Publishing.

Klobas, J. E., and Renzi, S. (2003). Integrating online educational activities in traditional courses: University-wide lessons after three years. In A. K. Aggarwal (Ed.), *Web-based education: learning from experience* (pp. 415-439). Hershey, PA: Information Science Publishing.

Klobas, J. E., and Renzi, S. (2005). Innovation in Web-enhanced learning at university. In C. Howard, K. Schenk, J. Boettcher, and L. Justice (Eds.), *Encyclopedia of online learning and technology*. Hershey, PA: Information Science Publishing.

Koschmann, T. (1996). Paradigm shifts and instructional technology: an introduction. In T. Koschmann (Ed.), *CSCL, theory and practice of an emerging paradigm* (pp. 1-23). Mahwah, NJ: Lawrence Erlbaum Associates.

Kreijns, K., and Kirschner, P. A. (2004). Designing sociable CSCL environments: applying interaction design principles. In J. Strijbos, P. A. Kirschner, R. L. Martens, and P. Dillenbourg (Eds.), *What we know about CSCL and implementing it in higher education* (pp. 221-243). Norwell, MA: Kluwer Academic Publishers.

Kreijns, K., Kirschner, P. A., and Jochems, W. (2003). Identifying the pitfalls for social interaction in computer-supported collaborative learning environments: a review of the research. *Computers in Human Behavior, 19*, 335-353.

Laurillard, D. (2002). *Rethinking university teaching: a framework for the effective use of educational technology* (2nd ed.). London: Routledge.

Laurillard, D. (2007). Modelling benefits-oriented costs for technology enhanced learning. *Higher Education, 54*(1), 21-39.

Leidner, D. E., and Jarvenpaa, S. L. (1995). The use of information technology to enhance management school education: a theoretical view. *MIS Quarterly, 19*(3), 265-291.

Liaw, S., and Huang, H. (2000). Enhancing interactivity in web-based instruction: a review of the literature. *Educational Technology, 40*(3), 41-45.

Lipponen, L., Hakkarainen, K., and Paavola, S. (2004). Practices and orientations of CSCL. In J. Strijbos, P. A. Kirschner, R. L. Martens, and P. Dillenbourg (Eds.), *What We know about CSCL and Implementing it in Higher Education* (pp. 31-50). Norwell, MA: Kluwer Academic Publishers.

Lucas, H. C., Swanson, E. B., and Zmud, R. W. (2007). Implementation, innovation, and related themes over the years in Information Systems research. *Journal of the Association for Information Systems, 8*(4), 206-210.

Northrup, P. (2001). A framework for designing interactivity in web-based instruction. *Educational Technology, 41*(2), 31-39.

OECD (2005). *E-learning in tertiary education: where do we stand?* Paris: Organization for Economic Co-operation and Development (OECD).

Orlikowski, W. J. (2000). Using technology and constituting structures: A practice lens for studying technology in organizations. *Organization Science, 11*(4), 404-428.

Palloff, R. M., and Pratt, K. (1999). *Building learning communities in cyberspace: effective strategies for the online classroom.* San Francisco: Jossey-Bass Publishers.

Renzi, S. (2008). *Differences in University Teaching after Learning Management System Adoption: An Explanatory Model Based on Ajzen's Theory of Planned Behavior.* Unpublished PhD Thesis, The University of Western Australia, Perth, Western Australia.

Rogers, E. M. (1995). *The diffusion of innovations* (4th ed.). New York: Free Press.

Rudestam, K. E., and Schoenholtz-Read, J. (2002). Overview: the coming of age of adult online education. In K. E. Rudestam and J. Schoenholtz-Read (Eds.), *Handbook of online learning: innovations in higher education and corporate training* (pp. 3- 28). Thousand Oaks, CA: Sage.

Schwarz, A., and Chin, W. (2007). Looking forward: toward an understanding of the nature and definition of IT acceptance. *Journal of the Association for Information Systems, 8*(4), 231-243.

Strijbos, J., Kirschner, P. A., and Martens, R. L. (2004). *What we know about CSCL and implementing it in higher education.* Norwell, MA: Kluwer Academic Publishers.

Wagner, E. D. (1994). In support of a functional definition of interaction. *American Journal of Distance Education, 8*(2), 6-29.

Wingard, R. G. (2004). Classroom teaching changes in Web-enhanced courses: a multi-instructional study. *Educause Quarterly, 27*(1), 26-35.

Woods, R., Baker, D. J., and Hopper, D. (2004). Hybrid structures: Faculty use and perception of web-based courseware as supplement to face-to-face instruction. *Internet and Higher Education, 7*(4), 281-297.

Zhang, S., and Fulford, C. P. (1994). Are interaction time and psychological interactivity the same thing in the distance learning television classroom? *Educational Technology, 34*(6), 58-64.

In: Faculty Training for Web Enhanced Learning   ISBN: 978-1-61209-335-2
Editors: Manuela Repetto and Guglielmo Trentin   © 2011 Nova Science Publishers, Inc.

Chapter 3

FIVE REASONS FOR THE RELUCTANCE OF ACADEMIC FACULTY TO EMPLOY A WEB-ENHANCED TEACHING[1]

Sarah Guri-Rosenblit

The Open University of Israel, Israel

ABSTRACT

Many far-reaching expectations have been echoed in the last decade as to the huge impact that the information and communication technologies might have on the academy and on the conventional ways in which professors teach and students learn. There has been a widespread belief that the new technologies will transform teaching and learning processes from being highly teacher-dominated to student-centered. However, many studies point to the fact that the applications of the advanced technologies in higher education settings worldwide are currently quite limited in the teaching domain. This chapter analyzes five major reasons for the reluctance of academic faculty to utilize the wide spectrum of possibilities embedded in a web-enhanced teaching: (1) Unbundling of the professional responsibility; (2) Work overload and burnout; (3) Lack of ongoing support systems; (4) Add-on functions rather than substitution; (5) Intellectual property concerns. It is of tremendous importance to comprehend the reasons underlying the reluctance of academic faculty to adopt a web-enhanced teaching in order to tackle the existing obstacles and pave the way for harnessing the immense possibilities offered by the advanced technologies for the benefit of both students and teachers in higher education institutions. The chapter concludes with some recommendations for respective higher education mangers of how to enhance the effective use of the digital technologies in academia.

---

[1] This chapter is based extensively on arguments presented in the book of Guri-Rosenblit, S. (2009). Digital Technologies in Higher Education: Sweeping Expectations and Actual Effects. New York: Nova Science.

INTRODUCTION

The information and communication technologies have penetrated in the last decade all levels of education from nursery to university level studies, and have challenged higher education institutions worldwide to redesign their administration and research infrastructures and redefine their teaching practices. Far-reaching expectations have been echoed in the last decade as to the huge impact that the new technologies might have on the academy and on the conventional ways in which professors teach and students learn. There has been a widespread belief that the advanced technologies will transform teaching and learning processes from being highly teacher-dominated to student-centered, and that this transformation will result in increased learning gains for students, creating and allowing opportunities for learners to develop their creativity, problem-solving abilities, communication skills, and other higher order thinking skills.

However, many studies point to the fact the applications of the digital technologies in higher education settings worldwide are currently quite limited. Face-to-face instruction in the classroom is familiar, effective, and well understood. Many academics feel wary about changing a well-tested paradigm of teaching. Adoption of the new technologies is perceived by many teachers as a risky, if not an intimidating change, and therefore quite often faculty members in many higher education institutions are not keen on participating in online initiatives. This chapter analyzes five major reasons for the reluctance of academic faculty to utilize the wide spectrum of possibilities embedded in a web-enhanced teaching: (1) Unbundling of the professional responsibility; (2) Work overload and burnout; (3) Lack of ongoing support systems; (4) Add-on functions rather than substitution; (5) Intellectual property concerns. It is of tremendous importance to comprehend the reasons underlying the reluctance of academic faculty to adopt a web-enhanced teaching, in order to tackle the existing obstacles and pave the way for harnessing the immense possibilities offered by the advanced technologies for the benefit of both students and teachers in higher education institutions.

UNBUNDLING OF THE PROFESSIONAL RESPONSIBILITY

One of the challenging demands of a web-enhanced teaching is associated with the unbundling of the professional responsibility of teaching any given course into discrete tasks undertaken by an array of academic, technical and administrative staff (Guri-Rosenblit, 2009; Paulson, 2002; Vrasidas and Galss, 2002; Williams, 2003). Within conventional classroom teaching, academics are responsible for the entire development and delivery process of their courses – they plan the content of their course and its relevant literature, they teach the course, decide on the nature of the relevant assignments and exams, and are usually also responsible for checking and grading the students' work. In large classes they are often supported by teaching assistants, who work under their close supervision and guidance.

When the large distance teaching universities were established in Europe in the early 1970s, Peters, the founding president of FernUniversität in Germany, argued that academics in the new distance teaching universities form a new species of professors, and that the traditional roles of professors have been challenged drastically: "It is a difficult task to switching from oral teaching to teaching by means of the written word and by merging traditional teaching techniques and modern technological ways of communication...The result is revolutionary in the sense that an academic teaching tradition of several hundred years had to be changed radically at once" (Peters, 1997, p.7100).

Peters was also the first to focus on the division of labor, inherent in large-scale distance education frameworks, as a basic ingredient of the industrialization theory (Peters, 1994, 2001). He highlighted mainly the impact of the division of labor on the planning of courses, the management and administrative organization, and the control measures of teaching large quantities of students. He emphasized the mechanisms of assembly line, mass production, standardization, objectification, concentration and centralization, typical of the development of self-study materials and of the monitoring of students' learning in distance education settings. Peters related also to the differential functions of academics teaching at a distance *vis-a-vis* university teachers in conventional universities, a differentiation which derives from breaking up the complete work process of teaching into discrete functions.

The distributed teaching responsibility characterizes nowadays also comprehensive web-enhanced teaching both in distance and in campus-based universities. Academics who teach online are frequently required to collaborate in a team framework with tutors, editors, instructional designers, computer experts, graphic production personnel in developing and delivering their courses. Such working conditions differ immensely from the sole and overall responsibility of professors of their courses which has characterized the academic teaching for over 900 years. Clearly, in a team framework, the professors' academic freedom in teaching is reduced in comparison to their being responsible for designing the overall learning/teaching process. Professors, who view the academic freedom in teaching as a sacred value of their profession, resist strongly the unbundling of their teaching responsibility and the participation in a team framework.

WORK OVERLOAD AND BURNOUT

An additional important reason explaining the reluctance of many academics to engage in a web-enhanced teaching relates to the fact that to design study programs for online teaching constitutes a complicated and demanding task. Teaching online, or even preparing some materials for online teaching, requires faculty to devote much more time to the preparation of study materials than they would for a face-to-face classroom presentation, both if they are required to operate within a team framework or undertake the overall design and teaching of their courses by themselves (Bates, 2005; Guri-Rosenblit, 2005, 2009). Many studies highlight the fact that academic faculty find that teaching online is time consuming, is more isolated and requires specialized skills (Arafeh, 2004; OECD, 2005; Paulson, 2002; Trucano, 2005; Zemsky and Massy, 2004). Even the use of the most simple e-mail function turns sometimes to be threatening for many academics. Potentially, teachers are expected to be attentive to students' queries and remarks with no time limits. Many professors view such reality as a severe penetration of their social and private life. In some studies it was found that professors decided to close their e-mails to students, since they felt that it 'vandalizes' their social and private lives (Guri-Rosenblit, 2009). Interestingly, not only teachers, but also students indicate sometimes that online or blended courses increase significantly their workload and study time (Aycock et al., 2002; Hong, 2008).

Many studies specify a long list of roles which teachers are expected to undertake when utilizing the new technologies in their teaching. For instance, according to Wilson et al. (2004), instructors teaching online are expected to: Provide infrastructure for learning (syllabus, calendar, communication tools, and instructional resources); model effective participation, collaboration and learning strategies; monitor and assess learning and provide feedback, remediation, and grades; troubleshoot and resolve instructional, interpersonal, and technical problems; and create a learning community in which learners feel safe and connected and believe their contributions are valid.

Abel claims that in online learning, faculty are asked to make the biggest changes, with unclear rewards (Abel, 2005). Zemsky and Massy (2004) indicated that many of the participating institutions in their study began to discover that they constantly had to make extra incentives available to faculty in order to involve them in e-learning. When the expenditures of those funds became too expensive, the institutions dropped the incentive programs and witnessed a general flattering of e-learning adoptions and experiments.

In addition, some faculty feel that the process of acquiring the knowledge and training to deliver effective online instruction and the actual teaching online constitutes a source of added stress and burnout. The overload put on professors who teach extensively online has been found in several studies to result in a higher burnout rate as compared to professors that do not teach online (Hislop and Ellis, 2004; Hogan and McKnight, 2007; Lackritz, 2004). Burnout is defined as both a psychological and physical response to workplace stress. Maslach and Leiter (1997) identified six major influences on burnout: (1) workload; (2) lack of control over establishing and following day-to-day priorities; (3) insufficient reward and the accompanying feeling of continually having to do more for less; (4) the feeling that relationships become impersonal; (5) the absence of fairness, in which trust, openness and respect are not present; and (6) conflicting value, in which choices that are made by management often conflict with their mission and core values. According to the Maslach Burnout Inventory-Educators Survey (Maslach et al., 1996) burnout is manifested in three dimensions: (1) emotional exhaustion – feeling of being emotionally overextended and exhausted by one's work; (2) depersonalization – a feeling of impersonal response toward students; and (3) a reduced sense of personal accomplishment - a loss of personal self-efficacy.

Research on burnout related to higher education faculty teaching online is sparse. Hislop and Ellis (2004) found that teaching online becomes a major workplace stressor leading to burnout symptoms. Shea et al. (2006) indicated that students studying online report higher levels of learning and teaching effectiveness in situations when they perceive higher levels of teaching presence, such as active directed facilitation and effective instructional design practices. One way for online instructors to be effective is to be online constantly, which leads quite often to burnout (Dunlap, 2005).

In a study conducted by Hogan and McKnight (2007) burnout has been identified as a significant factor among those in instructional positions using web-enhanced teaching. In this study 76 online instructors teaching at the undergraduate level within US universities were interviewed. The 76 university instructors who participated in Hogan and McKnight study were teaching courses in a technology-enhanced format. Data analysis revealed that online instructors possessed an average score on the emotional exhaustion subscale, high degree of depersonalization, and low degree of personal accomplishment. The final conclusion of Hogan and McKnight is that the online instructors were on the borderline of burnout showing signs of moving toward a high degree of burnout.

LACK OF ONGOING SUPPORT SYSTEMS

There is plenty of accumulated evidence that indicate that many professors most commonly use the new technologies for administrative tasks, such as record keeping, lesson plan development, information presentation, basic information searches on the Internet, but overall are less competent in using the technologies compared to their students. Many academics report that they do not feel confident in utilizing the advanced technologies, and this lack of confidence affects to great extent the way in which the learning/teaching processes are conducted. Ongoing and just-in-time support systems have been recognized as crucial for the use of technology in instructional delivery (Abel, 2005; Arafeh, 2004; Brindley et al., 2004; Carlson, 2002; Tait and Mills, 2003).

A large-scale OECD study had conducted an in-depth survey of e-learning practices in 19 tertiary education institutions in 13 countries in the Asia-Pacific region (Australia, Japan, New Zealand, Thailand), Europe (France, Germany, Spain, Switzerland, the United Kingdom), Latin America (Mexico, Brazil), and North America (Canada, the United States) (OECD, 2005). This study has clearly indicated that all of the participating institutions acknowledged the need to recruit a broader range of staff to complement academic staff, such as technologists, instructional designers, learning scientists, etc., in order to implement the technologies more effectively and establish more intensive support systems for the utilization of a broader web-enhanced teaching.

The study of Abel (2005) purported to provide insights into best practices for achieving success in online learning. It pulled from the experiences of 21 institutions across the Carnegie classifications in the United States. The 21 institutions included - five community colleges, seven BA/Master's institutions (five private, two public), and nine research doctoral institutions (one private, and 8 public). It included large to very small higher education institutions, such as Penn State University, which supports 62,000 students with online technology, on one hand, to Peirce College, which - while much smaller, generates 46% of its revenue from online programs, on the other hand. The most significant finding of Abel's study was that institutions that offer the entire degrees online are more successful than those that offer only a scattering of courses. The institutions which focused on putting full programs online were about four times as likely to perceive that they had achieved 'overwhelming success' compared to institutions that focused their efforts at the individual course level. Putting full programs online, when done correctly and focused on student learning, involves teamwork within the academic department among several units of the institution. Abel concluded that: "For online program to succeed, it must be thought through carefully and perhaps reengineered to serve students differently and, hopefully, better" (Abel, 2005, p. 76).

The most common success factors of those institutions implementing the 'programmatic approach' in the study of Abel included: Special support resources dedicated to the selected programs; new course and program formats to reflect the unique pedagogy of implementing the digital technologies into the various programs; program design sessions to help faculty leaders create an effective program. Institutions that adopted an overall policy of using the new technologies were doing a lot more than just posting course notes or syllabi online. However, many institutions which participated in Abel's study were still unclear about how the new technologies fit with their mission, and have found that achieving widespread adoption by the faculty is difficult. They have also found it challenging to achieve faculty use that truly enhances the learning interaction between faculty and students as opposed to simply posting materials online.

ADD-ON FUNCTIONS RATHER THAN SUBSTITUTION

The new electronic media were introduced into the academic world as a sudden thunderstorm without having sufficient time to define what are the purposes and functions that they are to fulfill or substitute (Guri-Rosenblit, 2009). The lack of clear problems had turned to be an acute problem in the adaptation process of the new technologies in universities and colleges. The impact of the technologies on learning and teaching is still unclear and open to much debate and research. In most higher education institutions, the new technologies are used mainly for add-on functions and not for substituting face-to-face encounters or for an intensive web-enhanced teaching. Using technology to supplement classroom teaching does not radically change teaching methods. It merely enhances what would be done in the classroom in any case, and it also might cost more than traditional face-to-face encounters or distance education through print and mass media, which undermines the potential attraction of harnessing the new technologies in an era of severe budget cuts.

The fact that the new technologies are used mainly to enhance on-campus learning, without substituting either the teacher or the classroom is well recognized in many studies (Bates, 2005; Garret and Jokivirta, 2004; Garret and Verbik, 2004; Guri-Rosenblit, 2009; Hong, 2008; OECD, 2005; Vest, 2007). Many studies point out that both students and academic faculty seem to like the traditional classroom encounters, even when given the opportunity to being exempt from attending a class, and provided with all the needed materials and assignments online (Guri-Rosenblit, 2009). Even when professors use e-learning products and devices, most of them still teach as they were taught - that is, they stand in the front a classroom providing lectures intended to supply the basic knowledge which the students need (Kurtz, 2008; Zemsky and Massy, 2004).

The fact that the change is slow, and not radical, was validated by an international survey of the Observatory of Borderless Education, which had been carried out both in developed and developing countries (Garret and Jokivirta, 2004; Garret and Verbik, 2004). This survey was conducted with the aim to test the widespread perception during the so-called 'e-education bubble' between 1997 and early 2000 that online learning would quickly and fundamentally rupture the conventional campus-based model of higher education. The conclusion from this survey was that online learning has had only a relative impact on campus and on distance education. Change has been relatively rapid as for modest online components and for institution-wide learning platforms. But a fundamental move away from on-campus provision has not been materialized.

In a wide-range study of Trucano (2005) it was clearly found that the new technologies are very rarely seen as central to the overall learning process. Trucano concluded that:

"Studies on the use of ICTs suggest that despite rhetoric that ICTs can enable new types of teaching and learning styles, for the most part they are being used to support traditional learning practices" (Trucano, 2005, p.35). This reflects the reality in both developed and developing countries.

In the comprehensive OECD study, aforementioned, it was found that provision with 'high' online presence accounted well under 5% of total enrolments at most OECD sample institutions (OECD, 2005, p. 12). Current institutional strategies do not back the assumption that tertiary institutions will gradually move their provision towards fully online delivery. The OECD and Observatory surveys clearly demonstrate that fully online provision at campus-based institutions will remain very much a minority in the short to medium term, and that e-learning is used mainly as supplementary to on-campus delivery at undergraduate level. The OECD study has highlighted the fact that skepticism about the pedagogic value of e-learning and staff development are probably the most challenging factors in the implementation of the digital technologies. In most examined institutions this factor was found to be stronger even than key barriers, such as lack of appropriate infrastructure and funding. One reason for the faculty skepticism probably lies in the fact that e-learning has not really revolutionized learning and teaching to date. Far-reaching, novel ways of teaching and learning, facilitated by the new technologies, remain nascent or still to be invented (ibid, p. 14).

INTELLECTUAL PROPERTY CONCERNS

Concerns about intellectual property rights may also be seen as a barrier for the implementation of web-enhanced teaching in academic environments. It seems of tremendous importance to clarify ownership of usage rights of intellectual property generated by and for teaching. Moreover, when rules of copyright become too stringent, and professors are not able to refer easily to other works in online settings, as they do regularly in classroom teaching, it deters them from utilizing the new technologies in their teaching.

The issue of copyright and privacy is a hot topic discussed in multiple books and research publications (Dupin-Bryant, 2006). Public policy and relevant legislation are gradually developing in this domain to protect individual rights. The most problematic area of widespread violations of academic work, enhanced greatly by the new technologies, relates to copyright. Gantz and Rochester entitled the phenomenon of violating academic copyrights on books, publication and other research artifacts as the 'Pirates of the Digital Millennium' (Gantz and Rochester, 2005). 'Copyright' is a legal concept, enacted by governments, giving the creator of an original work of authorship exclusive rights to it, usually for a limited time (of fifty to hundred years) after which the work enters the public domain. Most countries recognize copyright limitations, allowing 'fair use' exceptions to the creators exclusivity of copyright and giving users certain rights.

The development of the Internet, the digital media and the computer networked technologies, have introduced numerous difficulties in enforcing copyright and prompted reinterpretation of the meaning of 'fair use' in online teaching. Simultaneously, academic publishing houses, which depend to a great extent on copyright have advocated the extension and expansion of their copyright, and filed for stringent legal reinforcement (Dowd, 2006; Dupin-Bryant, 2006; Lindsey, 2003). Publishers and other content owners express fear that expanded exemptions for digital materials used in online learning will adversely affect the viability of their business. They fear that the digital content released in an educational setting will be widely redistributed by students. Some of the publishing houses hold a view that educators "want something for nothing" (Tanner, 1999).

Copyright laws in most countries do not prohibit all copying and replication. In the US, the fair use doctrine, codified by the Copyright Act of 1976, permits some copying and distribution without needing permission of the copyright holder or payment to him. The statute does not clearly define fair use, but instead defines four factors to consider in judging fair use: (1) The purpose and character of the use; (2) the nature of the copyrighted work; (3) the amount and substantiality of the portion used in relation to the copyrighted work as a whole; and (4) the effect of the use upon the potential market of the copyrighted work. Later legal acts amended the US Copyright law so that for certain purposes making 10 copies or more is construed to be commercial. The Digital Millennium Copyright Act prohibits the manufacture, importation, or distribution of devices whose intended use is to bypass an access or copy control put in place by a copyright owner.

Academics confront several dilemmas in relation to copyright laws in the digital millennium. On one hand, they are concerned as to losing intellectual property over their course materials, some of which include innovative ideas and original constructs. On the other hand, the stringent copyright laws initiated and formulated in the last decade as to the use of others' works in their ongoing teaching, as they do regularly in classroom teaching, might deter them from utilizing the new technologies in their teaching.

Michael Tanner, a professor of computer science in the School of Engineering at the University of California in Santa Cruz argued in favour of expanding the copyright law's existing exemptions for education. The great opportunities offered by the Internet for higher education requires that the exemptions currently offered for classroom teaching be extended to the networked environment. Tanner claimed that the publishing houses should not worry of losing their financial base, since academic faculty and institutions alike have strong interests in controlling who has access to online classes. The more interactivity is built into an online resource, the more care is given to protect the privacy of participants. The general public is usually not offered free access to online classes, if it is not intended to be an open source.

Tanner claimed in 1999 in his testimony before the Representatives of the US Copyright Office that: "We can assure copyright owners that material made available through educational exemptions will be contained within a limited community. We will cooperate with and respect limitations on copying and distribution. However, if such cooperation is unreasonably burdensome or intrusive, faculty will frequently choose not to use the material in question. Already, anxiety is high in academia about the kind of demands proprietors will make in exchange for allowing their copyrighted material to be transmitted to students over networks" (Tanner, 1999).

Tanner proposed to distinguish between two kinds of protection that must be in place to ensure that copyrighted material used under exemptions does not go into general circulation. First, measures need to be in place to ensure limited access, so that the transmitted material is available only to authorized users, such as students enrolled in a class. Second, it must be possible to prevent permanent storage and redistribution of the material. Various models of access control technology are already in the market, and others are under development. These include both hardware and software approaches and range from strong encryption to weak protections based on passwords and IP addresses. Determined assault should be deterred by criminal penalties.

Side by side with the ongoing discussions and actions in the last decade, both legal and public, on issues related to copyright in the academic world, an intriguing movement of open sources has emerged. Clearly, more open access to sources of scholarly information, libraries, and software codes benefit all participants in higher education, but most particularly it benefits teaching and research in those countries that suffer from severe shortages in adequate academic manpower and research facilities. The MIT's Open Courseware Project was one of the pioneers in promoting open source materials (Vest, 2007). Today, the open source movement is a wide-ranging phenomenon (Biltzer and Schroder, 2006; Guri-Rosenblit, 2009).

CONCLUSION

This chapter has examined five major reasons for the reluctance of academic faculty to utilize a wide-spectrum of web-enhanced teaching. However, it seems that in the near future the impact of the information and communication technologies will grow in academic teaching. Sir Arthur Clarke has phrased a most illuminating insight as to the adoption cycle of new technologies by the human mankind: "When it comes to technology, most people overestimate it in the short term and underestimate it in the long term" (in Twigg, 2004). This insight seems to hold true for the implementation of the digital technologies in higher education settings. Wilson stated that: "The e-learning revolution is not over. It is just entering a more intelligent and less self-indulgent phase" (Wilson, 2002, p. 5). Noble claimed that the story of e-learning is still unfolding, no one really knows what tomorrow will bring (Noble, 2001). Wilson and Noble echo the beliefs of many other researchers as to the future potential of the advanced technologies in higher education, in general, and in academic teaching, in particular.

It seems that policy matters greatly in enhancing the use of technologies. In the previous phase of the late 1980s and early 1990s, the role of policy may have been perceived as minor in the implementation process of the new technologies, in the sense that many initiatives were driven by innovators and early adopters (Zemsky and Massy, 2004). Nowadays, institutional policies play a crucial role in the adaptation process of the electronic technologies in educational settings. As Hoffman stated, for e-learning to become a dominant learning pattern - technology alone will not suffice (Hoffmann, 2005). The main challenge for both institutions and governments is now to develop more strategic policies on how the advanced technologies can be used for the different target groups that higher education is expected to serve in the knowledge economy in the 21st century. These target groups include traditional learners as well as lifelong learners from both within or outside national jurisdictions.

The study of Abel (2005) has clearly demonstrated that successful institutions in online learning had compelling reasons to support such learning. Many of them stated as their mission to serve working adults coupled with the strong need of these students to have more flexibility in receiving effective instruction. In all of these institutions there was a predominant leadership style that most likely contributed to the success in achieving mission alignment. The leadership elements were: A long-term commitment to the initiative;

investment of significant financial and other resources in the implementation process of the new technologies; prioritization of expenditures on high-impact programs; and a clear understanding by the academic faculty of why the institution is implementing online learning. In particular, the involvement of key leaders in prioritizing where to focus online learning development activities was critical and highly correlated with perceived success in these institutions.

Beaudoin emphasized the importance of leadership in implementing the information and communication technologies in higher education institutions: "Schools and colleges in the new millennium need leaders who have reflected on their experiences and internalized understandings about their own capacity to lead...Indecision and immobility during these tumultuous times could prove fatal to a number of institutions" (Beaudoin, 2006, p. 10). Individual faculty operating without any training or support and without adequate resources may become disenchanted with both the product and the process, and this reaction might naturally extend to their students. Such an outcome only reinforces the innate skepticism regarding the beneficial applications of the digital technologies in academe.

It is quite clear that there exists a burning need to develop incentives in order to promote effective teacher participation in various modes of online teaching. Of particular importance is an ongoing and just-in-time support. Many institutions acknowledge the need to recruit in the future a broader range of personnel to complement academic staff in order to implement the technologies more effectively.

The new technologies will require the academic faculty to assume new responsibilities and to develop a range of new skills. Academics will have to become in the future reconciled with the idea of collaborating with other colleagues and professionals in designing materials and in the teaching process. They will need to learn how to collaborate in a team framework with tutors, editors, instructional designers, television producers, computer experts, graphic production personnel, etc. in developing and delivering their courses. At the same time, teachers will have greater flexibility to choose the teaching styles better suited for their personal strengths and individual preferences. University leaders will have to deliberate how to prepare the new generations of academic faculty to operate in a world where blended courses and online teaching are an integral part of the academic teaching responsibilities.

REFERENCES

Abel, R. (2005). Implementing the best practices in online learning. *EDUCAUSE Quarterly, 28* (3), 75-77.

Arafeh, S. (2004). *The Implications of Information and Communications Technologies for Distance Education: Looking Toward the Future.* Arlington, VA: SRI International, Final Report, P11913.

Aycock, A., Garnham, C. and Kaleta, R. (2002). Lessons retrieved from the hybrid course project. *Teaching with Technology Today, 8* (6).

Bates, A.W. (2005). *Technology, E-Learning and Distance Education.* London: Routledge Falmer, 2nd edition.

Beaudoin, M. F. (2006). The impact of distance education on the academy in the digital age. In: M. F. Beaudoin (Ed.), *Perspectives on Higher Education in the Digital Age* (1-20). New York: Nova Science.

Biltzer, J. and Schroder, P. (Eds.) (2006). *The Economics of Open Source Software Development.* Elsevier.

Brindley, J. E., Walti, C. and Zawacki-Richter, O. (Eds.) (2004). *Learner Support in Open, Distance and Online Learning Environments.* Oldenburg: Bibliotheks-und Informations system der Universität Oldenburg.

Carlson, S. (2002). *The Missing Link in Educational Technology: Trained Teachers.* http://www.technowlogia.org/TKL_active_pages2/CyrrentArticles/main.asp?IssueNumbe r=18andFileType=PDFandArticleID=435.

Dowd, R. J. (2006). *Copyright Litigation Handbook.* Thomson West.

Dunlap, J. C. (2005). Workload reduction in online courses: Getting some shuteye. *Performance Improvement, 44*(5), 18-26.

Dupin-Bryant, P. A. (2006). Pervasive computing: The future of computers in higher education. In: Beaudoin, M. (Ed.), *Perspectives on Higher Education in the Digital Age* (35-47). New York: Nova Science.

Gantz, J. and Rochester, J. (2006). *Pirates of the Digital Millennium.* Prentice Hall.

Garret, R. and Jokivirta, L. (2004). *Online Learning in Commonwealth Universities: Selected Data from the 2004 Observatory Survey, Part 1.* Observatory on Borderless Higher Education. www.obhe.ac.uk/products/briefings.html.

Garret, R. and Verbik, L. (2004). *Online Learning in Commonwealth Universities: Selected Data from the 2004 Observatory Survey, Part 2.* Observatory on Borderless Higher Education. www.obhe.ac.uk/products/briefings.html.

Guri-Rosenblit, S. (2005). 'Distance education' and 'E-learning': Not the same thing. *Higher Education, 49,* 467-493.

Guri-Rosenblit, S. (2009). *Digital Technologies in Higher Education: Sweeping Expectations and Actual Effects.* New York: Nova Science.

Hislop, G. and Ellis, H. (2004). A study of faculty effort in online teaching. *Internet and Higher Education, 7* (1), 15-32.

Hoffmann, S. (2005). *Building E-Learning Organizations,* Presented at the Online EDUCA Berlin Conference, 29 November- 2 December, 2005.

Hogan, R. L. and McNight, M. A. (2007). Exploring burnout among university online instructors. *Internet and Higher education, 10* (2), 117-124.

Hong, L. (2008). Blending online components into traditional instruction in pre-service teacher education: The good, the bad, and the ugly. *International Journal for the Scholarship of Teaching and Learning, 2* (1).

Kurtz, G. (2008). *Technological Innovation in Teaching at Bar-Ilan University: Transfer from Experimental Phase to Ongoing Adoption,* Paper presented at a Symposium on Attitudes of Academic Faculty towards the Implementation of Technologies in Teaching. Raanana: Open University of Israel, 31 March 2008.

Lackritz, J. R. (2004). Exploring burnout among university faculty: Incidence, performance, and demographic issues. *Teaching and Teacher Education, 20* (1), 713-729.

Lindsey, M. (2003).*Copyright Law on Campus.* Washington State University Press.

Maslach, C., Jackson, S. and Leiter, M. (1996). *Maslach Burnout Inventory Manual.* Palo Alto, CA: Consulting Psychologists Press (3rd Edition).

Maslach, C. and Leiter, M. (1997). *The Truth about Burnout: How Organizations Cause Personal Stress and What to Do About It*. San Francisco: Jossey-Bass Publishers.

Noble, D. F. (2001). *Digital Diploma Mills: The Automation of Higher Education*. New York: Monthly Review Press.

OECD (2005). *E-Learning in Tertiary Education: Where Do We Stand?* Paris: Centre for Educational Research and Innovation.

Paulson, K. (2002). Reconfiguring faculty roles for virtual settings. *Journal of Higher Education, 73* (1), 123-140.

Peters, O. (1994). Distance education and industrial production: A comparative interpretation in outline. In M. Keegan (Ed.), *Otto Peters on Distance Education* (101-127). London: Routledge.

Peters, O. (1997). FernUniversität. In: I. Mugridge (Ed.). *Founding the Open Universities* (53-79). New Delhi: Sterling Publishers.

Peters, O. (2001). *Learning and Teaching in Distance Education: Analysis and Interpretations from an International Perspective*. London: Kogan Page.

Shea, P., Sau-Li, C. and Pickett, A. (2006). A study of teaching presence and student sense of a learning community in fully online and web-enhanced college courses. *Internet and Higher Education, 9* (3), 75-190.

Tait, A. and Mills, R. (Eds.) (2003) *Rethinking Learner Support in Distance Education: Change and Continuity in an International Context*. London: RoutledgeFalmer.

Tanner, M. R. (1999). *Testimony before Representatives of the United States Copyright Office,* February 10, 1999, Los Angeles, CA.

Trucano, M. (2005). *Knowledge Maps: ICTs in Education*. Washington D.C.: InfoDev, The Information for Development Program.

Twigg, C. (2004). A little knowledge is a dangerous thing. *The Learning Market Space,* Section 1, July 4, 2004, The Center for Academic Transformation.

Vest, C. M. (2007). *The American Research University from World War II to World Wide Web*. Berkeley: University of California Press.

Vrasidas, C. and Glass, G. V. (Eds.) (2002). *Distance Education and Distributed Learning*. Greenwich, CT: Information Age Publishing.

Williams, P. E. (2003). Roles and competencies for distance education programs in higher education institutions. *American Journal of Distance Education, 17* (1), 45-57.

Wilson, B. C., Ludwig-Hardman, S., Thornam, C. and Dunlap, J. C. (2004). Bounded community: Designing and facilitating learning communities in formal courses. *The International Review of Research in Open and Distance learning, 5* (3).

Wilson, J. M. (2002). E-learning: Is it over? *UMassOnline.net*. http://www.umassonline.net/news/shownews.cfm?news_ID=23.

Zemsky, R. and Massy, W. F. (2004a). *Thwarted Innovation: What Happened to E-learning and Why*. A Final Report for 'The Weatherstation Project' of The Learning Alliance at the University of Pennsylvania in Cooperation with the Thomson Corporation. University of Pennsylvania: *The Learning Alliance for Higher Education*.

In: Faculty Training for Web Enhanced Learning
Editors: Manuela Repetto and Guglielmo Trentin

ISBN: 978-1-61209-335-2
© 2011 Nova Science Publishers, Inc.

Chapter 4

TEACHER RESISTANCE TO NEW TECHNOLOGIES: HOW BARRIERS TO WEB ENHANCED LEARNING CAN BE OVERCOME

Steve Wheeler
University of Plymouth, UK

ABSTRACT

This chapter will address the question of how a transformation in teachers' use of information and communication technology can be achieved. There is evidence to suggest that the use of information and communication technology (ICT) in higher education can enhance and extend the learning experience. There is also evidence that although many teachers recognize this, many resist using ICT in formal education contexts, resulting in a shortfall in the adoption of technologies. An analysis of the barriers and constraints, and how they might be managed and overcome will feature during the discussion. A particular emphasis on Web Enhanced Learning (WEL) approaches will be made and strategies for university-wide adoption of social software (Web 2.0) tools and services will be presented.

INTRODUCTION

"In the times of rapid change, learners inherit the Earth, while the learned find themselves beautifully equipped to deal with a world that no longer exists." (Eric Hoffer).

Information and communication technology has taken a strong foothold in education. In most western universities, there are advanced networked services, digital presentation tools, and a large range of specialized software that enables teaching staff and students to search for, access, store and retrieve more knowledge than has ever previously been made available. Such opportunities to create new, innovative and stimulating learning environments are many, and the university it seems, has been the test-bed for new pedagogical approaches through new technologies for some time. Yet no matter how strong a desire institutions profess to adopting and exploiting the power of new technologies, it is the lecturer who must cause this adoption to take place and many are reluctant to make use of new technologies (Collis and Moonen, 2002). It is a strange paradox then to witness many academics avoiding, or even rejecting new technologies, in favour of older, more traditional methods, in an age of digital media and ubiquitous technology.

A few years ago, my colleague Ann Winter and I wrote about the issues surrounding teacher adoption of new technologies in the classroom (Wheeler and Winter, 2005). We identified several of the organizational and technological constraints that militate against widespread adoption of technologies in schools, but we also emphasized that there are social and psychological dimensions underlying teacher rejection or resistance to the adoption of technologies in education. We made the strong point that it is ultimately in the winning of hearts and minds of teachers that success resides.

From our research we showed that a number of problems emerge from situations where changes such as the introduction of new technologies are made in traditional educational settings. Although our study was set in a primary education context, it was clear than many of the issues we identified also existed in other education settings, due to the common underlying social and psychological factors. There is scope then to discuss those ideas and extend them to apply within a higher education context. This chapter dwells on teachers' uses of new technologies in the context of digital technologies and web based tools in a university education context. It also focuses on staff resistance to change, and presents some strategies that may be applied in attempts to overcome the barriers. Many of the issues and barriers to adoption of innovation in higher education are similar to those in primary and higher education. New technologies are constantly being introduced, and the social software applications in particular offer a new dimension to technology supported learning, but also bring challenges of unfamiliarity, perceptions of threat, the need to change work practices and the cost of extra time and energy spent re-learning and re-training. The new dimensions presented by approaches adopting Web Enhanced Learning (WEL) will therefore require further analysis.

The Nature of Change

Change is often painful, and most people avoid it if they can. This is human nature. People feel more comfortable with routines they have developed, and trust their own methods before they will trust those of another. Notwithstanding, Web Enhanced Learning (WEL) has the potential to revolutionize higher education at a number of levels.

At the pedagogical level – where we are concerned with how learning takes place – there are indicators that WEL and other technology enhanced approaches have the potential to transform the quality of learning. WEL provides a flexibility of pace and space that was previously unattainable. Further, WEL enables students to more directly participate in, and take control and responsibility over, their own learning processes.

Formal and Informal Learning

This emerges through formal and informal learner activities such as online discussion, user generated content, active social tagging and the sharing and exchanging of digital artifacts direct from user to user. We can observe this in the interpersonal dialogue that is common on social networking sites such as Facebook, in the user generated encyclopaedia pages of Wikipedia and on video and photo-sharing sites such as YouTube and Flickr. Not only do students enjoy using these tools informally, they also use them within formal education contexts, and often during lessons or for the purposes of completing their assignments. Engagement with learning at this level is a departure from the didactic, passive, instructional methods often seen in higher education. Students are now using WEL tools to engage more deeply and actively with their learning, and through their quick and easy to set up social networks, can call upon help and support to collaborate while they learn. It seems a shame that there appears to be a gulf growing between the expectations and activities of students within the social web, and the expectations and practices of university staff within the lecture room.

WEB 2.0 IN EDUCATION

Before we progress our discussion on the impact of WEL, we need to examine the emergence of the social web. The gradual evolution of the Web has seen a migration from institutional and corporate owned websites toward user generated content, social networking and open architectures which are commonly referred to as Web 2.0 (O'Reilly, 2005). Web 1.0 was characterized by websites that users could read from but not write to. Content was unchangeable, was unidirectional from the writer for the reader, and there was little room for interaction between the two. Web 1.0 sites were essentially similar in functionality to text books. Web 2.0 sites are different. They provide interactive tools such as wikis, blogs and social networking sites that afford users with the capability to create their own content and share it with a potentially global audience. Writers can now act as their own publishers, and musicians can play their music to worldwide audiences through the web. Such tools also present the teacher with opportunities to encourage greater student participation and deeper engagement in learning. There are many published accounts of students using social web tools to create and maintain their own course related content, invite comments and feedback, and update as required. Content can be tagged so that it is easily discovered, and RSS feeds alert users to any changes that are made in real time (Wheeler et al., 2008).

THE NEW DIGITAL LITERACIES

Users require an entirely new set of digital literacies to be able to effectively exploit the potential of Web 2.0 tools. The new literacies are also necessary for users to protect themselves, their resources and their reputations online. These include media literacy, or the ability to choose appropriate tools to communicate, share and create content, and information literacy, the skills related to interpretation, filtering and discernment of good or poor content found on the Web. There is also a keener awareness of the complexities of ownership, amidst a period of uncertainty when traditional legalities from the pre-digital age such as copyright laws are being eroded and supplanted by new digital age ethics of resource sharing, reasonable use and fair attribution such as Creative Commons and 'copyleft'.

There can be both positive and negative outcomes where new technologies are used in higher education. The problems usually stem from misuse or abuse of technologies. Students may become distracted by the use of laptops or other online technologies within the lecture room. Students may also visit inappropriate websites or disseminate materials that are objectionable. However, such behavior is thankfully rare, as most students are on campus to learn and gain good qualifications. Teacher responses to such errant behavior when it is detected should be measured according to the extent of the misdemeanour.

Far more widespread, and in some ways more problematic, is the gulf that grows ever wider between teacher expectations of student behavior, and the actual student behavior that emerges as a result of the prolonged and habitual use of new technologies. For example, some younger people tend to spend a great deal of time playing games online, and as a result, focus of concentration becomes piqued. The result in the lecture room is that such students become bored or distracted, and tend to disengage with learning. There is a view that the digital generation is characterized by short attention spans and an ability to multitask (Veen and Vrakking, 2006) due to their immersion within rich media environments (Prensky, 2005). Some also claim that due to continual use of digital media for recreation purposes, young people are ready to use the same technologies for formal learning purposes. However, this may be an oversimplification of an entire generation of learners who may not necessarily be as homogenized a generation of digital natives as is claimed (Bennett et al., 2008). Bullen (2010) for example argues that not all younger generation learners are as skilled as we think in the use of digital media. Not all are as goal oriented or as ready to apply familiar technologies to learning as has been claimed by Prensky and others.

REASONS TEACHERS FAIL TO ADOPT NEW TECHNOLOGIES

A spectrum of responses can be observed when new technologies are encountered for the first time. Teachers are working in a predominantly conservative environment where traditional values are espoused and where synchronization of behavior and disciplined approaches to the acquisition of knowledge are prized. There are many responses to change, whatever form it takes, but at the basest psychological level, any perception of threat can be translated into one of two responses – fight or flight.

Technophobia

Many academic staff respond enthusiastically, but at the far end of the spectrum there are those lecturers who react with anxiety or even fear. Such responses are psychological, says Brosnan (1998) and a large proportion of the populace may experience some feelings of technophobia at some time. Some lecturers are anxious about using new technologies because they may have had bad experiences with technology in the past (Wheeler and Winter, 2005) or because they fear that the equipment may be damaged in some way, or important data lost (John and Wheeler, 2008). Females tend to report higher levels of anxiety than males to technology (Brosnan, 1998) but some studies suggest that age need not be a problem with older people sometimes holding more positive attitudes to computers than their younger colleagues (Dyck and Smither, 1994). Rather, it appears that adverse and negative reactions to computers are context based. Minor reactions to computer technology, such as becoming annoyed or expressing frustration by shouting at the screen, when something goes wrong can be barriers to the effective use of new technology (Wheeler and Winter, 2005).

Lack of Confidence

Many lecturers lack the confidence to use Web 2.0 technologies. Often this is due to lack of familiarity with the features and functions of the new tools, but more than likely, lecturers fail to use technologies effectively, or even at all, due to a lack of time available to learn how to maximize their use of a tool, or how to integrate it into their curriculum. Some academic staff believe that their students know more than they do about new technologies, particularly those that relate to mobile or handheld technologies, games and music. These may indeed be true in many cases, because young people tend to be immersed in a rich media world that older lecturers may not have the same opportunities to become involved with. When faced with change and a perception of threat, many lecturers revert back to the methods with which they themselves were taught (Rogers, 2007, p.219). This may be the result of self-doubt or a loss of confidence in one's own abilities, but often, teachers avoid risk because they simply find it psychologically more comfortable. The bewildering variety of Web 2.0 tools found on the Internet may also confuse lecturers learning to further loss of confidence.

Time Constraints

Hard pressed university lecturers tend to spend most of their time on the preparation of teaching sessions, the creation of resources, teaching and marking and there is very little time available for learning new methods or tools. If a new technology or tool is irrelevant or useless in their work, teachers will reject it (Wheeler and Winter, 2005). The extent of usefulness of a new tool can only be demonstrated through trial within an authentic context, so realistically, teachers need to be given time to try out new tools before they accept their relevance and usefulness. Many university staff will claim that their time is fully taken up with day-to-day running of their programmes, and that little or no time is left for them to experiment with new technologies.

Yet such time is often taken up with other mundane activities such as creating and photocopying paper handouts for students, or writing copious notes on a display board, or the creation of other learning resources and display materials for use within lectures and seminars. Just about any of these tasks could be digitized so that paper and other artifacts are eliminated from teaching sessions altogether. Some Web 2.0 tools can be used to maximize time or even save it if applied appropriately. Delicious for example, can be used to store and tag all web resource bookmarks in one place so they are more easily retrievable. Slideshare is useful to store all slideshows so that students can access them at any time and leave questions or feedback. Using these tools, staff would then discover that there was actually time available for them to test out new technology. However, this is a tautology, because lecturers first need to be released from the mundane, in order to learn to use the new technologies which will ultimately ameliorate the mundane tasks.

Failure to See a Need

Some lecturing staff fail to see a need for new technologies, particularly Web 2.0 tools that have strange names. Some of the more seasoned professionals in a department may prefer to continue using the tried and tested methods they have always used. There is substance to this argument of course, as such teachers are generally very skilled and practiced in their chosen methods, and often have a proven track record of success. How does one encourage such experienced teaching staff to adopt and try new technologies within their professional practice? How does one convince them that there may be new dimensions to add to their teaching through the use of interactive technologies on the web?

One of the key arguments focuses on the needs and expectations of the learner: Opposing or restricting the introduction of new technologies into teaching can deny students access to new and rich experiences of learning which older technologies or methods may not be able to deliver. Teachers should therefore balance their own need to maintain their professional autonomy and status quo against the need to bring fresh impetus to the classroom, thereby inspiring young people to fall in love with learning.

Most teachers understand the need for more collaborative and interactive learning methods to be employed within the traditional learning environment so that dynamic, collaborative and active learning takes place. WEL can bring such outcomes to fruition through the appropriate application of new technologies, and as learning is more about making connections than storing facts and information (Rogers, 2007, p.38), many university lecturers can be persuaded that new approaches need new tools and technologies. We also need to consider the issue of professional practice and standards. If academics see no need to question their own practice or professionally update, they may reject new technology without even considering its relevance or usefulness (Preston et al., 2002). If however, they see the need to adapt their methods and adopt new technologies, they will discover that a whole new vista of opportunities will open up for them, and their students.

Loss of Ownership

People in organizations such as universities often work in teams, but they still operate as individuals. They may work concertedly toward a group oriented goal, but their perception and personal experience is that they toil individually, and invest their personal energies and thoughts into achieving that goal with their colleagues alongside them. Academics and professionals who believe that decisions are being made for them without any dialogue or that they are losing personal autonomy tend to resent those who impose those decisions, and sometimes resist. Consultation is often long and tedious, but managers will discover that the time and effort spent talking to teaching staff will ultimately be worth it, when all sides come to a mutual understanding of a joint set of goals.

Concerns over E-Safety

In schools, teacher must concern themselves about issues of safety and child protection. Understandably, many schools adopt a policy of restricted or heavily supervised access to children's free internet browsing. Filtering systems and site blacklisting are some of the countermeasures taken to ensure greater e-safety, but these are not always successful. In the adult education world of the university, many of the above issues are less problematic. However, e-safety is still a concern even in the university learning environment. Students and staff should be aware of a number of dangers of Internet use. In WEL students browse a multitude of websites, some of which may be unsafe.

Issues of cyberbullying occasionally rear their head in the popular press. Bullying through Web 2.0 services such as social networking services is on the increase, and such nefarious activities are not confined to school. Adults including university teachers and students may also fall victim. The posting of disparaging videos of lecturers on Youtube, or the creation of a Facebook site ridiculing a member of staff, may result in a lot of personal distress, loss of confidence and embarrassment. The reputation of the institution concerned may also suffer. Moreover, the content may remain 'out there' on the web, even though it may have been removed. The insidious aspect of cyberbullying is quite clear. Traditional bullying may take the form of an event or incident such as tripping someone deliberately in the corridor. With the advent of small video cameras and video sharing services, such incidents can be recorded, shared and perpetuated indefinitely on the Internet, causing the victim long term grief.

With the increase of WEL type activities a number of concerns around viruses and other malware attacks have recently emerged. Data loss, corruption of files, and damage to software and hardware, invasion of privacy and theft of personal data are all potential threats from malware infections. Further, spyware and hacking attacks are becoming more frequent as a result of students and staff freely surfing the Internet without adequate firewall and anti-virus software. It is difficult to police the personal technology students bring with them onto a university campus. Students are now able to use their own personal laptops, netbooks or handheld devices such as iPod Touches and mobile phones to access a university network. It is also easy for viruses to be spread from one computer to others through regularly used devices such as USB memory sticks. Many university lecturers are concerned about such issues of safety and tend to err on the side of caution when confronted with connected, networked systems. This in turn may lead to a rejection or over-cautious use which fails to capitalize on the full potential of web based tools and services.

Concern over Professional Standards

One criticism levelled at WEL based approaches such as technology mediated distance education, is that they are impersonal, and reduce tutor roles to those of supporter or facilitator. Some academics are concerned about the peripheralisation of the tutor role they perceive is brought about by the implementation of new technologies. Some have also suggested that in attempting to develop autonomous learners, universities open themselves up to criticism over what is perceived as a reduction in the delivery of content (Jarvis, 2007, p.227) leading to allegations of negligence. Conversely, there is also the problem that some students who learn through WEL approaches may demand more online time with their tutors to supplement a lack of face-to-face contact. Such demands are often quantitatively greater than the time demands imposed upon tutors in traditional learning delivery. Teachers who are already overburdened may not welcome such intrusions into their personal time or extended working hours with no tangible reward. Commentators such as Keen (2007) even go as far as to suggest that user generated content such as that found on Wikipedia tends to undermine the authority of subject experts, because now anyone can contribute toward the popular knowledge repositories. Others are more optimistic, arguing that the quality of such content can be assured, because there are enough contributing experts to ensure that errors and inaccuracies are quickly eradicated on these sites (Tapscott, 2008).

STRATEGIES FOR IMPLEMENTING SUCCESSFUL CHANGE

In his seminal exposition of innovation diffusion, Everett Rogers reflected on his experience introducing new ideas into conservative cultures. He recommended that in any context, opinion leaders should be drafted early into the process of change management (Rogers, 1962). Opinion leaders are those individuals who are generally highly regarded by their colleagues and have attained a high level of proficiency within their chosen profession. Such opinion leaders - if they are able to demonstrate best practice to their colleagues in new methods, the use of new tools and innovative approaches to practice - can often win their colleagues over.

Opinion leaders are often innovators in their field. They are good at convincing their peers to become early adopters of new ideas if enough evidence is shown for effectiveness. Such best practice modeling can also be introduced into training sessions to encourage new users to ask questions, visualize themselves using the tools and begin to acquire the necessary skills and confidence to use those new tools effectively. Any leader who wishes to seed innovation into an institution should therefore see the importance of identifying the opinion leaders – those innovators or 'technology champions' who are influential within the institution – and enlisting their support.

CHANGE MANAGEMENT

In an ideal world, change management should be conducted sensitively and with people in mind, but unfortunately this is not always the manner through which change is implemented. Where new technologies are introduced into traditional classroom settings, change is usually driven as an autocratic process, and from top-down management agenda. The success or failure of any change initiative will be typically dependent upon several key factors, but perhaps the two most vital components for success are good leadership and intelligent management of change. Change, when managed effectively, can overcome inertia and create a new impetus for institutions to move forwards, enabling its employees to achieve where previously they may have failed. Conversely, when change is managed poorly, results can be disastrous. Individuals within the institution suffer, reputations will fall, and in the case of education, students will fail. Good education leaders are acutely aware of these issues and will do all they can to avoid them.

One of the key reasons for the failure of change is that the end users – in this case the teachers – feel that they have no ownership of the process. Consultation is thus a vital feature of change management. Rosabeth Moss Kanter once said: *"It is a myth that people resist change. People resist what other people make them do, not what they themselves choose to do. That is why companies that innovate successfully year after year seek their people's ideas, let them initiate new projects and encourage more experiments"*. It is imperative that when change is required, managers and education leaders consult with their staff, even if it to merely ascertain the groundswell of opinion amongst colleagues. Consultation at any level is better than none, and teachers feel that at least they have had the opportunity to voice their views. Better still, if teaching staff are asked to come up with their own strategies to promote the change, and the ideas are good, managers would be wise to adopt these ideas if appropriate, to simultaneously achieve their goals and hand the ownership of the initiative to the staff. There are several other strategies education leaders can adopt to ensure innovation takes root.

Modeling Best Practice

Modeling of best practice by respected colleagues and opinion leaders can create a positive climate of change management where everyone becomes involved in the adoption of an innovation and all work together to achieve best results and best practice with the new tools. Consultation between those who wield the power to make the decisions and those who wield the tools to educate sounds a reasonable and logical proposition. However, due to a number of factors, including lack of time; management styles; poor communication across large institutions; and psychological factors such as mistrust, consultation does not always take place, and new technologies can be imposed upon teachers.

Staff Training

Training is also a vital part of the process of change management, for without it, academics and professionals would be left to their own intuition and creativity to find ways to use new tools. For many, the extra effort required for learning how to use new tools properly is deemed to be too much, and many simply give up or worse, actively resist and subvert the new technologies. Training should be specifically devised to meet the needs of the end user – a training needs analysis can be conducted to identify weaknesses or skill deficits. Training sessions will need to be built into the fabric of the working day if managers wish to avoid generating a resentful or absent work force. Authentic and situated training should be offered, providing realistic and relevant scenarios within which teachers can practice with new technology.

CONCLUSION

If there is one sure thing in higher education it is that change will always be with us. The manner in which that change is implemented varies across and within institutions. Some change promotion is successful due to visionary leadership, constructive consultation with staff, the modeling of best practice, and the provision of good and appropriate training and familiarization programmes. There will always be those in any organization who will oppose change no matter how it is presented. However, the majority of staff in any given institution are usually willing to work together to achieve change when they perceive it is necessary, and believe they have some ownership over the processes. Change should be managed sensitively, taking the working practices and cultures of the institution into consideration, and providing staff with time to adapt, practice new skills and evaluate their professional practice in the light of the changes.

REFERENCES

Collis, B., and Moonen, J. (2002). *Flexible Learning in a Digital World: Experiences and expectations.* Kogan Page: London.

Bennett, S., Maton, K., and Kervin, L. (2008). "The 'digital natives' debate: A critical review of the evidence. *British Journal of Educational Technology*, 39, 775-786.

Brosnan, M. J. (1998). *Technophobia: The psychological impact of information technology.* Routledge: London.

Bullen, M. (2010). *Net Gen Skeptic.*

http://www.netgenskeptic.com/ (Retrieved 15 March, 2010)

Dyck, J., and Smither, J. (1994). Age differences in computer anxiety: The role of computer experience, gender and education. *Journal of Educational Computing Research, 10*, 239-248.

Jarvis, P. (2007). *Adult Education and Lifelong Learning: Theory and Practice (3rd Edition).* London: Routledge.

John, P. D., and Wheeler, S. (2008). *The Digital Classroom: Harnessing Technology for the Future.* Routledge: London.

Keen, A. (2007). *The Cult of the Amateur: How today's Internet is killing our culture and assaulting our economy.* London: Nicholas Brealey.

O'Reilly, T. (2005). *What is Web 2.0?*

http://oreilly.com/web2/archive/what-is-web-20.html (Retrieved 20 January, 2010).

Prensky, M. (2005). Listen to the Natives. *Learning in the Digital Age*, 63, 8-13.

Preston, C., Cox, M. J., and Cox, K. M. (2002). *Teachers as innovators: An evaluation of teachers' motivation in the use of ICT.* A Report funded by the Teacher Training Agency, Oracle and Compaq, published by MirandaNet in collaboration with the Institute of Education, University of London.

www.mirandanet.ac.uk/pubs/tes_art.htm (Retrieved 12 January, 2010).

Rogers, A. (2007). *Teaching Adults (3rd Edition).* Maidenhead: Open University Press.

Rogers, E. (1962). *Diffusion of Innovations.* Glencoe: Free Press.

Rogers, J. (2007). *Adults Learning (5th Edition).* Maidenhead: Open University Press.

Tapscott, D. (2008). *Growing Up Digital*. New York: McGraw Hill

Veen, W., and Vrakking, B. (2006). *Homo Zappiens: Growing up in a digital age*. London: Network Continuum.

Wheeler, S., and Winter, A. (2005). Winning Hearts and Minds, in S. Wheeler (Ed.), *Transforming Primary ICT*. Exeter: Learning Matters.

Wheeler, S., Yeomans, P., and Wheeler, D. (2008). The Good, the Bad and the Wiki: Evaluating Student Generated Content as a Collaborative Learning Tool. *British Journal of Educational Technology, 39*, 987-995.

In: Faculty Training for Web Enhanced Learning   ISBN: 978-1-61209-335-2
Editors: Manuela Repetto and Guglielmo Trentin   © 2011 Nova Science Publishers, Inc.

Chapter 5

PROMOTING WEB-ENHANCED LEARNING IN UNIVERSITY TEACHING: CURRENT PRACTICE IN WEB-ENHANCED FACULTY DEVELOPMENT

Gail Wilson
Southern Cross University, Australia

ABSTRACT

Encouraging faculty's adoption of and innovation in teaching and learning with technologies continues to be a critical challenge for those responsible for faculty development in today's higher education institutions. This chapter examines current practice in Web-enhanced faculty development to promote Web-enhanced learning in university teaching. It begins by locating faculty development within the context of workplace learning and professional learning. Faculty development is seen as a continuum of formal and informal learning experiences offering a range of options. Critical questions are offered to assist the planning and implementation of faculty development to address the need for new learning models and pedagogy for the 21st century, followed by an overview of learning perspectives which dominate the design of faculty development to support adoption and widespread use of new technologies. Specific frameworks used to design faculty development to support Web-enhanced learning are explained and illustrated–technology adoption, skills acquisition, scholarly engagement, and the use of resources to support faculty learning. This chapter concludes with a summary of implications for faculty development practice.

INTRODUCTION

Faculty development is the provision of opportunities for faculty in higher education to engage in continuous improvement in relation to their role as teachers. This chapter examines faculty development conducted in the context of the university workplace aimed at facilitating faculty's understanding of and further competency in the application of technologies in Web-enhanced learning. The term faculty development is used synonymously with other terms in the literature such as academic development, educational development, continuing professional development, and staff development. Faculty development is cast as situated, workplace learning (Billett, 1999; Nicholls, 2001), defined as "learning from work, and learning through work" (Garavan et al., 2002, p. 61). Faculty development as workplace learning may be seen as a continuum combining a host of activities ranging at one end from informal learning, or the learning at work that is part of everyday actions of staff (Billet, 1999), to formally structured development activities at the other. It is a process by which faculty are afforded the opportunity to challenge their current academic practice and acquire, practice and adopt new knowledge (Anderson and Kanuka, 1997; Taylor, 1997). Faculty development also fosters knowledge development, a continuous process resulting from a problem-solving, collaborative, and guided approach to learning that includes the use of staff with relevant expertise aimed at maximizing the transfer of knowledge amongst peers. Knowledge development, in turn, supports the growth of organizational learning by leveraging the knowledge assets of the organization at the individual, work group and organizational levels for the benefit of the learner, with the aim of improving organizational performance overall (Boud and Garrick, 1999).

A wide range of professional learning options or "workplace affordances" (Billett, 2004, p.121) are available to faculty across this continuum - staff exchanges or temporary transfers; professional networking; peer support; formalized institutional-wide programs targeting individuals or groups of staff, sometimes with formal mentoring support; action learning projects undertaken by disciplinary or cross-disciplinary teams; and formal institutional programs of study such as diplomas, postgraduate certificates and masters degrees. Billet (2004) argues that the level of quality of these learning experiences and links to improvements in workplace performance are determined by the types of learning experiences made available to faculty, the design of those learning experiences and the support and guidance provided to faculty as learners.

This chapter concentrates on faculty development adopting Web-enhanced learning approaches to support the acquisition and expansion of knowledge and competencies in faculty's use of technologies. "Web-enhanced" is a position along a continuum of the use of the Web in faculty development which includes events which blend face-to-face and online components through to workshops, webinars (synchronous and asynchronous) and formal courses which may be offered fully online. It also includes the use of the Web to support faculty's learning about technology by providing a range of digital resources in the form of information and technology tools. This chapter begins with a review of the critical challenges facing faculty development in relation to technologies and offers advice concerning the planning and design of faculty development, followed by an exploration of learning perspectives that dominate current faculty development practice. Frameworks influencing the design of faculty development are explored with illustrated with examples of Web-enhanced faculty development in practice. This chapter concludes by drawing implications for professional practice for those responsible for faculty development within the institution.

CRITICAL CHALLENGES

As we begin the second decade of the 21st century, faculty development in relation to technologies continues to present considerable challenges to institutions and to those charged with the responsibility for planning and implementing faculty development within them. UK researchers have called for a re-thinking of pedagogy for the digital age (Beetham and Sharpe, 2007, p.3). The Horizon Report (2009, p. 6) listed the need for institutions to "adopt new learning models engaging to the younger generations" as one of the critical challenges facing universities. A recent Educause article (Diaz et al., 2009, p. 48) noted that "encouraging faculty adoption and innovation in teaching and learning with IT" persists as one of the most important challenges in teaching and learning. Despite the advances in the uses of technology in higher education in the last five years, the need for support for faculty continues in new areas–maintaining currency with rapidly changing technologies, enhancing the integration of technologies to enrich the student learning experience, and using the advantages of new technologies to broaden the ways in which student learning can be assessed. These new technologies are commonly referred to as Web 2.0 and include wikis, blogs, social networking and social bookmarking sites.

Web 2.0 applications provide the basis for what Australian researchers McLoughlin and Lee (2008) call "Pedagogy 2.0"–or the three principles (3 Ps) of participation, personalization and productivity–each of which capitalizes on the affordances of these and other Web 2.0 tools. The authors elaborate on each principle at length (McLoughlin and Less, 2008, pp.17-18). Participation emphasizes a decreased emphasis on prescribed curricula and a stronger focus on learning partnerships. These partnerships go beyond the teacher-student context as learners socialize and collaborate globally with experts, communities and peer groups. Personalization of learning is afforded through Web 2.0 and social software tools by offering learners more choice of resources, websites and tools to use, and expanding the forms of communication media available to them. Learners' productivity is enhanced through learner-generated content in e-portfolios, discussion forums and blogs, and learners are now more able to collect and share information and ideas with others from websites and online journals, magazines and news articles. Each principles is a lens through which faculty can re-examine course curriculum, content, communication, learning processes, learning tasks, learning scaffolds, and resources (McLoughlin and Lee, 2008, p.15).

A significant hurdle facing the widespread take-up of these three principles is that which faced the introduction of learning management systems in an earlier time–the provision of opportunities for faculty to experience the range and potential of these new tools and their demonstrable delivery of improved student learning outcomes. In examining how teaching and learning centers in North America have addressed the "tensions" of providing support for faculty in a constantly changing technological environment, Canadian researchers Thompson and Kanuka (2009, p. 159) concluded that "more substantive and strategic approaches are needed if an institution wants to move beyond pockets of innovation to more wide-spread organizational adoption". Some key questions shown in Table 1 can assist those who plan and design faculty development to respond to this newer set of challenges (Diaz et al., 2009; Wilson, 2006; Wilson, 2009).

Table 1: Key questions for faculty development planning and design

Issue	Question
Overall planning and design considerations	What is the local context in which faculty work? What level of support exists at the department/faculty level for staff to engage in extended learning opportunities such as team-based/project-based learning?
	What learning theories and frameworks will shape faculty development? What implications does adoption of a particular learning approach have on the design of programs, including duration?
	Are the goals of faculty development aligned with broader institutional goals related to student retention and access?
	What realistic measures of impact of the program can be used?
	Has there been input from academic units into the design of the overall program?
	Does the faculty development program provide flexibility in terms of its scheduling? Are different delivery modes offered?
	How will facilitators model the use of new technologies and their integration with teaching and learning methods?
	What institutional workload policies and/or reward systems are in place to support faculty as they engage with faculty development for Web-enhanced learning? What effect, if any, do they have on the design of faculty development?
	How is access to independent study by faculty and/or self-paced support facilitated after a program is completed? Are Web-based resources provided? If so, what criteria are important for choosing these resources?
Design of learning experiences	Are opportunities provided for faculty to consider their beliefs about teaching and learning and articulate their current teaching practices?
	Are opportunities provided for faculty to learn about the affordances of new technologies? Have different levels of use and experience amongst faculty been taken into account?
	What types of tasks are best suited to facilitate exploration by faculty of their new understandings about technologies with respect to their teaching practice and their role as a teacher?
	Are faculty provided with sufficient time to trial new teaching and learning methods using new technologies?
	Are faculty encouraged to share their new knowledge and skills with others and to learn from each other?
Institutional support for the program	What policies exist currently that support scholarly engagement within the institution about learning and teaching with technologies?
	How is proven innovation rewarded in the institution? Are there particular strategies for dissemination of successful technology innovations within the institution?
	How does the institutional culture help or hinder institutional support for teaching and learning with technologies?
	What is the role of the institution's teaching and learning centre in dissemination of technology-supported teaching innovation?

LEARNING PERSPECTIVES DOMINATING FACULTY DEVELOPMENT PRACTICE

Cognitive Learning Theory

Current approaches to faculty development practice for Web-enhanced learning such as reflective practice, action learning, and learning through learning communities or communities of practice draw on dominant learning perspectives. Cognitive learning theory arising from cognitive psychology and studies by German gestalt psychologists (Foley, 2000) underpins *experiential learning* theory, defined by Kolb (1983, p.38) as "the process whereby knowledge is created through the transformation of experience." Learning is more effective if it is based on the learner's own experience. Linked to experiential learning theory are two concepts found in current faculty development practice: *reflective practice* and *action learning*. Reflective practice is a process that allows individuals to reflect on their experiences as they engage in learning activities. Reflection was an important process in Kolb's experiential learning cycle, which was based on the work of Lewin (1948). Schön (1987) introduced the concept of the reflective practitioner, and distinguished between reflection-in-action and reflection-on-action. In the former, professionals draw *intuitively* on their practical experiences to deal with current complex situations. In contrast, reflection-on-action follows the action, and aims to probe the tacit or assumed knowledge professionals used (Roberts, 2002).

Advocates of reflective practice in faculty development contexts promote it as a way for teachers to advance their understanding of new practices (Donnelly and O'Farrell, 2006) and produce more effective practitioners in the application and use of ICT. Some use reflective practice as a meta-process embedded into online professional development workshops for teachers, where they can reflect on the possibilities of online learning and their use of new technology tools they progress through the workshop (Clegg, Konrad and Tan, 2000). Refection also underpins story-telling when teachers talk about their teaching (McDrury and Alterio, 2002), and is a common feature of exemplars or case studies of good teaching and learning practices in blended and online learning environments published on university websites.

A second concept widespread in current faculty development practice linked to experiential learning theory is action learning, a process whereby participants in small teams or groups engage in a cyclical process of planning, acting, observing, and reflecting, aiming to solve a particular real-life problem or task while learning from each other. This model has been used successfully for development of new teaching and learning approaches for the online environment within a single discipline group (Ellis and Phelps, 2000), or as a framework for a wider, institutional approach to changing staff attitudes towards the new technologies (Chism, 2004).

Constructivist Learning Theory

Constructivist learning theory encompassing cognitive learning theory dominates the literature associated with designing online learning environments and informs the design of many faculty development programs. Constructivists view learning as a continual process of constructing, interpreting and modifying representations of reality, based on experience. Four fundamental tenets of constructivism extrapolated from the literature can be defined as follows (Candy, 1991; Fosnot, 1989; Tam, 2000):

- Learners construct their own meaning and interpretations of teaching.
- Learning is an active process achieved through interaction with others, by testing ideas, perceptions and knowledge against those of others, posing questions, researching answers, in order for new constructions to be developed.
- Learners use their knowledge to solve problems that are meaningful and realistically complex. Problem solving occurs in learning environments that provide alternative ways to learners of viewing events and ideas, without being trapped by their own constructions.

- Teaching is a process of negotiating meaning with learners through dialogue with them, rather than solely the transmitting of content.

A distinction is made in the literature between *cognitive* constructivists and *social* constructivists. The former draw upon the work of Piaget (1954) and focus on individual constructions of knowledge discovered while interacting with the environment, while the latter draw on the work of Vygotsky (1978) and view learning as "connection with and appropriated from the socio-cultural context within which individuals are all immersed" (Bonk and Cunningham, 1998, p.32). Social constructivism underpins the use of collaborative and group learning using technologies. Cognitive constructivists and social constructivists share common ground in their emphasis on *active, generative learning* and the *role of the teacher as facilitator and guide* in the learning process.

Situated Learning Theory

Situated learning or situated cognition which can be attributed to the work of a number of researchers (Brown et al., 1989; Lave and Wenger, 1991; Scribner, 1985; Suchman, 1987) is another dominant learning theory influencing current faculty development practice. In this perspective learning and knowing are situated in physical and social contexts, are social in nature, and are distributed across individuals, other persons and the tools that they use (Putnam and Borko, 2000, p. 5). Learning activities also need to be authentic and conducted in a context that reflects the way the new knowledge acquired by the learner will be used. They should also provide opportunities for learners to access expert performances by those who are accomplished in the activities and who can model the desired processes. They must also provide multiple roles and perspectives for the learner and be designed to support the collaborative construction of knowledge by learners, supported by coaching and scaffolding at critical times (Herrington and Herrington, 2006). A series of seven strategies drawing on situated learning theory found useful by the author for devising authentic learning environments in Web-enhanced and online faculty development is provided by McLoughlin and Luca (2006, pp. 208-209).

Distributed Cognition

Distributed cognition sees learning as a distributed, or "going beyond the boundaries of an individual to include the (surrounding) environment" (Keller, Bonk and Hew, 2005, p. 337). Distributed cognition includes both a material dimension (use of artifacts) and a social dimension (involvement of other people) situated within a specific context and meaningful only in context (Keller, Bonk and Hew, 2005, p. 338). Learning communities, communities of practice, and discourse communities popular in the faculty development literature are based primarily on processes associated with distributed cognition. Learning communities can be face-to-face or virtual, where asynchronous discussion facilities and email (materials) enhance opportunities for interaction with greater numbers of staff (social) who can be geographically dispersed across and between institutions. Usually these communities develop as a result of shared interests and practices amongst teachers as they work on particular projects, and talk about their teaching and learning practices in relation to the use of technologies in their teaching. As individuals contribute particular knowledge and pedagogical expertise to these discussions, the collective wisdom of the community is advanced (Putnam and Borko, 2000).

Distributed Expertise

The situated perspective on learning, in particular the notion of *distributed expertise,* is also evident in the provision for use by faculty of digital resources featuring innovative uses of technologies in teaching. Representations of knowledge in this form are recognized in the literature to be potentially useful to faculty to help them change their current practices (Sharpe, Beetham and Ravenscroft, 2005). These authors point out that often such knowledge has been difficult to access, and that some ways of representing this knowledge may be more effective than others. Included as part of a wide-ranging list of types of representations of practice are stories, narratives, profiles and case studies accompanied by audio and/or video files that provide opportunities for faculty to see and hear others talk about and demonstrate their innovative uses of technology tools. Recent research (Sharpe and Oliver, 2007, p. 120) about the relationship of digital resource-based learning approaches such as the use of exemplars or case studies located on a website to the professional learning experiences of faculty stressed the importance of concentrating on the design of resources that can best facilitate the mediating of teachers' practices, or "moving from *representations to interventions*". A small study involving the author and her colleagues (Wilson, Thomson and Malfroy, 2006; Thomson and Wilson, 2007) based on the use and evaluation of digital resources for professional development of faculty in the area of assessment indicated that the biggest challenge was how to integrate and contextualize these resources with individual faculty member's everyday teaching practices. Possible solutions to this challenge lie in designing the resources to be more interactive, allowing staff to use and reuse them in different ways; or providing opportunities for staff to develop their own resources which they can share with their peers, debate, discuss and interact with in social contexts.

FRAMEWORKS FOR FACULTY DEVELOPMENT FOR WEB-ENHANCED LEARNING

The literature provides evidence of a diversity of frameworks supporting the design of faculty development focused on the adoption and embedding of Web-enhanced learning. These include technology adoption, skills acquisition (expertise), scholarly engagement, and resource-based learning frameworks (Wilson, 2006; Wilson, 2007). Faculty development drawing on one or several of these frameworks can be delivered either in Web-enhanced or fully online modes.

Technology-Adoption

In technology adoption frameworks for faculty development, Rogers's (2003) five attributes of an innovation - relative advantage, compatibility, complexity, trialability, and observability - have been a popular design framework for faculty development aimed at encouraging faculty members to take up Web-enhanced learning (Wilson, 2007). Use of the Rogers's attributes of an innovation in promoting adoption of an innovation is challenged by other technology adoption frameworks. An Integrated Technology Adoption and Diffusion Model (Sherry, Billig, Tavalin and Gibson, 2000) based on research with teachers in K-12 contexts matches professional development strategies to a staged process of technology adoption, in which teachers move from being learners to adopters of educational technology (Stages 1 and 2), to co-learners with their students (Stage 3), to a reaffirmation/rejection decision (Stage 4), and to Stage 5, where, as experienced teachers they are working with others to promote the innovation and assist others. At one Australian university (Benson and Palaskas, 2006) the RIPPLES model (Resources, Infrastructure, People, Policies, Learning, Evaluation and Support) (Surry, Ensminger and Haab, 2005) was employed to understand more clearly the factors that influenced the adoption and implementation of WebCT Vista™ across the institution. Influenced by Rogers (2003), Ely (1999), and Stockdill and Morehouse (1992) among others, this model focuses on integration of ICT into an institution. Similar to Rogers's emphasis on the attributes of an innovation to influence adoption of ICT, the RIPPLES model focuses the need for attention to the needs, hopes, values, skills and experiences of teachers. However, it differs from Rogers's approach in its highlighting of the links between the other components of the model that also impact on the provision of professional development of staff. This broader and at the same time more complex focus holds promise as a strategy to achieve embedding of a technology innovation.

Skills Acquisition (Expertise)

Institutions have framed their professional development for Web-enhanced learning using a skills acquisition model built on the work of Dreyfus and Dreyfus (1986) designed according to levels or stages moving from "novice" through to "expert". This framework is useful in focusing on skills in using particular technologies; in constructing a pedagogy focused on teaching and learning in the online environment, particularly in relation to design of learning activities that combine face-to-face and online features; in facilitating student learning; and in shifting the role of faculty from a didactic role to a more facilitative and collaborative role. In the higher education literature, the framework has become associated with effective course design for Web-enhanced and fully online learning environments because of its social and collaborative nature (Meredith and Newton, 2004), and its emphasis on learning about technology by learning with or through technology (Fitzgibbon and Jones, 2004; Forsyth, 2002; Hallas, 2005). A popular example of an expertise model of faculty relevant to Web-enhanced learning is found in Salmon's (2004) online course for prospective online teachers, or e-moderators. Based on research conducted in the Open University in the UK, Salmon's model offers a staged, developmental process along a continuum of five stages, extending over a period of five weeks, supported by experienced facilitators at each stage.

In New Zealand, the Manakau Institute of Technology (Kelly, 2006) has drawn on the skills acquisition framework to develop an institutional-wide plan for executing faculty development. Three broad levels of expertise required to accommodate Web-enhanced learning through to fully online learning across the institution were incorporated into a matrix which also included the IT, faculty development and other infrastructure support necessary to embed the skills staff required at any or all of the three levels. Faculty development at Level 2 and above involved faculty interacting in the online environment as both students and as facilitators of learning. This whole-of-institution approach to skills acquisition was complemented by the introduction of a fully online postgraduate qualification for faculty in applied e-learning.

Scholarly Engagement

Faculty development as scholarly engagement is situated within the actual practice of the faculty member. In this chapter it encompasses peer review of Web-enhanced and online teaching, and peer learning through faculty learning communities. Peer review and learning in online communities are both examples of faculty learning together, a key notion in the scholarship of teaching and learning (SoTL) whose principles as enunciated by Boyer (1999) and extended by Shulman (2004b) emphasize the *communal basis* of scholarly activity.

Peer Review of Web-Enhanced and Online Teaching

In Australia peer review of online teaching has been funded by two separate grants from the Australian Learning and Teaching Council (ALTC) – *Embedding Peer Review of Learning and Teaching in E-Learning and Blended Learning Environments* which is a collaboration of five Australian universities and the *Peer Review of Online Teaching and Learning Project* which is developing an online peer review instrument and companion website that can be accessed by faculty to either facilitate initial development or redevelopment of courses as well as have current Web-enhanced or fully online courses evaluated against the same set of criteria. The peer review instrument itself centers on four key dimensions: instructional design, interface design, use of media, and technical aspects. Each dimension has a link to further information including key literature. Users can add, remove or modify criteria at any time. New technologies can be added, and there is allowance for customization. A project Wiki allows interested faculty to contribute to developing the instrument. Further information about these projects is available from the Australian Learning and Teaching Council's website at <http://www.altc.edu.au/>.

Faculty Learning Communities

Advocates of faculty learning communities (FLCs) see them as quality faculty development practice contributing to sustainable individual and organizational change over time and enabling innovative learning and teaching practices to be extended to large numbers of teaching staff (Cox, 2001; Ingram and Gilding, 2002; Lefoe and Albury, 2002). Faculty learning communities in the 1990s were mainly face-to-face but technology has enabled these communities to expand activities and reach beyond a single institution to an extended community, supplement or replace face-to-face meeting using synchronous and asynchronous communication tools and provide a suite of online resources. Sherer, Shea and Kristensen (2003) suggested an online FLC portal that includes community management tools, workspaces, best practices, faculty development opportunities, a Frequently Asked Questions (FAQ) page, and links to other related communities. An example of a portal FLC website developed by Milton Cox at Miami University in the United States explaining a FLC and associated resources relevant to establishing and maintaining one or several such communities is located at <http://www.units.muohio.edu/flc/index.php >. Recent research (Thompson and Kanuka, 2009, p. 157) into FLCs and the role teaching and learning centers play in their establishment and sustainability, stressed the importance of context, clear purpose and the need for an institutional champion. They also emphasized the requirement for these communities to be embedded "within the values priorities, traditions, culture, and academic plan of the institution".

Communities of Design

A variation of the learning communities approach to faculty development called *communities of design* (Mishra, Koehler and Zhao, 2007) has also surfaced in the literature, where *community* is a team of faculty, technology, and educational design specialists working together and learning to solve an authentic pedagogical problem associated with the integration of technology into teaching. The framework underpinning communities of design is known as *technological pedagogical content knowledge* or TPCK (Ferdig, 2006; Mishra and Koehler, 2006; Mishra, Koehler and Zhao, 2007) which integrates three sources of teachers' knowledge: technology, pedagogy and content. The framers of this model have added knowledge about the technology and its use to Shulman's (2004a, p. 228) concept of *pedagogical content knowledge* (PCK) which identifies

> ...the distinctive bodies of knowledge for teaching...the blending of content and pedagogy into an understanding of how particular topics, problems, or issues are organized, represented, and adapted to the diverse interests and abilities of learners, and presented for instruction.

Community of Inquiry

Canadian researchers Garrison and Vaughan (2008) offer a variation on the learning communities model for faculty with limited time to engage in face-to-face faculty development – a blended "community of inquiry" (CoI) approach which models Web-enhanced or blended learning experiences by integrating face-to-face, Web-based and independent learning activities within a faculty development program. This model builds on the original CoI model (Garrison, Anderson and Archer, 2000) which represents a process of building and sustaining learning environments through the development of three interdependent elements – social presence, cognitive presence and teaching presence. The CoI model is well suited to guiding faculty through a course redesign process for Web-enhanced learning environments and these researchers argue that adopting CoI to frame the design of a faculty development program has the potential for a "transformational shift" (Garrison and Vaughan, 2008, p. 52) in faculty's approach to teaching by providing time for faculty to "re-examine and reflect on their course curriculum, teaching practice, and use of information and communication technologies" (p. 53).

Resources to Foster and Encourage Professional Learning

Resource-based learning frameworks support faculty development by providing a variety of Web-based resources to foster and support professional learning. In the context of this chapter the focus is on digital resources described by Hill and Hannafin (2001) as "media, people, places or ideas that have the potential to support learning...data points organized by an individual or individuals to convey a message" (p. 38). A single resource, such as a digitized text, a DVD/CD-ROM, a podcast or video clip, and a website is seen as a "collection of knowledge objects" (p. 41) to be used and re-used in different ways by different groups of learners. Digital resources can accommodate a wide range of faculty interests, experiences, learning styles, needs and ability levels. Resources to support faculty learning may be located either on an institution's teaching and learning center website and made open to the public, or within an institution's resources repository accessible only to faculty working within the institution.

Websites

Websites for faculty development can be resource-focused, offer a range of good practice features and/or provide online opportunities for formal study in the area of Web-enhanced and/or online learning The rationale for most of these websites is to create a "one-stop-shop" where staff can access information and resources relevant to the application of new technologies to teaching and learning. Workshops and courses provided in the online environment are generally framed by the need of the designers to immerse staff in the environment in which they will be teaching, and for staff to understand what it is like to learn in the online environment. The use of communication tools that enable discussion and collaboration amongst learners is seen as an opportune way for faculty to develop as communities of learners, focusing on their development as online teachers. Recent research (Maor and Volet, 2007) has indicated a need for continuing investigations into effective pedagogical approaches for online professional development that can deliver these desired outcomes.

Hundreds of examples of institutional websites supporting faculty in their adoption of Web-enhanced learning exist. An example from each of the US (Regent University), Australia (Deakin University) and the UK (The Higher Education Academy) is provided by way of illustration of different uses of websites to support faculty development.

Regent University Centre for Teaching and Learning (US)< Http://Www.Regent.Edu/ Admin/Ctl/>

In 2009 Regent University won the Sloan-C Award for Excellence in Faculty Development for Online Teaching. This university's teaching and learning center provides a single space facilitating easy access by faculty to a wide range of supports, including online faculty development. A Web-based video magazine brings faculty up to date with current and future offerings and provides demonstrations of updated software enhancements available to faculty. A blog space provides tips, tricks and online tutorials on a range of social software and tools available for Web-enhanced teaching. In addition, faculty can access "just-in-time" skills in the use of their institution's learning management system through a Quick Tutorials Library. A twice-monthly online newsletter eNews provides a vehicle for faculty to publish their teaching projects, as well as their best practices, viewpoints, and work related to technology enhancements for teaching and learning.

Deakin University's Contemporary Online Teaching Cases Site (Australia) <Http://Www.Deakin.Edu.Au/Itl/Teach-Learn/Cases/Index.Htm>

This site features a singular-focused approach to the use of Web for faculty development r through the work of over 70 faculty who have adopted and embedded technologies into their teaching. The cases are divided into a number of categories: approaches to learning and teaching; use of graduate attributes; study level; categories of Web use (either extended online or wholly online); particular online features; and use of various technology tools. The cases can be browsed by discipline, faculty, and individual case participant. Users can listen to the teacher's voice through links to audio files, and/or read the transcript of each case. Each case has links to other related cases from within the site. The site is an example of a strong link between the use of technologies and the wider policy framework that supports technology adoption by the university.

The Higher Education Academy (UK)<Http://Www.Heacademy.Ac.Uk/>

The Higher Education Academy is an independent organization funded by four UK higher education funding bodies in England, Scotland, Wales, and Northern Ireland, plus subscriptions from universities and special initiative grants. The publications page of this large public site provides up-to-date resources for faculty and faculty developers on technology enhanced learning. A full description of and links to all resources focused on enhancing learning and teaching through technology useful for both faculty and faculty developers is provided in the (2009) online report Enhancing learning through technology: A guide to resources provided by the Academy and the JISC collaboration network produced by the Academy in collaboration with the Joint Information Systems Committee (JISC) and its collaboration network.

CONCLUSION

This chapter has examined current practice in faculty development for promoting Web-enhanced learning in university teaching. Emphasis has been placed on workplace-based faculty development aimed at facilitating faculty's understanding of and further competency in the application of current technologies in Web-enhanced learning. Implications for faculty development practice and those responsible for faculty development within their institution drawn from this chapter include the following:

- Faculty continue to require support in order to maintain currency with rapidly changing technologies in teaching and learning and their implications for different pedagogical models to better engage students and support student learning. Calls for a "new pedagogy" for the 21st century are influenced by technologies which support the sharing and creation of new information amongst learners and the adoption of different roles for learners and their teachers from those that existed previously.

- In planning faculty development to address these challenges, give attention to key questions to guide the planning and designing of faculty development, and be cognizant of nature and level of institutional support that exists in the institution as part of the planning process.

- Current faculty development practice is influenced by a range of learning perspectives–among them distributed cognition and distributed expertise–to inform the use of faculty learning communities and the use of exemplars and case studies about good practice in Web-enhanced teaching and learning.

- Technology adoption, skills acquisition, scholarly engagement and resource-based learning are frameworks influencing current faculty development practice for Web-enhanced teaching and learning. Peer review of online teaching and the use of faculty learning communities both emphasize the communal basis of scholarly activity in relation to faculty development.

- Different types of websites can support faculty in their acquisition of skills and knowledge in relation to pedagogy for Web-enhanced learning and the use of a range of technology tools. This support may include online faculty development, "just-in-time" tips, examples of good practice across disciplines, and research supporting technologies-in-use.

REFERENCES

Anderson, T., and Kanuka, H. (1997). On-line forums: New platforms for professional development and group collaboration. *Journal of Computer Mediated Communication* 3(3). http://jcmc.indiana.edu/vol3/issue3/anderson.html.

Beetham, H., and Sharpe, E. (2007). *Rethinking pedagogy for a digital age. Designing and delivering e-learning*. London: Routledge.

Benson, R., and Palaskas, T. (2006). Introducing a new learning management system: An institutional case study. *Australasian Journal of Educational Technology, 22*(4), 548-567.

Billett, S. (1999). Guided learning at work. In D. Boud and J. Garrick (Eds.), *Understanding learning at work* (pp. 151-164). London: Routledge.

Billett, S. (2004). Learning through work. Workplace participatory practices. In H. Rainbird, A. Fuller, and A. Munro (Eds.), *Workplace learning in context* (pp. 109-125). London: Routledge.

Bonk, C., and Cunningham, D. (1998). Searching for learner-centered, constructivist, and sociocultural components of collaborative educational learning tools. In B. Bonk and K. King (Eds.), *Electronic collaborators: Learner-centred technologies for literacy, apprenticeship and discourse* (pp. 25-50). Mahwah, NJ: Lawrence Erlbaum Associates.

Boud, D., and Garrick, J. (1999). Understandings of workplace learning. In D. Boud and J. Garrick (Eds.), *Understanding learning at work* (pp. 1-11). London: Routledge.

Boyer, E. (1999). *Scholarship reconsidered. Priorities of the professoriate*. San Francisco: Jossey-Bass.

Brown, J. S., Collins, A., and Duguid, P. (1989). Situated cognition and the culture of learning. *Educational Researcher* (January-February), 32-42.

Candy, P. (1991). *Self-direction for lifelong learning*. San Francisco: Jossey-Bass.

Chism, N. (2004). Using a framework to engage faculty in instructional technologies. *Educause Quarterly, 27*(2), 39-45. http://net.educause.edu/ir/library/pdf/eqm0424.pdf

Clegg, S., Konrad, J., and Tan, J. (2000). Preparing academic staff to use ICTs in support of student learning. *The International Journal for Academic Development, 5*(2), 138-148.

Cox, M. (2001). Faculty learning communities: Change agents for transforming institutions into learning organizations. In D. Lieberman (Ed.), *To Improve the Academy*, Vol. 19 (pp. 69-92). Bolton, MA: Anker Publishing Company.

Diaz, V., Garrett, P., Kinley, E., Moore, J., Schwartz, C., and Kohrman, P. (2009). Faculty development for the 21st century. *Educause Review, 44*(3), 46-55. http://ww w.educause.edu/EDUCAUSE+Review/EDUCAUSEReviewMagazineVolume44/Faculty Developmentforthe21stCe/171776.

Dreyfus, H., and Dreyfus, S. (1986). *Mind over machine*. New York: The Free Press.

Donnelly, R., and O'Farrell, C. (2006). Constructivist elearning for staff engaged in continuous professional development. In J. O'Donogue (Ed.), *Technology supported learning and teaching. A staff perspective* (pp. 146-159). Hershey, PA: Information Science Publishing.

Ellis, A., and Phelps, R. (2000). Staff development for online delivery: A collaborative, team based action learning model. *Australian Journal of Educational Technology, l6*(1), 26-44. http://www.ascilite.org.au/ajet/ajet16/ellis.html.

Ely, D. (1999).Conditions that facilitate the implementation of educational technology innovations. *Educational Technology, 39*(6), 23-27.

Ferdig, R. (2006). Assessing technologies for teaching and learning: Understanding the importance of technological pedagogical content knowledge. *British Journal of Educational Technology, 37*(5), 749-760.

Fitzgibbon, K., and Jones, N. (2004). Jumping the hurdles: Challenges of staff development delivered in a blended learning environment. *Journal of Educational Media, 29*(1), 26-35.

Foley, G. (Ed.). (2000). *Understanding adult education and training* (2nd ed.). Sydney: Allen and Unwin.

Forsyth, R. (2002). Making professional development flexible: A case study. *Open Learning: The Journal of Open and Distance Learning*, 17(3), 251-258.

Fosnot, C. (1989). *Enquiring teachers enquiring learners*. New York: Teachers College Press.

Garavan, T., Morley, M., Gunnigle, P., and McGuire, D. (2002). Human resource development and workplace learning: Emerging theoretical perspectives and organisational practices. *Journal of European Industrial Training, 26*(3/4), 60-71.

Garrison, A., Anderson, T. , and Archer, W. (2000). Critical inquiry in a text-based environment: Computer conferencing in higher education. *The Internet and Higher Education, 2*(2-3), 87-105.

Garrison, R., and Vaughan, N. (2008). *Blended learning in higher education. Framework, principles, and guidelines*. San Francisco: Jossey-Bass.

Hallas, J. (2005). Getting started in flexible learning: Perceptions from an online professional development workshop. In A. Brew and C. Amar (Eds), *Higher Education in a Changing World. Research and Development in Higher Education (Vol 28). Proceedings of the 2005 Annual International Conference of the Higher Education Research and*

Development Society of Australasia (pp. 57-66), University of Sydney, Australia. Milperra, NSW: Higher Education Research and Development Society of Australasia.

Hill, J., and Hannafin, M. (2001). Teaching and learning in digital environments: The resurgence of resource-based learning. *Educational Technology Research and Development, 49*(3), 37-52.

Ingram, D., and Gilding, A. (2002). Centralised decentralised professional development models: Supporting the long term use of information and communication technology (ICT) in higher education. In G. Williamson, C. Gunn, A Young, and T. Clear, T. (Eds.), *Winds of Change in the Sea of Learning, Proceedings of the l9th Annual Conference of The Australasian Society for Computers in Learning in Tertiary Education (ASCILITE)* (pp. 299-308). Auckland, New Zealand: UNITEC Institute of Technology.

Johnson, L., Levine, A., and Smith, R. (2009). *The 2009 Horizon Report.* Austin, TX: The New Media Consortium. http://wp.nmc.org/horizon2009/

Keller, J., Bonk, C., and Hew, K. (2005). The Tickit to teacher learning: Designing professional development according to situative principles. *Journal of Educational Computing Research, 323*(4), 329-340.

Kelly, O. (2006). Moving to blended delivery in a polytechnic: Shifting the mindset of faculty and institutions. In M. Bullen and D. Janes (Eds.), *Making the transition to e-learning: Strategies and issues* (pp. 33-46). Hershey, PA: Information Science Publishing.

Kolb, D. (1983). *Experiential learning: Experience as the source of learning and development.* New York: FT Press.

Lave, J., and Wenger, E. (1991). *Situated learning. Legitimate peripheral participation.* New York: Cambridge University Press.

Lefoe, G., and Albury, R. (2002). Creating new learning environments off campus in the Faculty of Arts: What impact on teaching and learning on campus? In A. Williamson, C. Gunn, A. Young and T. Clear (Eds.), *Winds of Change in the Sea of Learning. Proceedings of the 19th Annual Conference of the Australasian Society for Computers in Tertiary Education (ASCILITE)* (pp. 369-378). Auckland, New Zealand: UNITEC Institute of Technology.

Lewin, G. (1948). *Resolving social conflict: Selected papers on group dynamics.* New York: Harper and Row.

Maor, D., and Volet, S. (2007). Interactivity in professional online learning: A review of research based studies. *Australasian Journal of Educational Technology, 23*(2), 269-290.

McDrury, J., and Alterio, M. (2002). *Learning through storytelling. Using reflection and experience in higher education contexts.* Palmerston North, NZ: The Dunmore Press.

McLoughlin, C., and Lee, M. (2008). The three P's of pedagogy for the networked society: Personalization, participation and productivity. *International Journal of Teaching and Learning in Higher Education, 20*(1), 10-27.

McLoughlin, C., and Luca, J. (2006). Applying situated learning theory to the creation of learning environments to enhance socialisation and self-regulation. In A. Herrington and J. Herrington (Eds.), *Authentic learning environments in higher education* (pp. 194-213). Hershey, PA: Information Science Publishing.

Meredith, S., and Newton, B. (2004). Models of eLearning: Technology promise vs. learner needs literature review. *The International Journal of Management Education, 4*(1), 43-56.

Mishra, P., and Koehler, M. (2006). Technological pedagogical content knowledge: A framework for teacher knowledge. *Teachers College Record, 108*(4), 1017-1054.

Mishra, P., Koehler, M., and Zhao, Y. (Eds.)(2007). *Faculty development by design. Integrating technology in higher education.* Charlotte, NC: Information Age Publishing.

Nicholls, G. (2001). *Professional development in higher education.* London: Kogan Page.

Piaget, J. (1954). *The construction of reality in the child.* New York: Ballantine Books.

Putnam, R., and Borko, H. (2000). What do new views of knowledge and thinking have to say about research on teacher learning? *Educational Researcher, 29*(1), 4-15.

Roberts, B. (2002). Interaction, reflection and learning at a distance. *Open Learning, 17*(1), 39-55.

Rogers, E. M. (2003). *Diffusion of innovations* (5th ed.). New York: The Free Press.

Salmon, G. (2004). *E-moderating. The key to teaching and learning online* (2nd ed.). London: Kogan Page.

Scribner, S. (1985). Knowledge at work. *Anthropology and Education Quarterly, 16*(3), 199-106.

Sharpe, R., Beetham, H., and Ravenscroft, A. (2005). Active artefacts: Representing our knowledge of learning and teaching. *HERDSA News*, 27, 8-11.

Sharpe, R., and Oliver, M. (2007). Supporting practitioners' design for learning: Principles of effective resources and interventions. In H. Beetham and R. Sharpe (Eds.), *Rethinking pedagogy for a digital age. Designing and delivering e-learning* (pp. 117-128). London: Routledge.

Sherer, P., Shea, P., and Kristensen, E. (2003). Online communities of practice: A catalyst for faculty development. *Innovative Higher Education, 27*(3), 183-194.

Sherry, L., Billig, S., Tavalin, F., and Gibson, D. (2000). New insights on technology adoption in schools. *T.H.E. Journal Online*(February 2000).

Shulman, L. (2004a). Knowledge and teaching. Foundations of the new reform. In Wilson, S. (Ed.).*The wisdom of practice. Essays on teaching, learning, and learning to teach* (pp. 219-248). San Francisco: Jossey-Bass.

Shulman, L. (2004b). Teaching as community property. Putting an end to pedagogical solitude. In Wilson, S. (Ed.).*The wisdom of practice. Essays on teaching, learning, and learning to teach* (pp. 455-462). San Francisco: Jossey-Bass.

Stockdill, S., and Morehouse, D. (1992). Critical factors in the successful adoption of technology: Checklist based on TDC findings. *Educational Technology, 32*(1), 57-58.

Suchman, L. (1987). *Plans and situated actions. The problems of human machine communication.* New York: Cambridge University Press.

Surry, D. W., Ensminger, D., and Haab, M. (2005). A model for integrating instructional technology into higher education. *British Journal of Educational Technology, 36*(2), 327-329.

Tam, M. (2000). Constructivism, instructional design, and technology: Implications for transforming distance learning. *Educational Technology and Society, 3*(2). http://ife ts.ieee.org/periodical/vol_2_2000/tam.html

Taylor, P. G. (1997). Creating environments which nurture development: Messages from research into academics' experiences. *International Journal for Academic Development, 2*(2), 42-49.

The Higher Education Academy and the Joint Information Systems Committee (JISC) Collaboration Network (2009). *Enhancing learning through technology: A guide to resources provided by the Academy and JISC Collaboration Network.* Heslington, YO: The Higher Education Academy. http://www.jisc.ac.uk/media enhancinglear ningthroughtechnology.pdf.

Thompson, T., and Kanaka, H. (2009). Establishing communities of practice for effective and sustainable professional development for blended learning. In E. Stacey and P. Gerbic (Eds.), *Effective blended learning practices. Evidence-based perspectives in ICT facilitated education* (pp. 144-162). Hershey, PA: IGI Global.

Thomson, R., and Wilson, G. (2007). Promoting staff learning about assessment through digital representations of practice: Evaluating a pilot project. In R. Atkinson, C. McBeath, S.K. A. Soong, and C. Cheers (Eds.). *ICT: Providing choices for learners and learning. Proceedings of Ascilite Singapore 2007.* (pp. 1024-1028). Centre for Educational Development, Nanyang Technological University, Singapore. Retrieved May 21, 2010, from http://www.ascilite.org.au/conferences/singapore07/procs/Thomson.

Vygotsky, L. (Ed.). (1978). *Mind in society.* Cambridge, MA: Harvard University Press.

Wilson, G. (2006). New skills and ways of working: Faculty development for e-learning. In M. Bullen and D. Janes (Eds.), *Making the transition to e-learning. Strategies and issues* (pp. 121-138). Hershey, PA: Information Science Publishing.

Wilson, G. (2007). *Using information and communications technology in higher education.* Unpublished PhD folio. Deakin University, Geelong, Victoria.

Wilson, G. (2009). Case studies of ICT-enhanced blended learning and implications for professional development. In E. Stacey and P. Gerbic (Eds.), *Effective Blended Learning Practices: Evidence-Based Perspectives in ICT-Facilitated Education* (pp. 239-258). Hershey, PA: Information Science Publishing.

Wilson, G., Thomson, R., and Malfroy, J. (2006). Gathering online representations of practice about assessment for use as a professional development tool: A case in progress. In L. Markauskaite, P. Goodyear, and P. Reimann (Eds.), *Whose Learning? Whose Technology? Proceedings of 23rd Annual Conference of the Australasian Association for Computers in Learning in Tertiary Education (ASCILITE) Conference* (Vol 2, pp. 893-897). Sydney: Sydney University Press.

In: Faculty Training for Web Enhanced Learning
Editors: Manuela Repetto and Guglielmo Trentin

ISBN: 978-1-61209-335-2
© 2011 Nova Science Publishers, Inc.

Chapter 6

BEGINNING TO BEGIN

Kim Floyd[1], Cathy Galyon Keramidas[1], Sharon Judge[2] and Tara Jeffs[3]

[1]West Virginia University, USA
[2]Darden College of Education, USA
[3]Loudoun County Public Schools, USA

ABSTRACT

This chapter is geared toward faculty members new to Web Enhanced Learning (WEL), as well as the seasoned faculty seeking to incorporate WEL into their traditional classroom settings. The chapter begins with the importance of community within the WEL, especially for the students that are far away from the institute of Higher Education. We discuss current research on the importance of social presence in regards to student learning, feelings of acceptance, and the retention of students at a distance as well as including tips creating a community of learners and sustain this community through the course. Essential elements of Universal Design for Learning are presented with examples provided for each of the three tenets of this approach to instruction (Multiple Means of Expression, Multiple Means of Engagement, and Multiple Means of Presentation). With one of the daunting facets of teaching through web enhanced activities and learning environments is the amount of time needed to effectively teach, respond, and interact with students, this chapter suggests tips and strategies to assist with the time demands needed for course management. Some of these tips will include how to effectively manage emails, posting announcements for maximal effect, using tools within the system such as time and conditional releases, and methods for creating student independence within the WEL environment. Additionally, suggestions for maintaining academic integrity within course activities and work submissions are given. With the increase of students with varying abilities (e.g., visual impairments, hearing impairments, physical impairments, learning disabilities) enrolling in institutions of Higher Education, WEL environments must be accessible to all learners. The chapter closes with preplanning and course design ideas which meet the needs of a variety of learners.

INTRODUCTION

The face of higher education is changing. Today's learners have a plethora of educational opportunities and educational systems. Competing in a global learning market, institutions of higher education are working to meet the needs of their consumers. The diversity of needs and backgrounds of the students entering institutions of higher education create the need with the diversified modes of instruction, allowing students for any time learning. Therefore, the necessity for on line instruction is undeniable. We must create learning environments and communities that will provide high quality instruction in a virtual learning setting. This chapter is geared toward faculty members new to Web Enhanced Learning (WEL), as well as seasoned faculty seeking to incorporate WEL into their traditional classroom settings.

The chapter will present the importance of community within the WEL, especially for the students that are learning from a distance (Beuchot and Bullen, 2005). We will discuss current research on the importance of social presence in regards to student learning, feelings of acceptance, and retention of students at a distance (Conaway, Easton and Schmidt, 2005). Further we will discuss the benefits and challenges of problem based learning and providing anchored instruction throughout the learning activities. Universal Design for Learning principles and challenges faced by accessibility of students will be addressed and suggestions for seamless inclusion of these guidelines during the development stage will aid as you plan and prepare for your course layout, design, and dissemination. As you move throughout this chapter, you will glean strategies and approaches that will support both the quality of your instruction and the learning experiences of your students.

ON-LINE COMMUNITIES

Having a feeling of belonging and connectedness to classmates and the instructor are important factors that contribute to the building of a community of learners (Aragon, 2003; Rovai, 2002). Further, Aragon (2003) suggests that the development of social presence must be established in order to facilitate optimal online learning. Social presence may take different forms in different settings, but one leading definition posited by Rourke, Anderson, Garrison, and Archer (1999), par. 3 is "the ability of learners to project themselves socially and emotionally in a community of inquiry". In WEL environments, the interactions of students occurs in an on line environment with limited peer to peer contact and discussion unless required or prompted to do so. Therefore, incorporating interdependence within the learning community will assist in supporting critical thinking, social presence, and cognitive growth (Picciano, 2002).

Implications from research from Jiang and Ting (2000) stress the importance of clear and distinct expectations for the form, quality, and quantity of student-instructor contact. Increased presence by the instructor supports student learning as well as establishing a framework for dialogue between students. Providing timely, positive, and supportive comments aid in the student's feeling of success and presence within the course.

Picciano (2002) suggest that online discussions may not be the ideal mechanism for convergent thinking from the learning community. Thus, utilizing multiple aspects of course supports while creating a community of learners is critical for a well rounded learning experience tapping into both the instructor directed inquiry as well as convergent thinking. Providing activities that require small group interaction and collaboration while providing grading rubrics supporting more cognitive efforts, self-testing, and consistent feedback from peer and instructor increase interaction, trust, and a feeling of presence within the community of learners.

PROBLEM-BASED LEARNING

Research has consistently demonstrated that students retain information gained while engaged in real life experiences more than simply text-based activities (Sendag and Odabasi, 2009). Therefore, creating this opportunity in WEL environments is essential, while also challenging. One way to obtain these experiences while in different geographical locations is through case based or problem based learning (PBL) activities. PBL provides an anchor or common experience for the students since so many students enter traditional and virtual classrooms from varied background. PBL is the use of real life situations in which students, alone or in groups, work to develop solutions to issues, circumstances, or conditions common to their field of study (Andrews and Jones, 1996). PBL allows information gained in the course to be applied immediately to real life situation for better understanding of new material and concepts without losing content in a course that might be presented in a more traditional lecture-type format (Beers, 2005; Capon and Kuhn, 2004; Chung and Chow, 2004).

Problem-based learning (PBL) is not new having been used in the Harvard business school since 1911 (Bhandari and Erikson, 2005), however, many programs are seeing promise in the use of problem based learning in online coursework as well. PBL is a learner-centered approach where the learner(s) is given a real-life problem or issue that may have multiple "answers," and time to discover solutions that will potentially lead to problem solving skills in that subject area (Barrows and Tamblyn, 1980). PBL also is referred to as case-study method in the literature. Andrews and Jones (1996) describe PBL as a bridge from theory to practice, and PBL has many advantages in to those in new learning situations, particularly in a WEL environment.

Instructors often use PBL in at least two ways in a course: as information provided in an individual assignment or information provided in a group assignment. PBL often uses an anchor to assist in learning the materials. Bransford, Sherwood, Hasselbring, Kinzer and Williams (1990) were the first to coin the term "anchored instruction" referring to the use of videos of real-life situations to allow learners to explore solutions to the situations presented in a video. Today, anchored instruction has come to mean scenarios, role-playing, videos, and other methods used to giving learners a real-life situation, and is a common way to present the problem in PBL. In WEL, video or scenarios are often the preferred anchor in PBL. For an individual, PBL gives a real-world experience in which s/he can apply theories and other information provided in a course. For groups, PBL provides an anchor for all learners to work on at the same time, even though in WEL they may be in different geographical locations. It gives a common experience that they can all understand and build upon. The benefit for both individuals and groups is that PBL allows each to attempt different solutions to a problem, even if the learner has not had that real world experience personally. PBL allows information gained in the course to be applied immediately to real life situation for better understanding of new material and concepts without losing content in a course that might be presented in a more traditional lecture-type format (Beers, 2005; Capon and Kuhn, 2004; Chung and Chow, 2004: Hang Wong and Day, 2009). For this reason, PBL is a good method to use with individuals who are new or who have never been in situations that the PBL anchor covers. PBL is a particularly good strategy to use in applied fields and has been successfully used in accounting (Ballantine and Larres, 2004), nursing (Beers, 2005), pharmacology (Cheng, Alafris, Kirschenbaum, Kalis and Brown, 2003), psychology (Connor-Greene, 2002), the medicine (Tufts and Higgins-Opitz, 2009), engineering (Rojas, Prats, Montlaur and García-Berro, 2008), physical/occupational therapies (Vogel, Geelhoed, Grice and Murphy, 2009), and special education (Fitzgerald et al., 2009) to name just a few. Sternbeg (2008) argues that problem-based learning would be beneficial in multidisciplinary courses, too.

Many WEL courses containing content in the areas of studies listed above, as well as other areas of study, use PBL. Since anchors used in PBL can be in the form of videos, learners often have a richer experience with the problems presented in a WEL learning environment. Instructors can use various types of media to present the problem, and learners have a variety of resources to research information and present possible answers to the problem. Research shows there are positives and negatives in using PBL. Some of the positives are that PBL is effective with different learning styles (Andrews and Jones, 1996), and it can increase critical thinking skills (Sendag and Odabasi, 2009); however, some negatives can be that the PBL does not provide enough depth in the anchor provided (Andrews and Jones, 1996), the tasks involving PBL can create much more work for the learner (Ballantine and Larres, 2004), lower-achieving learners may need guidance to learn how to learn using this method, (Jeong and Hmelo-Silver, 2010), and learners may not have been taught the necessary information to be successful in learning using this method (Yun-Jo and Reigeluth, 2008). Additionally, there also are some positives for the instructors of WEL courses that incorporate PBL. The instructor can gauge if the learner understands the basic materials of the course, can see how the learner is applying presented materials, and how the learner comes to a solution. Andrews and Jones (1996) caution that using a PBL does not ensure the learner can apply the materials to a real life situation, but it does give the learner experiences that might lead to better decision making on that problem after coursework is finished.

UNIVERSAL DESIGN FOR LEARNING

The applications of universal design, although well established in architecture and product development, are relatively new in higher education. Universal design is defined as "the design of products and environments to be usable by all people, to the greatest extent possible, without the need for adaptation or specialized design" (Center for Universal Design, 1997, para. 3). Thus, universal design focuses on removing barriers through initial designs that consider the needs of diverse people, rather than overcoming barriers later through individual adaption (Rose et al., 2006). Universal design for learning (UDL) is one part of the universal design movement. Initially many higher education faculty perceived that the focus of UDL was to reduce the barriers to access for students with disabilities in higher education, but it is now realized that UDL should be considered for all possible students. Thus, UDL focuses on removing barriers to learning for all types of learners rather than just students with disabilities. As a result, students from other historically underrepresented populations are likely to experience a more welcoming learning environment. Universal refers not to the traditional "one size fits all" approach to curricula; rather, it encourages universal access to learning for all students. UDL offers a blueprint for designing flexible curriculum methods, materials, and assessments that meet the needs of diverse learners with diverse experiences (Rose, Meyer and Hitchcock, 2005).

The three UDL principles focus on learning and calls for a kind of flexibility that will support individual differences relating to one of these sets of networks: differences in how students recognize essential cues and patterns, master skillful strategies for action, and engage with learning (Meyer and Rose, 2005). The first principle is to provide multiple means of representation (the "what" of learning) thus reflecting that there is no one way of presenting information or transferring knowledge that addresses diverse learners needs (Rose et al., 2006). Principle 1 suggests that the instructor provide multiple representations of the same information, such as digital text read by text-to-speech software (Rose and Meyer, 2002).

While the first principle focuses on representation, the second principle is to provide multiple means of expression (the "how" of learning) (CAST, 2008). This principle encourages instructors to differentiate the ways that students can express what they know. For example, many students are able to adequately demonstrate their knowledge through writing text while others may be more adept at creating PowerPoint or other multimedia presentations to demonstrate their knowledge. Additionally, technology enables text-to-speech capabilities, voice activated transcription of responses, and automated translations across languages including Braille. This principle reflects that there is no one means of expression that is optimal for all students, therefore, options for expression is critical.

The third principle of UDL is to provide multiple means of engagement (the "why" of learning) thus reflecting that students differ greatly in the ways in which they are engaged or inspired to learn (Rose et al., 2006). This principle advocates tapping into students' interests, offering appropriate challenges, and increasing motivation. One of the most successful ways of engaging students is by providing them with choices and opportunities for personal control (CAST, 2008). For example, students can be provided choices in the tools used for information gathering or production or the context or content used for practicing skills. This principle not only focuses on extrinsic means but also points toward developing students' intrinsic abilities for self-regulation. According to Rose et al. (2006), "not all students are engaged by the same extrinsic rewards or conditions, nor do they develop intrinsic motivation along the same path" (p. 137). Thus, alternative ways to engage students are essential.

Applying UDL Principles to Web Enhanced Learning

WEL is uniquely capable of supporting students with regard to the UDL principles. The number of devices that can access the Web has grown immensely. Thus, it is even more important that Web pages are accessible by everyone. The World Wide Web Consortium (W3C), which develops and maintains protocols to ensure interoperability of the Web, has always been committed to UDL. One of the primary goals of W3C is to make the Web "available to all people, whatever their hardware, software, network infrastructure, native language, culture, geographical location, or physical or mental ability" (http://w

ww.w3.org/Consortium/mission). The W3C develops Web standards and guidelines to assist site developers with the creation of accessible Web pages. The Web Accessibility Initiative (WAI) developed guidelines for the accessible design of Web sites. The guidelines are organized around four principles that lay the foundation necessary for anyone to access and effectively use Web content. The Web Content Accessibility Guidelines (WGAG) 2.0 and quick tips are listed in Figure 1.

The WAI (Web Accessibility Initiative, 2005) promotes universal as well as accessible design pointing out that Web accessibility also benefits people without disabilities. For example, a key principle of Web accessibility is designing Web sites that are flexible to meet different user needs, preferences, and situations. Such flexibility benefits people with disabilities, but also those without disabilities, such as people using a slow Internet connection, people with "temporary disabilities" such as a broken arm, and people with changing abilities due to aging.

Web pages can be tested for accessibility by using special validator programs and by accessing the pages with a variety of monitors, computer platforms, and Web browsers and with sound and graphic capabilities turned off and a keyboard alone (World Wide Web Consortium, 1999).

Despite the international efforts to make the Web accessible, many Web sites in higher education remain inaccessible to faculty, staff, students, and visitors with disabilities (Hackett and Parmanto, 2005; Schmetzke, 2001, 2003; Thompson, Burgstaher, and Comden, 2003). Adding to this problem are Webmasters' and administrators' lack of knowledge of legal obligations to provide accessible content, of barriers created by their Web sites, of guidelines for designing accessible sites, and of the benefits of UDL for all Web users. This confirms that continued effort is needed in order to educate administrators, faculty, and web designers about the need for web accessibility and the techniques for implementing it.

With Web accessibility in mind, developers of WEL need to design flexible, customizable materials with built-in adaptations. Building upon the work of the Center for Applied Special Technology (CAST) and the University of Washington's Disabilities, Opportunities, Internetworking, and Technology (DO-IT) Center, the Equity and Excellence in Higher Education (E and E) project developed Universal Course Design (UCD) to be more responsive to course design, instruction, assessment, the environment, and the culture of each student. Behling and Hart (2008) argue that "the academic, social, and conceptual differences among elementary, secondary, and postsecondary schools often make it difficult for college faculty to relate easily to the K-12 focus common to UDL" (p. 111). As a result, the E and E project has created UCD instructional strategies based on the ideas and tools that faculty developed and used through their work with this project. Comprehensive strategies requiring technology in the areas of course curriculum, instruction, assessment, and environment can be found at http://www.eeonline.org/ucd-strategies. Some of these strategies include using a speech-to-text software to record lectures that can be posted on a course website, providing a link to video presentation with closed captioning on, having students conduct webquests around a topic they are interested in that relates to the course, and creating and monitoring online debates between groups.

In sum, applying UDL principles to WEL by supporting the learning of all students by providing them with multiple means of acquiring information and of expressing what they have learned, and by allowing students to engage with a course in different ways. Allowing students to choose from several different ways to complete the same assignment is one way to give each student the opportunity to demonstrate learning in his or her own way. Resources such as CAST's UDL online modules at http://udlonline.cast.org/home provide examples of applications that can be used by higher education faculty.

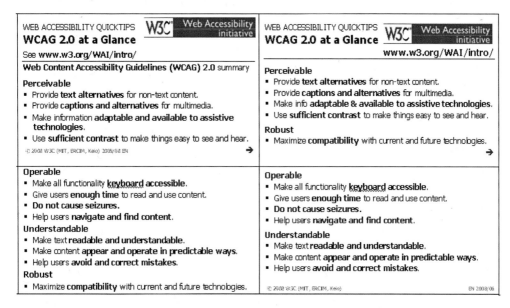

Figure 1. Web Content Accessibility Guidelines (WCAG 2.0) and Quicktips[1].

TIPS FOR COURSE MANAGEMENT

It is estimated that preparation and instructional time for an online or web enhanced course is almost double to that of traditional courses preparation (Coppola, Hiltz and Rotter, 2002). With this type of time commitment, it is no wonder that faculty at institutes of higher education often chose NOT to create online courses. Many who already teach online are investigating their own methods of managing an online curse to find short cuts and ways to save time. A (2007) article by Keramidas, Ludlow, Collins, and Baird, the authors provide many tips on managing a course online. Below are some of those tips along with other ideas to keep a course more manageable, along with others to assist an online instructor.

Prepare materials in advance. When a course is in progress, it is difficult to manage the interactions on a course (e.g., lectures, discussion boards, emails) and create materials too. A well thought-out, well-planned course with all materials, prepared, uploaded and ready to go can save time for the instructor while the course is ongoing. Also, while a course is ongoing, keeping notes as to what need to be edited, changed, deleted, etc., can assist the instructor to make the necessary changes quickly when a course is re-offered.

Practice efficient file management. Many online course management tools (e.g., Blackboard, Moodle, Learning Management Systems) have a built-in file managing system that needs to be set up by the instructor. Finding a system that works for you will allow you to

---

1 Source: WCAG 2.0 at a Glance edited by Shawn Lawton Henry and Wayne Dick. Copyright© (2008) World Wide Web Consortium. (MIT, ERCIM, Keio) Reprinted with permission. http://www.w3 .org/Consortium/Legal/2002/copyright-documents-20021231.

manage an online course more effectively and efficiently. Some online instructors set up their files to have only certain types of documents within a file (e.g., all Word documents in one file, all adobe documents in another, PowerPoint documents in another, etc.). Other online instructors set up the files by content (e.g., all assignment documents in one file) all lecture materials in another, etc.), and there are probably other ways to set up the file system. This is an area of the course the students will not see and can be set up to meet the needs of the instructor –whatever system works best for them.

Make expectations in the course clear. This is particularly important in discussion boards, where the point of the discussion and how it will be graded is often unclear to learners. Learners do better when they know upfront what is expected of them. One way to make expectations clear that assists the leaner as well as the instructor is the use of grading rubrics, which are a tool to assist an instructor in grading that has fixed standards and a rating of the quality of a student's work (Popham, 1997). Instructors can use grading rubrics for many assignments and tasks in an online course such as discussion boards, assignments, and exams. Students report that students find a grading rubric helps them complete assignments and know the expectations of the instructor (Saam, 2007), and Stevens and Levi (2004) found that use of grading rubrics allowed instructors to grade more efficiently and efficiently.

Discussions do not have to include all learners in a course. Creating one discussion area in the course and expecting all participants to participate in the one discussion area can be difficult for the learners to read and discouraging for them to participate in as well. For the instructor it also can be difficult to manage. Discussions are often more easily managed when there are 4-8 participants. This might mean the instructor/designer creates more than one discussion group, and that each group might be simultaneously discussing the same topic. This might also mean each group of 4-8 learners is involved as a group with a series of discussion boards throughout the course. The learners get more interaction on a discussion board with fewer participants, and the discussion can be more meaningful to all involved.

Set timelines for discussion boards. It can be difficult for learners in a course participate in different discussions at the same time. The discussion can be disjointed and not meaningful if learners are going at their own pace on different boards at different times than other learners. Often, working on one question at a time, with set beginning and ending dates, creates a more cohesive, thoughtful discussion amongst the participants. It can make grading such discussions easier for the instructor as well.

Establish a separate discussion (area) *for off-topic comments.* Creating an off-topic area allows learners to have a place for informal conversation, and it also can assist learners in staying on-topic in the discussion boards created for particular topics. In an off-topic discussion board, the instructor may or may not want to participate, depending on what is shared. Often, this type of discussion board is a place for students to express frustrations and questions within the course. Interestingly, this area becomes a discussion of related materials/information or continuation of conversations that were initiated elsewhere.

Effectively manage email. Email within a course can get overwhelming! Checking email at least daily cuts down on massive amounts of email, and it allows the student to receive a more timely response. Filing emails, once answered in another area such as a file can assist the instructor in knowing what email has been answered and what has not. The file can be labeled 'read email" or some instructors find it useful to label individual files with the names of every student in a file and emails from exact students can be found more quickly. Also, it can be more time efficient to have a "standard " answer that can be copied and pasted into a reply when an instructor has requested specific information be given in an email. For example, "I approve of this position paper topic. You may begin your paper." Could be a standard email for when an instructor asks for students to email a paper topic for approval.

Use existing tools in the course management system to do things more efficiently. Course management systems often already have time saving features. For example, in Blackboard, an instructor can sort the discussion board postings by date or by learner. Depending on how the instructor is grading that area one specific course utility tool may be more efficient than other and should be utilized accordingly. Also, in the Blackboard assessment tool, the instructor has the option of grading one learner's exam at a time or one question on all learners' exams at a time. The second option of grading 1 question of all exams at a time can allow the instructor to think about answer for that question only, causing grading to not only be faster for the instructor, but the students receive more consistent grading.

ACADEMIC INTEGRITY

Academic Integrity is a growing concern across higher education, and the increase of distance education further exacerbates the issues with the ease of copying and pasting information from websites directly into word processing computer programs (Baron and Crooks, 2005). The Internet, however, also facilitates instructors in catching instances of cheating, plagiarism, and fraud. Therefore, it is imperative to address the potential of academic violations up front in the planning and design of the WEL environment. Pavela (1978) notes several different types of academic dishonesty: 1) cheating or using materials/information for an assignment that is not allowed (typically in testing situations), 2) fabrication or intentional falsification of information on an assignment, 3) facilitating academic dishonesty or helping another student cheat, and 4) plagiarism or taking someone else's ideas/work, using it as your own, and not citing the other person. Yardley, Rodriguez, Bates, and Nelson (2009), found in a study of over 600 learners, 81% self-reported academic dishonesty in their major courses and 99.5% self-reported academic dishonesty in courses outside their major. Some studies show academic dishonesty to be higher in WEL (Kennedy, Nowak, Thomas, and Davis, 2000), while others show it to be similar to what occurs in traditional face-to-face courses (Black, Greaser and Dawson, 2008). However, instructors have more tools than ever to assist learners to understand academic integrity, methods to decrease academic dishonesty, and methods to find instances of academic dishonesty – especially plagiarism.

The first line of defense in stopping academic dishonesty is to educate the learner. Every institute of higher education (IHE) has policies on academic dishonesty. Discussing these policies and consequences of infractions makes students aware of what constitutes academic dishonesty as well as what might occur if they engage in dishonest practices. These polices should be included in the syllabus of the course as well. Many IHEs have tutorials that can be accessed even if you are not affiliated with that IHE. The tutorials often have quizzes associated, and instructors of WEL can direct learners to these resources, requiring either proof of completion of tutorials or an honor statement of understanding of what constitutes academic dishonesty.

After ensuring that learners are aware of what is academic dishonesty, the instructor can design assignments to decrease the likelihood that infractions occur. One such method is to have an assignment occur in stages. For example, if learners are writing a research paper, the instructor could require that drafts or different portions of the paper be turned in at different times. Also, requiring editing sessions where learners assist each other in editing can decrease the chances of plagiarism. For exams, instructors need to make sure the exams in their courses are changed often. Many course management systems have tools that decrease the ability of the learner to cheat. Course Management systems can often randomize questions, randomize answers on questions, limit the time an exam is open, restrict the leaner from opening other windows while taking the exam, not allow the learner to return to a question once it has been seen and can work from a question pool so that learners receive different questions.

Just as it is easy for learners to commit acts of academic dishonesty, it also is easy for instructors to catch it. Regardless of education and precautions, some learners will still choose to engage in dishonest academic practices, however, an instructor does not have to be suspicious of everyone. One tool available to instructors that many IHEs subscribe to is Turnitin. Turnitin is a service that learners and/or instructors can submit written work to and have that work checked for plagiarism against online materials only (Turnitin: Home: Welcome to Turnitin, n.d.). It does not compare learners' work to printed materials. Some instructors think that it deters academic dishonesty, however, others have submitted known plagiarized documents that were not shown to be plagiarized. Turnitin is a good tool to use, but it is only on tool.

One of the best tools in catching academic dishonesty is the judgment of the instructor. When grading, it has been the experience of the authors that a plagiarized paper sounds and often looks different. View the submitted work critically and ask questions like,

- Does the work sound like the learner talks?
- Does the work read too smoothly?
- Is the work too choppy or unintelligible?
- Is the work written well but the transitions are not?
- Is there a verb tense change in places?
- Do the personal pronouns change from "they" to "me" "I" or "we?"
- Does the paper change font styles and/or size in various places?
- Is there an extra wide left margin?
- Does the work sound familiar?

If the answer to any of these questions is "yes" then there is a reason to check more closely for plagiarism. Search engines such as Yahoo and Google are other good tools to use to find sources that are not cited. Choosing phrases or sentences that are rare and pasting them into the search engines often can provide results as to where they are used in online documents. Also, Library databases such as Ebscohost can be searched in the same way to yield similar results.

ACCESSIBILITY

In terms of development, e-learning is moving from the stage of infancy to adolescence. As more and more learners want the convenience of learning online more pressure is placed on the university and its instructors to assure that all students have equal access to the learning environment and materials. Legislative such as Section 508 of the Vocational Rehabilitation Act, and the Americans with Disabilities Act mandates that electronic and information technology must be accessible to individuals with disabilities. Can you rest assured that your online classes and educational materials are easily accessed by all your students so that learning can take place?

Approximately seventeen percent of the total student population on any given campus acknowledges a disability (Stodder, Whelley, Chang and Harding, 2001). While new technologies can broaden access they can also create barriers. Accessible e-learning starts with a close examination of the university's virtual infrastructure. Such items would include selected courseware or course management systems, library resources, text documents, presentations, and multimedia. Once an accessible infrastructure is in place then instructors can begin to meet the learning needs of their diverse learners. In order for this to occur, instructors must provide multiple pathways to learning online to ensure learner access and success. This requires instructors to understand how students learn and use technology and as a result provide educational supports where they are needed and position the challenge appropriately for each learner.

Common Learning Tools

Web-based learning materials can present barriers to people with different kinds of disabilities. Such disability types include individuals with visual disabilities, hearing disabilities, physical disabilities and cognitive or neurological disabilities. Common tools for each of the disability types will be briefly described.

Visual Disabilities

People who are blind or visual impaired use multiple access methods in acquiring computer-based information. For example, a screen reader is a software program that reads aloud everything on the computer screen and including some elements such as menu and formatting codes that are hidden or provided behind the screen. Screen readers can be used separately or in combination of other assistive technologies such as screen magnifiers, and Braille output devices. Common challenges that users face when using these tools are: a) reading images that do not have a description or an alternate text tag to describe what is seen in a picture; b) text layout that does not make sense when a screen reader reads straight across the page reading from left to following a single line/row on the computer screen. This is often caused by text formatted in multiple columns or tables without headers; c) pixilation of text that is embedded in an image, such as a picture of a sign with words; and d) the use of color to differentiate information (i.e. an information screen with two identically shaped buttons- one colored green and one colored blue and the user is to suppose to select the green button to continue).

Hearing Disabilities

Individuals with hearing disabilities are faced with challenges related to multimedia use. Synchronized captions for auditory content are most beneficial. If captioning software is not available for video or audio clips then a transcript of the content should be provided.

Physical Disabilities

Accessing the computer for individuals with physical disabilities can be quite challenging. Tools such as voice recognition, head mouse or wand, expanded keyboards, or switch access are commonly used to move and interact within an e-learning environment. Challenges and issues that arise often revolve around keyboard access, timed response, and selecting target areas on the web page.

Cognitive and Neurological Disabilities

Individuals with mild cognitive or neurological disabilities often have difficulty acquiring information due to difficulty with memory, association, or attention. These individuals are challenged by text only pages that require reading and focus. Animations used can distract or cause a lack of concentration. Users with cognitive and neurological disabilities can benefit greatly from illustrations and graphics as well as from properly organized content with headings, succinct lists, and visual cues.

Accessible Course Content

> "When designing my courses, I think about learning styles but I have never considered that an individual with a visual impairment or any other disability for that matter would actually take an online course. In my mind, I was thinking that would be insane. But then it hit me, they could and some will and they're not afraid of the challenge. So it is my job to make sure that I set up my course so they can navigate it easily and be able to access all the materials."
>
> *Interview of Elementary Education Faculty Member after an accessibility workshop*

Traditionally, what we have done in education is to accommodate individual needs without changing our courses. For example, we have told deaf students to arrange for a sign language interpreter or blind students to acquire Braille versions of printed material. This is no longer acceptable or possible to accommodate the online learner with disabilities. Preplanning and designing accessible courses and related learning materials are much easier than adapting a course retrospectively. Ensuring that materials can be interpreted by screen readers and other assistive technologies can save an instructor time when considered before a course is offered. It is not as difficult as it seems. The following checklist may be helpful.

Course Navigation

Is navigation consistent on every page?
Is information on the page clear, concise and in manageable chunks?
Have I removed flicker, flashing or unnecessary motion (triggers seizures and distracts)

Are animations necessary and do they add meaning to the presentation?

Are links provided? If so, are they descriptive?

Text

Is the font clear and easy to read?

Have I used high contrast between text and background?

Do my tables include column and row headings?

Is the language as clear and concise as possible to get the point across?

Can all written material be read by a screen reader, text to speech software or transferred to Mp4 format?

Is real text used rather than text embedded in a graphic or photo?

Images

Are diagrams labeled so that they are not dependent on color?

Can the user understand the page without color?

Do all images in my Power Points and documents contain ALT tags for description of pictures?

Do all visuals have a written counterpart or explanation?

Multimedia

Have I provided transcripts or the option to turn on or off caption?

Have I included a text-only version of the content?

Is audio clear and easy to understand?

Other Considerations

Have I provide other options for a user to request more time to complete a response.

Do I provide students with choices in acquiring information or demonstrating knowledge?

Do I provide all necessary plug ins needed to review information on my webpage?

Have I included the University's ADA statement?

Have I considered the Priority 1 checkpoints of ADA section 508?

Have I checked my page with Section 508 checker http://www.section508.info/ and/or WAVE http://wave.webaim.org/ ?

When looking at accessibility for your students, the bottom line is that it is your responsibility to ensure that no student is disconnected from any part of your course due to his or her functional impairment. It is essential to assure pathways to learning access and success. To learn more about assistive technology or accessibility explore the following links:

- Guide to Accessibility http://lab.dotjay.co.uk/notes/assistive-technology/videos/
- Access Technology Higher Education Network http://www.athenpro. org/
- Understanding assistive technologies in higher education . athenpro. org/wiki/Assistive_Technology

CONCLUSION

Although there is no clear cut, prepackaged design of WEL that will work for every student, this chapter provided an overview of techniques, suggestions, and questions that need to be in the forefront of the preplanning process. In higher education, the question is no longer will I ever need to teach in a nontraditional platform, but rather when will I be asked to provide WEL to the changing needs of the students. All the planning, time, and work that are supplied prior to the first day of delivery, will save you considerable time and work as you move through the delivery of the course. Therefore, embrace the challenges and address the pitfalls during the development stage versus the implementation of the course itself.

REFERENCES

Andrews, M., and Jones, P. R. (1996). Problem-based learning in an undergraduate nursing programme: A case study. *Journal of Advanced Nursing, 23,* 357-365.

Aragon, S.R. (2003). Creating social presence in on line environments. *New Directions for Adult and Continuing Education, 100,* 57-68.

Ballantine, J. A. and McCourt Larres, P. M. (2004) A critical analysis of students' perception of the usefulness of the case study method in an advanced management accounting module: the impact of relevant work experience, *Accounting Education, 13*(2), 171-189.

Bhandari, A. and Erikson, L. (2005). Case studies can fill a critical need in environmental engineering education. *Journal of Environmental Engineering. 131*(8), 1121-1121.

Baron, J., and Crooks, S. M. (2005). Academic integrity in web based distance education. *TechTrends: Linking Research and Practice to Improve Learning, 49*(2) 40-45.

Beers, G. W. (2005). The effect of teaching method on objective test scores: Problem-based learning versus lecture. *Journal of Nursing Education, 44(7),* 305-309.

Behling, K., and Hart, D. (2008). Universal course design: A model for professional development. In S. Burgstaher, and R. C. Cory (Eds.), *Universal design in higher education* (pp. 109-125). Cambridge, MA: Harvard Education Press.

Beuchot, A. and Bullen, M. (2005). Interaction and interpersonality in online discussion forums. *Distance Education, 26,* 67-87.

Bransford, J., Sherwood, R., Hasselbring, T., Kinzer, C., and Williams, S. (1990). Anchored instruction: Why we need it and how technology can help. In Nix, D. and Spiro, R. (Eds.). Cognition, education, and multimedia: Exploring ideas in high technology, 163-205. Hillsdale, NJ: Lawrence Erlbaum Associates.

Capon, N., and Kuhn, D. (2004). What's so good about problem-based learning? *Cognition and Instruction, 22,* 61-79.

CAST (2008). *Universal design for learning guidelines version 1.0.* Wakefield, MA: Author.

Center for Universal Design (1997). *About universal design.* http://www.design.ncsu. edu/cud/about-ud/about_ud.htm.

Cheng, J.W.M, Alafris, A., Kirschenbaum, H.L., Kalis, M.M., and Brown, M.E. Problem-based learning versus traditional lecturing in pharmacy students' short –term examination performance, *Journal Pharmacy Education, 3*(2), 117-25.

Chung, J. C. C., and Chow, S. M. K. (2004). Promoting student learning through a student-centred problem-based learning subject curriculum. *Instructions in Education and Teaching International, 41,* 157-168.

Conaway, R. N., Easton, S. S., and Schmidt, W.V. (2005). Strategies for enhancing student interaction and immediacy in online courses. *Business Communication Quarterly, (68)*1, 23-35.

Connor-Greene, P. A. (2005). Problem-based learning. In W. Buskist and S. F. Davis (Eds.), *The handbook of the teaching of psychology* (pp. 70-77). Malden, MA: Blackwell.

Coppola, N. W., Hiltz, S. R., and Rotter, N. G. (2002). Becoming a virtual professor: Pedagogical roles and asynchronous learning networks. *Journal of Management Information Systems, 18*(4), 169-189.

Fitzgerald, D., Koury, K., Mitchem, K., Hollingshead, C., Miller, K., Park, M. K., et al (2009). Implementing Case-Based Instruction in Higher Education Through Technology: What Works Best? *Journal of Technology and Teacher Education, 17*(1), 31-63.

Greaser, J., Black, E. and Dawson, K. (2008). Academic dishonesty in traditional and online classrooms: Does the "Media Equation" hold true? Journal of Asynchronous Learning Networks.

Hackett, S., and Parmanto, B. (2005). A longitudinal evaluation of accessibility: Higher education Web sites. *Internet Research, 15*(3), 281-294.

Hang Wong, K. K., and Day, J. R. (2009). A comparative study of problem-based and lecture-based learning in junior secondary school science. *Research in Science Education, 39*(5), 625-642.

Jeong, H., and Hmelo-Silver, C. E. (2010). Productive use of learning resources in an online problem-based learning environment. *Computers in Human Behavior, 26*(1), 84-99.

Jiang, M., and Ting, E. (2000). A study of factors influencing students' perceived learning In a web-based course environments. *International Journal of Educational Technologies, 6*(4), 317-338.

Kennedy, K., Nowak, S., Thomas, J., and Davis, S. (2000). Academic dishonesty and distance learning: Student and faculty views. *The College Student Journal, 34*(2), 309.

Keramidas, C. G., Ludlow, B., Collins, B. C., and Baird, C. M. (2007). Saving your sanity when teaching in an online environment: Lessons learned. *Rural Special Education Quarterly, (26)*1, 28-39.

Meyer, A., and Rose, D. H. (2005).The future is in the margins: The role of technology and disability in educational reform. In D. H. Rose, A. Meyer, and C. Hitchcock (Eds.), *The universally design classroom* (pp. 13-35). Cambridge, MA: Harvard Education Press.

Pavela, G. (1978). Judicial review of academic decision- making after Horowitz. *School Law Journal, 55*(8), 55- 75.

Picciano, A.G. (2002). Beyond student perceptions: Issues of interaction, presence, and performance in an on line course. *Journal of Asynchronous Learning Networks, 6*(1).

Popham, J. W. (1997). What's wrong—and what's right—with rubrics. *Educational Leadership, 55*(2), 72–75.

Rojas, J. I., Prats, X., Montlaur, A., and García-Berro, E. (2008). Model Rocket Workshop: a Problem-Based Learning Experience for Engineering Students. *International Journal of Emerging Technologies in Learning, 3*(4), 70-77.

Rose, D. H., Harbour, W. S., Johnston, C. S., Daley, S. G., and Abarbanell, L. (2006). Universal design for learning in postsecondary education: Reflections on principles and their application. *Journal of Postsecondary Education and Disability, 19,* 135-151.

Rose, D. H., Meyer, A., and Hitchcock, C. (2005). *The universally designed classroom.* Cambridge, MA: Harvard Education Press.

Rourke, L., Anderson, T., Garrison, D.R., and Archer, W. (1999). Assessing social presence in asynchronous text-based computer conferencing. *Journal of Distance Education, 14*(2).

Rovai, A.P. (2003). A practical framework for evaluating online distance education programs. *Internet and Higher Education, 6*(2), 109-124.

Saam, J., Sorgman, M., and Calhoon, S. K. (2007). Uncovering students' perceptions of rubrics. *Journal on Excellence in College Teaching 18*(3), 39–53.

Schmetzke, A. (2001). Accessibility of the homepages of the nation's community colleges. Stevens Point: University of Wisconsin-Stevens Point. http://library.uwsp.edu/aschmetz/Accessible/nationwide/CC_Survey2001/summary_CCC.htm.

Schmetzke, A. (2003). Web accessibility survey home page. Stevens Point: University of Wisconsin-Stevens Point. http://library.uwsp.edu/aschmetz/Accessible/websurveys.htm.

Sendag, S., and Odabasi, H. F. (2009). Effects of an online problem based learning course on content knowledge acquisition and critical thinking skills. *Computers and Education, 53*(1), 132-141.

Sternbeg, R. J. (2008). Interdisciplinary Problem-Based Learning. *Liberal Education, 94*(1), 12-17.

Stevens, D. D., and Levi, A. (2004). *Introduction to rubrics: An assessment tool to save grading time, convey feedback, and promote student learning.* Sterling, VA: Stylus.

Stodden, R., Whelley, T., Chang, C., and Harding, T. (2001). Current status of educational support provision to students with disabilities in postsecondary education, *Journal of Vocational Rehabilitation,16*, 189-198.

Thompson, T., Burgstahler, S., and Comden, D. (2003). Research on Web accessibility in higher education. *Journal of Information Technology and Disabilities, 9*(2). http://people.rit.edu/easi/itd/itdv09n2/thompson.htm

Tufts, M. A., and Higgins-Opitz, S. B. (2009). What makes the learning of physiology in a PBL medical curriculum challenging? Student perceptions. *Advances in Physiology Education, 33*, 91-97.

Vogel. K., Geelhoed, M., Grice, K., and Murphy, D. (2009). Do occupational therapy and physical therapy curricula teach critical thinking skills? *Journal of Allied Health, 38*(3),152-157.

Yun-Jo, A. and Reigeluth, C. (2008) Problem-based learning in online environments. *Quarterly Review of Distance Education, 9*(1),1-16.

Web Accessibility Initiative (2005). Introduction to Web accessibility. Cambridge, MA: World Wide Web Consortium. http://www.w3.org/WAI/intro/accessibility.php.

World Wide Web Consortium (1999). Web content accessibility guidelines 1.0: W3C recommendation 5-May-1999. Cambridge, MA: Author. http://www.w3.org/TR/WAI-WEBCONTENT/.

In: Faculty Training for Web Enhanced Learning
Editors: Manuela Repetto and Guglielmo Trentin

ISBN: 978-1-61209-335-2
© 2011 Nova Science Publishers, Inc.

Chapter 7

CHANGING TECHNOLOGIES/RENEWING PEDAGOGIES: IMPLICATIONS FOR UNIVERSITY TEACHING AND LEARNING

Karen Starr, Elizabeth Stacey and Lauri Grace
Deakin University, Australia

ABSTRACT

This chapter describes a project that researched the use of Web Enhanced Learning (WEL) with postgraduate students from rural and remote communities who were studying through two Australian universities. We examine, in detail, the experiences of a university teacher using WEL in an off-campus course for the first time. As with many academic teachers, she was willing to use new technologies and integrate these into her teaching but required time, technical support and professional development to achieve this. Using a design-based methodological approach, the experiences and frustrations in introducing WEL are described from the teacher's perspective through her progressive reflections at stages throughout the course. The findings and their implications for university policy and leadership are detailed with conclusions about how teachers and students are best supported in their engagement with WEL.

INTRODUCTION

Most Australian university courses rely on Web Enhanced Learning (WEL) methods, with teaching and learning no longer reliant on the traditional model of face-to-face lectures and tutorials. Australia's low population distributed over a large geographical area has meant that many students have long studied by distance and most universities now offer courses off-campus and online. WEL can apply to traditional face-to-face classes, blended modes of course delivery or fully online or distance classes that draw on resources made accessible to students online through the internet whether these are text based or multimedia. WEL applications change rapidly as new enhancements become readily available and broadly accessible through improved technological infrastructure. An implicit assumption in higher education is that teachers and students are familiar, or will become familiar, with these applications.

While university staff may have access to up-to-date technologies and applications, the time and resources for professional learning and associated pedagogical changes are usually limited. Much relies on the personal interest and technological expertise of individual staff members, with varying results for both teaching and learning. It is recognized that "institutions that require teachers to teach ...fully online ... classrooms are obliged to offer professional development to support teachers making this transition" (Wiesenberg and Stacey, 2009, p. 217), but this is often not the case, or at least in a suitable form (Samarawickrema, 2009; see also Wilson, 2009). While teachers have always used available educational technologies to enhance their teaching, in this instance, the university - which is a long-time leader in distance education - now offers a far greater range of courses using only WEL approaches. What is clear is that higher education teachers and students who are not familiar and comfortable with WEL are severely disadvantaged with deleterious results for both being highly likely.

In Australia such a situation has important ramifications since considerable emphasis is now placed on students' evaluations of their learning experiences and the teaching they encounter. Online student evaluation surveys are compared nationally, with both funding and reputational implications – so teaching has to be effective, no matter what form it takes. Furthermore, universities in Australia are becoming increasingly conscious of cost-efficient teaching and learning methods as funding becomes scarce and students are enrolling from the world over. WEL approaches appear promising on all counts and are becoming increasingly prominent as competition for students and funding increases.

This chapter provides a case study of the triumphs and tribulations of teaching an off-campus university course using WEL for the first time. It discusses the experiences of a middle-aged but early career researcher with an overloaded teaching allocation as she grapples with using WEL. Though comfortable with a basic course design using the university learning management system, enhancing this with a number of optional web technologies was a first-time experience. In a very frank personal account our case study participant reflects on what she learned through the experience. Hence this chapter considers what we believe may be the broad implications of WEL approaches for individuals and institutions in higher education settings, providing information that is likely to be applicable in other such contexts.

Our research results emerged from a small scale collaborative research project funded jointly by two Australian universities with a common interest in providing higher education access to students from rural and remote locations within Australia, as well as from overseas.

DESIGN-BASED RESEARCH

While following a grounded theory building approach generally, we chose to adopt design-based research methodology specifically for this project. We made this decision because design-based research is becoming increasingly popular in the field of technology-supported learning, due to its fundamental premises about the functions and purposes of research in developmental areas. In particular, the characteristics of good design-based research described by the Design-Based Research Collective (2003) closely matched our research purposes. That is, the central goals of designing learning environments and developing theories of learning were intertwined through all our deliberations; the development and research took place through continuous cycles of design, enactment, reflection / analysis and redesign; we wanted to develop shareable theories to communicate relevant implications to practitioners and other educational designers; we accounted for how designs functioned in authentic settings; we documented both successes and failures and interactions that refined understanding of learning issues; and lastly, we documented all aspects of the research to increase capacity in WEL innovations.

Consistent with Meier's (2007) description of Wiggins and McTighe's nine-stage process, this project began with a meaningful, real-life problem and involved collaboration between the researchers and practitioners at all stages of the research. From a basis of theory about learning and teaching, a literature review and needs analysis, research questions were generated and an educational intervention designed by researchers and teachers to respond to problems they identified together. This design process was implemented, revised and evaluated by the project team through an iterative process and reported to inform the educational field.

Hoadley (2004, p. 204) suggests that design-based research serves innovation and experimentation. In this project, the research involved a close relationship between all members of the research team, including the researchers, teachers and technical support staff. This relationship consciously blurred the "objective" researcher-subject distinction. As a small project, this design-based research uses tentative generalization, with the results being shared without the expectation that universality will hold (although, as noted below, the fieldwork data reported here resonated strongly with the experience of all members of the research team). In this project, the researchers and teachers frequently followed new revelations where they led, tweaking both the intervention and the measurement as the research progressed. Finally, as design-based researchers, we documented what was designed, the rationale for that design, and the changing understanding over time of both the teachers and the researchers of how each particular intervention embodied or did not embody the hypothesis that was being tested. In short, the theoretical fidelity of the interventions developed and implemented in the project was initially treated as suspect, and the subsequent reporting broadly documents the intervention to catch all relevant, but unanticipated, consequences.

Taking this approach the research involved teachers and students who were surveyed and interviewed about their WEL experiences. Two teachers in two regional universities and ten students located in rural and remote areas agreed to be involved in this small scale research project. Interviews were semi-structured, and all participants were invited to participate in online reflection as part of the project. In this chapter we focus on the experiences of one teacher - working in an Education Faculty - chosen because her involvement in the project incurred considerable new personal, professional and technological learning, providing insights into how a newcomer to WEL adapts to these new working circumstances. For purposes of retaining her anonymity, we shall call her Linda.

Throughout this research project we held several workshops with a large reference group, who considered the findings in light of their own experiences as university teachers. Through our field notes and the recording of anecdotes throughout the project, we report on the responses of Linda in particular, since she is, we believe, a fine example of a common case.

In other words, many others who worked with us in a different capacity throughout the project, but who considered they had encountered similar experiences and feelings about initial WEL usage agreed with the survey and interview feedback we received.

We look beyond the technical ramifications (which were considerable), to explore personal, philosophical, pedagogical and professional consequences, while also considering the implications of these experiences for future practice and professional learning elsewhere. The project was conducted in 2009.

DESCRIPTION OF THE PROJECT

The project researched a WEL environment that was designed to enhance student engagement and improve the learning outcomes of postgraduate learners from rural and remote communities who are studying by distance. Linda, a member of the academic teaching staff, was offered support in using WEL approaches to improve pedagogical effectiveness in her course for Masters level students who were studying the management of flexible modes of teaching and learning for training, vocational and higher educational contexts. The students were drawn from a range of postgraduate Education courses and those who volunteered for this project were all located in regional or remote parts of Australia. The course was designed to be delivered through the university learning management system supported by traditional distance education resources including print materials such as a reader and a study guide. The research focused on the integration of new information and communication technologies with traditional teaching and learning practices with technical and pedagogical guidance and support. Both the teachers and students were asked to reflect on their course engagement through using the WEL environment. As Linda described early in the program:

> The unit I am using for this project is formally structured as an entirely asynchronous online unit. I've selected it (and indeed volunteered to participate in the project) because: a) I have long wanted to introduce more varied uses of technology into the range of units I teach that explore teaching in FODE (Flexible, Online and Distance Education); and, b) my online students in these FODE units have recently been indicating that they would like some technology-based opportunities for synchronous interaction or more personal face-to-face style materials such as podcast lectures. (Linda, July 2009)

Linda rated herself as part of the mainstream majority who Rogers (1995) categorizes as "pragmatic or conservative, risk averse, and (who) seek proven applications of the use of technology in teaching" (cited in (Wilson and Stacey, 2004, p.34)). Linda rated herself at Level 3 using Wilson and Stacey's (2004, p. 42) levels of needs of academic staff to content of staff development. At this level, teachers are willing and ready to use new technologies and try to integrate these into their teaching but may have limited skills and confidence to be innovative without support. They require technical one-to-one assistance, hence the trend of universities to provide web pages as support instead of personal intervention was a concern that Linda anticipated. In her initial response to our questions she wrote:

> I'll have to be convinced about whether this represents best use of the human and time resources. A key reason I haven't introduced these strategies in the past is the time it takes to

set up and learn new technology, overcome technical glitches, etc. Much will depend on whether the level of support 'promised' in this project is able to be achieved. (Linda, July 2009)

During the year in which the project took place Linda was involved in the following stages:

- In May she attended an orientation session to introduce the project after which she was supported in setting up the WEL environment in the design of her course. She was provided with technical and pedagogical guidance and support to integrate the use of information and communication technologies with her traditional teaching and learning practices and she was asked to complete the first phase of an online survey.
- In July, before the course began, Linda identified students from rural and regional locations who were asked to volunteer to participate in the project. Linda helped run a preliminary online workshop for students to explain the WEL process through a one hour synchronous session using Elluminate Live, (eLive, a synchronous communication tool which enables participants to talk over the Internet, text chat online, share video, whiteboards, multimedia files and applications in one connected space and where moderators of eLive sessions can choose to record them and make them available for later review)as well as an asynchronous discussion over one week. Linda also recorded a vodcast introducing herself and the project to her students which she uploaded to her website on the university learning management system.
- Over the semester Linda was supported as she integrated new web-based technologies into her course. She scheduled four bi-weekly one hour eLive sessions with her students, usually mid week in the evening to suit their working hours, which were also saved for later review by her students. She recorded a lecture that included reference to resources on the web and a PowerPoint presentation which were uploaded to her web site for downloading as a streamed podcast. She recorded another final vodcast discussing her WEL process and reflections on the project which was also uploaded to her site. Throughout the semester she maintained a regular and responsive interaction with her students through online discussion and monitored their involvement in online scenario discussions and use of online print-based resources. At the end of the semester she was asked to respond to reflective questions about these aspects through emailed questions.
- Linda was interviewed about her perspectives on the use of the WEL and the students' engagement in the course.
- At the end of the year Linda was invited to participate in a dissemination workshop where the findings of the project were presented and discussed.

RESEARCH FINDINGS

At each point in the semester described above, as Linda reflected on her WEL usage and experiences, she shared her thoughts and experiences with the research team. We found that Linda's responses could broadly be categorized under three main themes – time, technical support and professional learning, and pedagogical change and student engagement, which are discussed below.

Time

Linda's greatest frustration was finding extra time to trial and implement WEL innovations. As she explains on being asked what difficulties she encountered:

> Time – getting my head around how the technology works and how I can use it; also the considerable time and frustration involved in dealing with student questions when the technology DOESN'T work. The more time I put into being engaging and innovative in this unit, the less time I have available for providing the levels of support and engagement that I normally expect myself to provide in my other (teaching) units. This is probably easy to justify to students in this unit – (but) less easy to justify for students in other units … To be honest, if I am to use this technology more widely in my units, I need to find a way that doesn't involve shifting the available resources (i.e. my time) away from the bulk of my students towards a small number in one unit. (Linda, September 2009)

This comment was made in the context of Linda explaining her heavy workload, exacerbated by having to pick up additional courses and students through the retirement of a colleague, and through agreement to become involved personally in another research project with people who were beginning to make unreasonable demands, making her working week much longer and less enjoyable. In many ways this is a common story. Through all kinds of demands and changing circumstances, academic work can be extended and altered unexpectedly, while much of it remains both atomistic and invisible to colleagues who are experiencing similarly work intensive lives. Of special concern to Linda was her frustration about the necessity of producing research outputs in the form of publications in time-strapped contexts in an environment characterized by pressure and competition. But involvement in our project added stress and work, and at times Linda's emails and survey responses expressed her regret about agreeing to be involved. During these times we had discussions with Linda about her participation, and she agreed to continue without being pressured, simply because she knew that ultimately she would have to come to grips with WEL. We felt very concerned, none-the-less, about the extra pressure Linda was feeling through encountering new WEL technologies in her teaching, on top of myriad other commitments. She stated in her emails:

> Frankly, if I hadn't had to do this for this project - if I hadn't been made to (learn new technological uses) - I wouldn't have done it. I'm too busy and it would have been too hard. That's the reality - I've come a bit, kicking and screaming.
>
> I am currently drowning in work, all of which seems due by the end of September. Working in a Faculty that has abolished staff support, every time you ask for advice you're told to find it on the website. I don't have time for this. (Linda, July 2009)

Linda's outbursts of frustration, however, did keep us alert as to how much pressure we were placing on her, and we tried to be more helpful than demanding. However, Linda counter-balanced her own arguments somewhat through her personal understanding about how useful and time saving WEL approaches could be, and how student learning could be enhanced through their usage. Furthermore, she understood the need for her own ongoing renewal as a teacher and relished the opportunity to experiment with WEL practices.

Technical Support and Professional Learning

Fortunately the research project provided technical support for Linda but such support should be accessible to any teacher attempting to use technology for the first time, which is often not the case. However, the technical support was not always provided at the time or in the form that Linda required. At the researched universities technical support is mostly available through a telephone hotline, with academic service requests queued for response, which in itself can be a time-consuming process. Furthermore, not all queries are adequately or satisfactorily resolved. Hence Linda was appreciative of the one-on-one, face-to-face support she received through her participation in the project, (although even that was not available at all times):

> The support provided by (the team and their contacts) for the eLive sessions has been fantastic. There is no way I could have managed the access problems that arose when we first started out in this project, and not being able to address those raises fundamental questions of equity about building course components that only some students can benefit from. (Linda, September 2009)

As this comment demonstrates, Linda was concerned that her own lack of technical skill in using some web-based technologies raised issues about equitable learning provision for students – for example, students who encounter teachers who are less technologically competent may be disadvantaged compared to those whose learning experiences are enhanced through their teacher's in-depth familiarity with a wider range of web-based applications. This raises questions about the effect of WEL aptitude and performance on teachers' professional identities.

Even trying to find technical equipment to record podcasts was initially a problem, although when overcome Linda was delighted with her informal introduction to her students, recorded from her desk through a webcam. And although feedback from technical staff indicated that this wasn't of good enough quality, Linda and her students were very happy with this simple way of introducing themselves through a personalized message on the web site. Linda felt she had accomplished something quite significant along her WEL journey.

The university provided streamed recording equipment accessed and organized through a website and although this appeared efficient to the ICT staff, it was again a frustration to Linda who needed someone to show her how to use this technology. The research team provided the support required and Linda has since vowed to use it in all her future online courses due to its ease and simplicity. The support provided in person at the time of need enabled a much easier use of technology as Linda expressed:

> In this marvelous world where mainstream staff support seems to be addressed by providing URLs and reassurances that it's all easy, I have become very hesitant to try new technologies. … I simply don't have the available time or the headspace to start downloading

instructions and working things out for myself - especially when my forays into technology using (university) systems leave me with little confidence that what I'm trying to do will actually WORK! ...Without the additional (and highly valued) support provided by staff involved in the research project I would not have gone anywhere near trying the few things I've tried in this unit. (Linda, September 2009)

Linda found that students also expected support for using new technologies such as eLive and she was expected to provide this while the technical support provided to her by the university's IT services was insufficient to her needs.

Some difficulties are bound to exist, especially when people engage with technologies for the first time. But for Linda, there were occasions when mistakes and shortcomings should not have been expected, such as:

> ... the satisfactory migration of course materials, the usual late notice for course change in universities, the lack of human support when you need it, the nuisance of clunky online environments, infrastructure inadequacies, having to use course templates that don't suit everyone's needs, unsatisfactory support services, keeping up with online course chat functions.... And then I wonder, is the learning curve too steep for increasingly time-strapped academics? What happens with casual staff – or when staff (members) leave? (Linda, November 2009)

According to Linda, there is a strong sense amongst her colleagues that until adequate support and professional learning are provided, academics can expect to "go it alone and find (their) own way through the woods", which is an unsatisfactory situation.

Linda was also adamant that higher education teachers cannot simply present WEL through the likes of web links without considering student engagement in the course. As a result, Linda went to considerable effort to learn how to use the technologies described above, particularly vodcasting and eLive, to engage more fully with her students and their learning. Students in turn, appreciated this, with highly positive comments made about Linda's teaching through the annual *Student Evaluation of Teaching Units* (SETU) survey – which were much more favorable, in fact, than those received in most other courses. Students stated they "could feel Linda's presence as a teacher", felt as if they knew her better, and perceived her genuine interest in them and their learning experiences. This feedback provided considerable satisfaction and made Linda's efforts all the more worthwhile in her own eyes. (And since this time, due in part to her foray into WEL, Linda was nominated for and awarded a quality teaching honor!)

Our research supports the findings of Wilson and Stacey (2004) who argue that competent, confident online academic teaching can still not be assured even if teachers have used computers for considerable years in their daily lives, are competent computer users and enthusiastic learners and teachers. Specifically, Linda found the roles of technologist, course designer, process facilitator, WEL teacher and learner (Goodyear et al., 2001) to be areas that created extra anxiety and feelings of lack of confidence.

Pedagogical Change and Engagement

Web 2.0 social and technological infrastructure supports a great range of participatory teaching and learning activities achieved through virtual means. WEL extends traditional conceptions of the "classroom" to "enable hybrid learning spaces that travel across physical and cyber spaces according to principles of collaboration and participation" (Greenhow et al., 2009, p. 247). Linda found WEL enabled and assisted inquiry based learning and increased student sharing and engagement whilst learning off campus but online. She found that WEL provided greater choices and empowered learners.

The research project enabled Linda to explore the advantages and disadvantages of different technologies and through the students' data collected she was able to realize the most appropriate technologies for her needs and plan her future courses using WEL. As she says:

> I embarked on this project with the aim of using it as a pilot to explore opportunities for using ICTs that I had not been using ... I made this decision in large part in response to feedback from students that they wanted more sense of (a WEL site) as a place where real people meet – they wanted faces and voices as well as text-based interaction. When I started I had some ideas about things I wanted to try. Looking back, I feel I have tried most of those things. Some worked as I'd hoped, some did not. I don't actually feel that I've made as big an impact on the delivery of THIS ... as I'd hoped, BUT I do very much feel that I've made significant progress in that I now appreciate some of the benefits and some of the limitations of using interactive blended learning technologies. ... I have developed a plan for using the technologies that worked for me ..., and building a series of student transition support iLectures and voicepoint / videoconference seminars to be conducted for a particular cohort of students across a number of Masters units. This proposal has been very well received by all who I have discussed it with, and it looks like it might be adopted more widely in the Masters program. Based on my experience with the time, energy, and limitations of eLive, I am not planning to use this particular technology on an ongoing regular basis. I MAY look at using it with some of my research students. I certainly plan to create an informal sitting-at-my-desk podcast / vodcast (which IS the right term???) as my introduction in all my online units. And that, after all, is what a pilot is supposed to achieve. (Linda, November 2009)

While seeing the very positive benefits of WEL, the comment above also reveals difficulty with fast-moving technological terminologies, which indicate a further need for ongoing professional learning and support. Even a minor matter such as whether there is a difference between podcasts and vodcasts, was considered a consequence of Linda's increasing intensification of her workload. She simply did not have the time to find out whether the terminology described a difference between the two.

IMPLICATIONS

There are many implications that can be derived from these themes. These implications relate to learning for students and teachers, policy, resources, support, leadership, and evaluation. However, from what we have read and researched in this field, it appears that too few lessons have been learnt and translated to transformative policy and practice in Australian tertiary institutions. We discuss these implications in the interests of this design-based research having broader applicability and to aid future research and discussion in this area, in line with our original intentions.

Learning

The constant proliferation of WEL continues to transform teaching and learning and organizational cultures in higher education. There are enormous expectations on teachers' ability to remain interested and committed in order to teach using WEL to increasing levels of sophistication. Clearly WEL requires certain desirable technological competencies amongst teachers and learners.

Like any teaching and learning situation, both are improved through the efforts of individuals. Linda believes that although her initial investment in time to become familiar with new applications was onerous, eventually – after much frustration, it paid off. Linda is therefore aware of her own growing respect for the possibilities that WEL offers for her as a professional, for her students and for the learning community they create together.

Hence from our findings WEL is as much, if not more, about teacher learning as it is about enhancing student learning.

Academic staff members do not embrace technological change and developments at the same rate (Wilson and Stacey, 2004). This study demonstrates a continued need for higher education institutions to provide greater access to professional learning in WEL. Such provision would include one-on-one and face-to-face instruction, an immediate response help line, personal assistance when experimenting for the first time, and some easily described (user-friendly) notes for future reference. Opportunities for staff to work together to share knowledge, ideas and experiences would also be useful.

Higher education institutions should understand and be mindful about the factors that influence WEL adoption and familiarity rates. Clearly a number of individual factors come into play, yet some common concerns could be more readily addressed and resolved to ensure steady, ongoing improvements in teaching and learning. Similarly, the take-up of WEL beyond a cursory, foundational level appears to be very much an individual decision. If WEL requirements were embedded into course requirements and probationary and performance reviews, we assume take-up and proficiency rates would increase. However, while professional learning and support provisions are perceived as inadequate, this would be highly unfair. Students may also require similar support in learning about WEL while undertaking their coursework.

As some WEL applications proved more useful than others, we see the need for further investigation into which WEL social networking and virtual environment features best assist temporally and spatially separated teachers and learners. We also wonder how learning connections can be made between different applications (Zhang, 2009) and how learning across applications can be calibrated to demonstrate those that are more effective than others for both teachers and students.

In our study Linda found trade-offs for her extra work through improved SETU (student evaluation) results, even though this was not her motivation for trialing WEL. We believe the benefits of using WEL should be highlighted to off-set the difficulties people will experience at the beginning of their WEL engagement. Professional learning support is as important as technical support. Clearly professional learning and training in WEL is a key element to improve the quality of university teaching and, consequently, the pedagogical sustainability of WEL itself.

Resources

The most obvious resource implications of WEL concern costs associated with constant technological upgrades in hardware and software to capture the extent and potential of WEL. As major hubs of learning internationally, university resource allocations to ICTs and WEL will continue to expand. As we found, part of this resource allocation should be spent on face-to-face, one-on-one professional learning, in addition to online and timely helpdesk sources of information.

The design of WEL resources is also a strong consideration for improved university teaching and learning. While university teaching and learning takes WEL for granted, the design of web-based resources makes for greater or lesser degrees of usability, usefulness and interactivity. This feature, according to Linda, is commonly overlooked, with many teachers failing to give sufficient attention to how WEL environments can be used for optimum interactivity, participation, creative capabilities and knowledge production. Too often WEL is used in courses at a base level only.

There is a huge requirement for technological and professional learning resources which, as Linda explained, need to be direct and one-on-one rather than impersonal. The lack of support in these two areas was Linda's largest source of frustration and disappointment. Linda was in no doubt, that the university needed to improve most in these areas to be of greatest support to her as a teacher, and subsequently, to students. These support and learning resources are costly and have been easy targets for 'cost efficiencies' and personnel downsizing exercises, as university budgets have become increasingly stretched over the past two decades (Marginson, 2002). This policy is having deleterious effects, according to Linda, who would like to see reversals on false economies on resources and funds.

Leadership

We have found that implications of ICT and WEL reforms and improvement for educational leadership in higher education are rarely raised. In this study, Linda found few leaders within her faculty, formal or informal, who took responsibility for problems, future developments or technological capacity building amongst academics. These matters are obviously assumed at a centralized level, but decision makers and policy makers appear to be unknown, remote and inaccessible, such that few teachers would be aware of their names or roles. Certainly, remaining abreast of developments is an individual matter, and never had Linda been asked about her needs, ideas or opinions before new learning management systems have been implemented. Leadership per se, was absent or invisible.

Policy

Attached to the above comment about leadership, it appears that universities are such mammoth organizations that ICT policy development and involvement is not within the realm of teachers at the grassroots level. In Linda's case, she had never been consulted about policy or practice, yet was expected to adjust to policy and attendant changes to practice – some of which were major, second order changes – irrespective of any significant personal and professional repercussions. One example was the removal of human, face-to-face problem solving technicians and WEL support personnel from faculties, to be replaced with a university-wide hotline service available via phone or email, with resultant time delays, misunderstandings and the frustrations of DIY over-the-phone repairs and assistance with online space building. Hence there is a call and need for policy in WEL and ICT in general to be developed from the grassroots up - from the perspectives of the core users - university teachers and students.

Evaluation

While teachers and teaching are evaluated through the likes of SETU which includes questions such as how students' technological capabilities had been developed through the course - the technology, its infrastructure, policies, resources and support services are not evaluated by teachers or in-house users. Linda was not required to provide constructive feedback to the university's IT division as to how the technology or technology services could be improved or to explain what professional learning and support she desired. This she perceived as unfair, yet Linda conceded that having such a question in student evaluation surveys did inspire her to explain to students in a podcast the technology "experiments" she was trialing in order to improve her service by responding to their feedback. From the student data gathered it was found that this honesty and a sense that Linda was 'listening' to their requests was greatly appreciated by students.

Had Linda had the chance to evaluate IT services in general and WEL in particular, she would have indicated how her experiences as a teacher could have been better assisted, supported and enhanced.

CONCLUSION

Tertiary teachers and students have no choice but to engage with WEL, although their levels of commitment and competence cannot be pre-determined. Our study demonstrates many inadequacies in current policies, practices and provisions. Unless these many-faceted issues are embraced for resolution by individuals from all levels and positions within universities, they are likely to remain as impediments to fruitful, robust and full engagement with all the learning possibilities that WEL entails. The findings of this small study can be summarized thus:

- higher education teachers require a thorough understanding and constant, up-to-date professional learning experiences in WEL applications – especially in what to use and how to use them;
- teachers' personal attitudes, fears and emotions about new technologies and web-based learning approaches influence their experiences in using WEL;
- lack of professional learning support or technological back-up with the concomitant time consumed in do-it-yourself problem-solving is a common experience for many higher education teachers, including our case participant;
- for many higher education teachers, use of WEL is as much about teaching others (subject matter) while learning oneself (in WEL applications);
- effective higher education teachers do not assume that students have access to or can use WEL. They carefully explain to students how to use WEL (through applications such as podcasts or posted instructions, for example). Linda found that some of her students were as unfamiliar with using WEL as she was;
- competency levels in WEL may influence higher education teachers' sense of identity, their own professional standing and confidence in light of students' complaints and questions to which those unfamiliar with WEL may have few or no answers;
- learning how to use WEL through do-it-yourself methods such as an online help facility can create stress and anxiety in already time-strapped contexts such as universities, where much academic work occurs outside working hours and / or remains hidden and
- initial WEL engagement can be stressful and anxiety-provoking for teachers unless they have access to effective and timely support, usually of the "behind the shoulder" kind.

An over-riding issue is the need for leadership in WEL at the institutional level. Given the enormous potential for learning and teaching, equity, access and the ability to transcend barriers of time and space, WEL developments should assume a greater priority in higher education as usage becomes increasingly expected, assumed and demanded. Teachers such as Linda certainly hope that universities develop a range of much needed, but currently under-developed, services around WEL adoption, usage and improvement.

REFERENCES

Design-Based Research Collective (2003). Design-based research: An emerging paradigm for educational inquiry. *Educational Researcher, 32(1)*, 5–8.

Goodyear, P., Salmon, G., Spector, J.M., Steeples, C., and Tickner, S. (2001). Competencies for online teaching: A special report. *Educational Technology Research and Development, 49*(1), 65-72.

Greenhow, C., Robelia, B., and Hughes, J. E. (2009). Learning, teaching, and scholarship in a digital age. Web 2.0 and classroom research: What path should we take now? *Educational Researcher: An Official Journal of the American Educational Research Association, 38*(4), 246-259.

Hoadley, C. M. (2004). Methodological Alignment in Design-Based Research. *Educational Psychologist, 39*(4), 203-212.

Marginson, S., and Rhoades, G. (2002). Beyond national states, markets, and systems of higher education: a glonacal agency heuristic. *Higher Education, 43*(3), 281–309.

Meier, E. (2007). *Understanding by Design Wiggins and McTighe: A Brief Introduction* (Presentation).   http://iearn.org/civics/may2003workshop/Understanding%20by%20 Design% 20Teaching%20Ellen%20Meier%20CTSC.pdf.

Rogers, E.M. (1995). *Diffusion of Innovations* (4th ed.). New York: Free Press.

Samarawickrema, G. (2009). Blended learning and the new pressures on the Academy: Individual, political and policy driven motivators for adoption. In E. Stacey and P. Gerbic (Eds.), *Effective blended learning practices: Evidence-based perspectives in ICT-facilitated education,* pp. 222-238. Hershey, PA: Information Science Reference.

Wiesenberg, F. and Stacey, E. (2009). Blended learning and teaching philosophies: Implications for practice. In E. Stacey and P. Gerbic (Eds.), *Effective blended learning practices: Evidence-based perspectives in ICT-facilitated education,* pp.204–221. Hershey, PA: Information Science Reference.

Wilson, G., and Stacey, E. (2004). Online interaction impacts on learning: Teaching the teachers to teach online. *Australasian Journal of Educational Technology, 20*(1), 33-48.

Wilson, G. (2009). Case studies of ICT-enhanced blended learning and implications for professional development. In E. Stacey and P. Gerbic (Eds.), *Effective blended learning practices: Evidence-based perspectives in ICT-facilitated education,* pp.239-258. Hershey, PA: Information Science Reference.

Zhang, J. (2009). Toward a creative social web for learners and teachers. *Educational Researcher: An Official Journal of the American Educational Research Association, 38*(4), 274-279.

In: Faculty Training for Web Enhanced Learning   ISBN: 978-1-61209-335-2
Editors: Manuela Repetto and Guglielmo Trentin   © 2011 Nova Science Publishers, Inc.

Chapter 8

ECOMPETENCE TO MOVE FACULTY TOWARDS A SUSTAINABLE USE OF LEARNING TECHNOLOGIES IN HIGHER EDUCATION

Dirk Schneckenberg
ESC Rennes School of Business, France

ABSTRACT

Based on a theoretical framework for the concept of eCompetence of academic staff, this chapter develops explores principles for the design of faculty development measures. It carries out a literature review that identifies key components and combines them into a model of action competence, which serves as point of departure to develop a concept for eCompetence. We define eCompetence in higher education context as the motivation and capability of faculty members to use information and communication technologies (ICT) in the classroom. This general view on eCompetence is specified by contextual factors that teachers face in eLearning scenarios. A discussion of portfolio models, which aim to increase the motivation of faculty to use learning technologies for their teaching and learning activities, is concluding this study. Main conclusion of this work is that universities have to create holistic portfolios for faculty development which extend considerably both the scope and the breadth of traditional training measures, and they have to offer institutional incentives to increase the motivation of faculty to sustainably use learning technologies for their courses.

INTRODUCTION

eCompetence for lecturers and academic staff is taken up in the current eLearning discussion as one element in wider strategic objectives of universities to sustainably implement eLearning into their institutional structures and work processes. The eCompetence perspective posits that faculty plays a crucial role for the sustainable integration of eLearning in higher education. It assumes that human factor is one important aspect within technology-driven innovation, and the potential of learning technologies to enhance teaching and learning in higher education is seriously restrained by both organizational barriers and knowledge gaps of faculty members. Two of the key questions that this chapter will discuss are: (1) What is eCompetence of faculty? And (2): How can we develop their eCompetence with coherent measures?

This chapter develops a theoretical framework for the concept of eCompetence, and it investigates principles for the methodical design of competence development measures for academic staff. A specific research focus of this study is placed on innovative competence development concepts and measures which go beyond traditional training for academic staff in universities. Two preconditions determine the active involvement of faculty in eLearning innovation: faculty members have to become aware on technology-driven changes and the potential of eLearning in higher education teaching and learning processes; and faculty members need to develop eCompetence to make persistent use of ICT in their personal work routines and teaching practice (Euler and Seufert, 2004; Johnson, 2003).

Learning technologies offer a wide range of options to enhance communication and interaction between teachers and students in universities. ICT can be used to realize innovative educational concepts and teaching and learning scenarios. Amongst other things, ICT can help to organize mass lectures through the storage and dissemination of electronic learning material; they have the potential to enhance flexible learning modes by providing students with permanent access to course resources and by widening their learning options independent from place and time; and they can help to raise quality standards and to create a culture of excellence in teaching and learning by adding digital communication channels for increased collaboration to course settings.

Faculty members face as a result of the rapid technology development a growing demand to offer more flexible, technology-enhanced teaching courses. This demand derives from students, who develop a changing learning style; and it derives from university management, which is pushing for a reduction of costs and an exploration of additional income sources. This demand includes for academic teachers the pedagogical challenge to design innovative learning environments which respond to the changing needs of technology-savvy students, and which apply ICT efficiently in order to extend the flexibility of educational services. To cope with these challenges, academic teachers need to enhance given and to acquire new competences that enable them to know and to judge why, when and how to use ICT in education.

Certainly, individual teachers may develop these competences through self-directed, non-formal learning processes. But if universities as educational institutions want to act in an organized way to improve the range and the quality of their educational services, they have in consequence to define coherent strategic frameworks for eLearning. These strategic frameworks need to include the creation of adequate support units and measures which foster the development of ICT-related competences of academic staff. This focus on competence development for faculty is one important factor for the sustainable integration of eLearning into higher education establishments - a strategic innovation objective which so far remains a major organizational challenge.

A number of surveys (Collis and Van der Wende, 2002; OECD survey, 2005; Open and Distance Learning Paper, 2004) confirm that many universities have neither fully recognized nor systematically exploited the innovative potential of learning technologies. Barrios and Carstensen (2004) have found that only 5% of the active faculty in German-speaking universities use learning technologies for their courses - a threshold for eLearning integration which a recent confirms at international level. Zesty and Massy (2004) report similar disappointing numbers for the US higher education context. They have consequently dubbed eLearning in their report a 'thwarted innovation'. This finding fits well the results of (Latchem et al., 2007) which show that eLearning in Japanese higher education advances at the leisurely speed of a tortoise. By summing up these studies, we can resume that the integration of eLearning in universities has so far been disappointing both at the macro-level of their strategic options and at the micro-level of their educational work processes.

While it is evident that technology development outpaces strategic thinking and pedagogical design in universities, the essential role of faculty in the slowdown of eLearning innovation seems so far to remain underestimated. Kerri's et al. (2005) argue that faculty members are the process owners and gate keepers of research and teaching in universities. Faculty members define the (subject) curricula, they plan study programs and individual courses, and they communicate and interact with students in teaching and learning scenarios. While this key role of faculty in universities has not changed, the pervasive nature of ICT has driven the evolution of eLearning as strategic issue for the innovation of higher education. Faculty is nowadays facing new pedagogical challenges; they have to design learning environments which respond to the changing needs of technology-savvy students; and they have to integrate ICT into their courses to extend the flexibility of educational services in universities. But does faculty have the competencies to respond to these challenges?

This chapter explores a range of key areas that are situated around the topic of eCompetence. It takes the perspective that an inadequate level of eCompetence of the majority of faculty members is one reason for the slow adoption of eLearning in higher education. The human factor is one important aspect within technology-driven innovation, and the concept of eCompetence needs to be well clarified to overcome both organizational barriers for eLearning and to close knowledge gaps of faculty members. Section two of the chapter explores the concept of action competence; section three proposes a model for eCompetence discusses shortcomings of traditional ICT trainings; section four outlines institutional frameworks for the strategic integration of eLearning; section five introduces portfolio models for competence development of faculty; the conclusions present some managerial implications, specify limitations of this chapter and propose directions for future research.

A CONCEPTUAL FRAMEWORK FOR COMPETENCE

Before we can think about eCompetence, we have to clarify the competence term. Competence is a complex research subject and a certain level of incertitude about the competence concept can be found in many related studies and discussions. Definitions of competence are as manifold as their use in various contexts. Winterton (2005) characterizes the concept of competence in current research as fuzzy and he states that it is impossible to identify or impute a coherent theory or to arrive at a definition capable of accommodating and reconciling all the different ways that the term is used. Authors like Weinert (2001) and Erpenbeck and Heyse (1999) confirm this assessment, as they observe just in the German research literature a range of contradicting definitions for competence. The research literature on competence is as vast as it is diverse, and he level of complexity makes it almost impossible to define a generic competence concept which would represent all inherent theoretical aspects in an adequate way.

We can nonetheless identify a group of key components for competence which are used in a number of definitory approaches. These components include terms like knowledge, motivation, skills, abilities, aptitudes, values, performance, cognition, learning, proficiencies, and dispositions. Remarkably, most of these key terms within the competence concept are complex terms by themselves - they contain additional implications which need to be further clarified to understand what they represent within competence definitions. And, with reference to different approaches to competence, the nomination, the grouping, the hierarchical structure, the interrelation, and the interdependence between these key components is changing.

North and Reinhard (2003) have assigned the contributions from different science disciplines for competence research into two wider categories: (1) cognitive sciences, including psychology, pedagogy, philosophy, linguistics, neuro-, and computer science; and (2) social sciences, including sociology, organizational studies, business science, public management science. Weinert (1999) identifies at least eight different and mutually exclusive concepts for competence, and a common framework to harmonise these different approaches does not exist. The research on eCompetence in this chapter relies on the concept of action competence. Its key components are briefly outlined in this section.

Van der Blij (2002) defines action competence as the "... the ability to act within a given context in a responsible and adequate way, while integrating complex knowledge, skills and attitudes". Similar definitions of action competence are given by a number of other researchers (Dejoux, 1996; Erpenbeck and Heyse, 1999; Euler and Hahn, 2004; Weinert, 1999); The concept of action competence combines cognitive and motivational components into one holistic system of knowledge, skills, and attitudes. It assumes a learning process at the core of competence development and it puts an emphasis on action or on performed behavior. The largely cognitive and mental nature of these dispositions results in the dilemma that we cannot directly measure competencies; instead, competencies have to be measured through the assessment of performed action. Apart from cognitive dispositions, action competence includes individual, role-specific, and collective conditions for the successful development of competencies within a group or an institution. Action competence represents in this perspective the ability to react in an adequate way to challenges that occur in complex situations.

Weinert (2001) notes that the research literature tends to be fuzzy about the distinction between skills and competencies. Competence always implies that a sufficient degree of complexity is required in the act of performance to meet given demands and tasks. Those dispositional factors, which can be in principle automatized in performance situations, are more adequately characterized as skills. Therefore, the competence term can only be adequately applied to those task-solving activities which contain a high degree of complexity.

Motivation is a final key component for the understanding of action competence. It explains the difference between the ability to act and the concrete action. Potential actions of individual actors depend on their motivation to act. Only if substantial motivational drivers trigger an adequate performance in a specific situation, the ability to act – as a potential – will the ability to act be translated into adequate action.

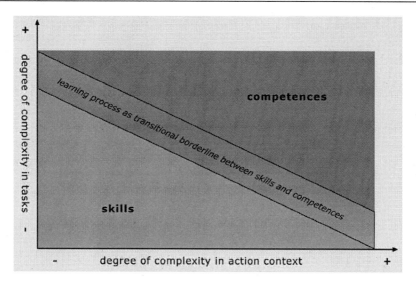

Figure 1. From Skills to Competencies.

Figure 2 gives an overview of the action competence model, as it has been described above. We can identify the following components as main building blocks for action competence: (1) learning at the inner core of the model; (2) a system of dispositions including knowledge, skills, and attitudes; (3) the four key competencies, which combine into performance; (4) the visible outer action competence shell; (5) the independent factor of intrinsic and extrinsic motivation; and (6) the context of performance..

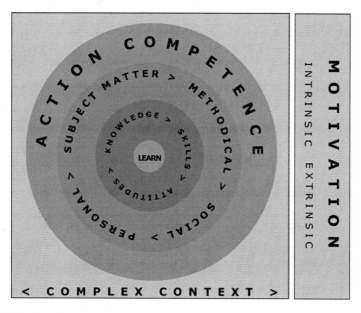

Figure 2. Model of Action Competence.

The action competence model serves as background for our subsequent conceptualization of eCompetence. Table 1 summarizes the basic assumptions for each key component of the action competence model.

Table 1. Components and Assumptions for Action Competence

Key Component	Basic Assumption
Learning	At the core of the action competence model – there is no competence development without learning.
System of Dispositions	The basis for goal-oriented, adequate action in complex contexts. The system of dispositions makes competent action possible.
Motivation	The essential condition for competence-based performance. A person can be competent, but if he or she shows no motivation to act, there will be no action at all. Motivation is not considered as an integral component of competence; it is supposed to be an independent influence factor.
Performance	The visible manifestation of 'hidden' dispositional competence components in specific social contexts. Assumptions on implicit competencies have to be validated and interpreted by the observation of real performance.
Context	The particular context of performance defines and specifies competencies which are necessary to act adequately in a given situation. It is not possible to specify competencies without an analysis of contextual action requirements. Furthermore, the degree of complexity within performance contexts triggers learning processes through which learners aim to acquire new competencies to handle the complexity.
Key Competencies	The typology of subject matter, methodical, social, and personal competence specifies the visible outer layer or shell of performance. The typology provides a conceptual substructure for the component of performance; the four combined key competencies integrate into action competence.

KEY DIMENSIONS OF ECOMPETENCE

The educational context, in which the competence of academic teachers to apply ICT in teaching and learning becomes manifest, sets the focus for defining eCompetence. Although eCompetence is using a technological point of view, the required competencies for academic staff are not limited to the 'e', the electronic component of the term. eCompetence needs to be interpreted in a wider mode. It includes not only technical aspects, it is understood as the educational ability to use ICT in teaching and learning in a meaningful way. Here we focus on individual eCompetence for discussing on how to diagnose and to measure this competence type of the individual teacher.

eCompetence is a verbal specification of competence. It is a sub-class of the competence concept that relates the ability for adequate action to complex electronic contexts (Phelps, 2005). eCompetence defines in general terms the ability to use ICT in a meaningful way. The personal eCompetence of faculty describes in the context of eLearning integration in universities their ability to use learning technologies for teaching and course delivery. The eCompetence of faculty deals from institutional perspective with the role of the human factor for a sustainable integration of learning technologies into universities.

The following model includes a range of layers for eCompetence which is at the micro-level part of the general action competence of academic staff members. The ability of faculty to use learning technologies at meso-level of the institution is influenced by competence development measures that universities create to foster the adoption of eLearning; and the motivation of faculty is influenced by wider institutional eLearning rewards, which universities establish to encourage the use of learning technologies. The portfolios of direct and indirect competence development measures for faculty are part of institutional innovation strategies at macro-level of universities which aim to exploit the pervasive potential of ICT for educational purposes.

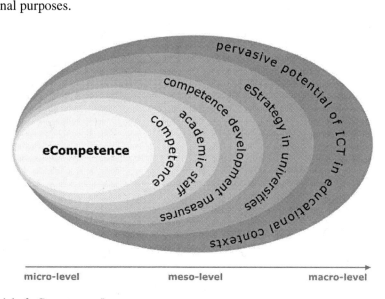

Figure 3. Model of eCompetence Layers.

Based on this argumentation, we subsequently propose a generic model for eCompetence, which takes the potential performance options of teachers in digital learning environments into account. Considering closer a potential structure for the concept of individual eCompetence, one can identify the following key components: the university teacher - which bears the competence as his or her general cognitive disposition to act, and the teaching and learning scenarios - which embed or rely on the use of ICT as the particular context in which the performance of the university teacher is situated.

The first key component is the competence of the individual university teacher. The action competence definition sets its focus on the performance dimension of the academic teacher. So the approach here discussed is tying the dispositional dimension - as individual prerequisites of a teacher to act in an adequate way, and the performance dimension - as the combination of key components of the competence of the teacher in observable action, together. In the preceding section we have explored a model that defines and integrates the key competencies personal, social and communicative, methodical and subject-specific competencies into action competence. This action competence model and its inherent implications are used for the discussion of the eCompetence model.

The second key component of eCompetence are teaching and learning scenarios which embed or rely on the use of ICT as the particular context in which the performance of the university teacher is situated. The eCompetence construct can only be inferred in a meaningful way from the specification of the situate context as the dimension in which the performance occurs. The eContext determines as contextual environment the options of the lecturer to perform in a given situation. The variables are included in this eContext serve to identify, which competencies are required by teachers to adequately act in given teaching and learning scenarios (Cattaneo, 2006; Phelps, 2005).

The specification of eContexts combines two key influence factors. The first key influence factor is the pedagogical design of the learning environment, and the second key influence factor is the technological design of the learning environment, in which teacher and learners interact and communicate with each other. Both key influence factors determine in their combination the potential action patters of the academic teacher in the learning environment. The pedagogical design of the learning environment can vary according to the pedagogical model that the teacher applies. Teachers can select design principles from a spectrum of pedagogical models for teaching and learning which foster interaction with students in specific learning environments (Wildt, 2004; Viebahn, 2004).

Teachers also need to select ICT tools that are adequate for use in given pedagogical scenarios. The available ICT options represent a spectrum of electronic variables which range in their complexity from simple electronic documents - for example the storage of pdf files on a website for download, to highly complex electronic learning environments - for example the setup and use of a virtual classroom with complex applications for interaction and communication. In an ideal pedagogical design scenario, university teachers select ICT options for their learning environments on basis of suitable pedagogical models. An economic sciences teacher who needs to cope with a mass lecture in front of a thousand students has different pedagogical concepts and ICT options in mind than his colleague in philosophy who plans a discussion seminar with a small work group. In practice, the selection process of teachers takes place on a pragmatic basis, combining both pedagogical models and the ICT options which are available within the universities in a simultaneous way.

To sum up, we assume that the eContext in the concept of the university teacher's individual eCompetence is determined by two key influence factors, which are the pedagogical and the technological design of the learning environment. Both key influence factors can be illustrated in form of a spectrum, which arrays the choices teachers can make on pedagogical and technological design options: pedagogical design options are represented in a spectrum of pedagogical models for the learning environment; and technological design options are represented in a spectrum of electronic variables for the learning environment.

The final component for the model is the eCompetence of the students that interact with teachers or with each other's in specific teaching and learning scenarios. Each student brings in a specific level of ICT-experience, which can be conceptualized in a similar way as we have inferred the eCompetence of teachers. The main difference between teachers and students is not contained in the dispositional dimension, but in the performance dimension of the competence concept that is determined by the context. The primarily goal of the teacher is to teach, the primarily goal of the student to learn. One important aspect within this relation is the fact that the efficiency of a specific course setting is largely dependent on the degree, in which competencies of teachers and students interrelate in teaching and learning processes (Sáiz, 2006).

So the roles in the interaction between teacher and student are situated at opposite sites of the teaching and learning process, but they need nonetheless to complement each other. The personal eCompetence of individual students describes their ability in using ICT in their learning activities. And the combined individual eCompetencies of students in a particular course sum up to the group dispositions of the student class to adequately use ICT in their learning.

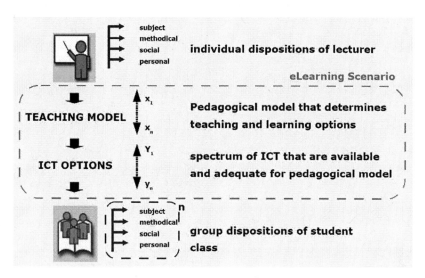

Figure 4. Generic Concept of eCompetence.

The next section investigates which implications the eCompetence concept has for the design of portfolio measures for faculty.

ECOMPETENCE DEVELOPMENT WITH THE PORTFOLIO APPROACH

The current eLearning discussion is gradually converging around strategic approaches for technology-driven educational innovation within universities. Authors like Duderstadt et al. (2003), Euler and Seufert (2004), Bremer and Kohl (2004), Vom Brocke (2005) and Boezerooij (2006) propose distinct pathways to develop these strategic approaches. Nonetheless, all authors finally argue for one common objective - to develop eStrategies as institutional innovation frameworks which guide the efforts that universities undertake to sustainably integrate ICT into their work processes. Bates (2000) as well as Collis and Van der Wende (2002) emphasize in their respective works that eLearning can only find its way into the mainstream of the university culture if it is rethought as part of wider strategic concepts for educational innovation. The specific role of eLearning within these strategic concepts needs to be based on the analysis of crucial integration factors for the deployment of learning technologies. University management has to identify the main target groups for eLearning within the student population and to think about the added value that learning technologies offer these target groups. This way, eLearning will not any longer be perceived as a separate area of innovation and as a means to itself; it can instead be applied as a technology-based toolset that enhances the portfolio of educational services within universities.

Many contributions that discuss eLearning strategies refer to Rogers (2003) model for the diffusion and adoption of innovations. Ely (1999) has specified Rogers' model for educational contexts and extended it with a specific implementation focus. He has identified conditions which determine successful implementations of educational innovation. Ely sees the combination of personal traits - like dissatisfaction, knowledge, commitment, and leadership, and institutional traits - like time, resources, rewards and participation as interrelated functions that assure the performance of educational institutions and influence their innovation capabilities. Cook et al. (2009) argue in a similar line that a well-balanced combination of intrinsic and extrinsic motivators drives faculty participation in institutional eLearning efforts.

This article assumes with reference to the above outlined strategic perspective that a successful implementation of eLearning in universities depends on the capabilities of leadership management to actively involve faculty in organizational change. The insufficient level of eCompetence in faculty is one inhibiting factor for educational innovation in universities. But the development of new competencies for faculty is not primarily achieved by conventional ICT training programs - it relies on wider organizational contexts and conditions. The motivation of academic teachers to acquire eCompetence and to make use of learning technologies is influenced by portfolios of competence development measures and institutional incentives that universities offer.

Recent findings in eLearning research (Bates, 2000; Euler and Seufert, 2004; Hagner and Schneebeck, 2001; Johnson, 2003; Kerres et al., 2005; Allen and Seaman, 2007) indicate that traditional training courses for teachers are not sufficient in scope and impact to generate ICT competencies for academic staff members. Accordingly, we have to identify and to analyse innovative approaches for eCompetence development within universities. Elements of these innovative approaches can be, for example, a well-balanced combination of formal training courses and additional measures for non-formal competence development - measures, which are embedded into the immediate work environment of the individual teacher; or measures, in which academic teachers interact and develop ICT-related competencies on-the-job or near-the-job in communities of practice, peer groups or networks.

Portfolio models combine formal and informal learning with organizational incentives; they aim to develop not only cognitive, but also motivational and attitudinal competence levels of faculty to use ICT and to engage into eLearning. Portfolios of direct and indirect competence development measures extend the training delivery model, where faculty attends 2-3 days seminars on pedagogical and technical aspects of eLearning - traditional training approaches that have shown major flaws in efficiency (Carraher and Schliemann, 2002; Saks, 1997; Lave, 1988). Adding to the training transfer dilemma, several eLearning authors like Bates (2000), Euler and Hahn (2004), Hagner (2001), Kerres and Voß (2006) and Salmon (2004) argue that existing ICT qualification tend to be expensive, time-consuming, limited in scope, and they are not directly linked to real teaching and learning contexts of faculty.

This holistic vision of learning activities in portfolio approaches, which aims to increase both the scope and the efficiency of learning interventions, fits well with the conceptualization of action competence, as it includes not only subject matter knowledge, but also skills and attitudes as dispositional competence components. A number of researchers (Erpenbeck and Heyse, 1999; North and Reinhard, 2003; Weinert, 1999 and 2001) emphasize the importance of non-formal or informal learning processes for the acquisition of competence. The portfolio perspective for faculty development also fits better the specific work culture in academia, as high degree of autonomy of faculty in universities is one dominant trait of the academic learning culture (Light, 1974; Weick, 1976; Prosser and

Trigwell, 1999; Becher and Trowler; 2001) The competence development of faculty is driven by the readiness of staff members to engage in self-directed learning to stay up-to-date in their discipline domains.

These institutional peculiarities of universities have implications for the design of appropriate eCompetence measures. Kerres et al. (2005) have developed a typology of eight different types of direct and indirect measures. The four direct measures are: (1) to provide information; (2) to foster positive attitudes; (3) to organize educational supplies; (4) to offer consulting support. The four indirect measures are: (5) to increase action readiness; (6) to establish learner-active quality development ; (7) to foster dialogue and collaboration; and (8) to make innovation mandatory. This typology of measures is basis for the analysis of effective eCompetence practices in a large-scale International survey. The case study findings are presented here in summarized form. A more comprehensive presentation of the case study methods and survey findings can be found in Schneckenberg (2008).

PRACTICAL EXAMPLES FOR ECOMPETENCE MEASURES IN UNIVERSITIES

Part of the European eCompetence Initiative, a European research project that has involved eLearning experts from 23 higher education institutions, has been the execution of a survey on faculty development measures. We have used a standardized web questionnaire to capture the expert knowledge of eLearning stakeholders. With reference to Wengraf (2001) the survey has been drafted, pilot-tested with a focus group to sharpen the research questions, and distributed to respondents. A total of 31 descriptions of eCompetence practices have been submitted to the database. Subsequently, a number of semi-structured case study interviews have been carried out with eLearning experts in partner institutions to gain in-depth insights of their faculty development activities. The resulting case study interviews as well as a collection of secondary data from all responding universities have been used as complementary sources of evidence for the analysis of the eCompetence practices.

For most eCompetence practices it has been possible to carry out a triangulation of data sources to make the findings more reliable (Mayring and Gläser-Zikuda, 2003). The eCompetence practices have been analyzed in comparative and longitudinal perspective to categorise key patterns and processes of each case (Yin, 2003). The evidence gives detailed insights into institutional strategies of universities to foster eCompetence of their faculties and indicates both inter-institutional similarities and differences in their approaches. The pattern matching approach helps to decide if and to what extent the theoretical implications of the portfolio model for eCompetence development have been implemented into organizational practice.

The findings show that eCompetence practices in the survey provide not a single example for a truly integrative portfolio of faculty development of this design and scope. Nonetheless, a number of universities have developed advanced strategies for eLearning, as they have created several types of measures that they try to combine to an integrative portfolio framework. The positive experiences that have been reported with the combination of several types of measures indicates that integrative approaches should be more extensively taken into consideration and explored in future research and practice of faculty development. A variation of types of measures and their coherent combination into institutional portfolios for faculty development are likely to produce more efficient learning outcomes than the knowledge delivery mode of traditional staff trainings.

The survey data also confirms earlier research findings of Hagner (2001), Euler and Seufert (2004), and Zemsky and Massy (2004) that faculty splits into different types of innovation adopters with distinct abilities, opportunities, motivations and interests to get involved into eLearning. Speaking in terms of Rogers' (2003) adopter categories, technology-savvy early adopters have other eLearning needs and support expectations than the more critical late majority. Accordingly, the design of competence development measures has to be tailored to learning styles and levels of expertise of these different faculty types and provision of learning options should fit their main interests and needs. eLearning stakeholders which are involved into faculty development need to know the differing motivational backgrounds of different faculty types, when they think about appropriate raining measures. Rather than to simply follow a supply-driven 'one size fits all' approach, they should consider an expansion of training formats towards a 'fit of measure to target groups' approach; this requires a demand-driven design of tailored competence development measures for the different eLearning adopter types within universities.

The meaning of eCompetence varies according to specific contexts of performance - the required abilities of teachers in lecture-centered eLearning scenarios are different from the abilities of teachers in interactive and collaborative eLearning scenarios. This finding, which the comparative perspective of the case studies reveals, is not surprising. The definition of feasible competence profiles depends on specifications of contextual performance requirements in different scenarios - 'team competence' in a philosophy department is for example quite different from its meaning in an US marine corps. This way, eCompetence is rooted in an underlying set of basic competencies in eLearning contexts, like the basic pedagogical competence of academic teachers. Nonetheless, specific contexts of performance result in the differentiation of faculty competence profiles for different eLearning scenarios. When we take this key finding from the comparative case analysis into account, it is unlikely that a generic definition of eCompetence which represents a global profile for a wide range of different contexts will evolve.

The case interviews with eLearning experts also indicate that different kinds of competence development measures produce differing degrees of impact on the dispositional key components of action competence. This variation translates into the following assumptions: (1) The provision of information has mainly an influence on the knowledge disposition of faculty's action competence; (2) The organization of educational supplies influence both knowledge and skills of faculty; And (3) measures like peer exchange in communities of practice influence in addition to knowledge and skills the attitudes of faculty.

This rating of measures could be used in an ideal scenario for training designs in a taxonomy of scales which indicates different values for the impact of specific interventions on the dispositional core components of action competence. Table 2 below is a short draft proposal of such a taxonomy of scales for developing knowledge, skills and attitudes.

Does this kind of taxonomy of scales and the holistic training perspective propose a feasible approach to explain the impact of learning interventions on competence dispositions? We have at the current stage of competence research no scientifically proven impact scales, we can only assume variations of significance in correlations between different types of competence development measures and levels of increase of action competence dispositions.

Table 2. Taxonomy for Impact of Competence Interventions on KSA

		Dispositions		
		Knowledge	Skills	Attitudes
Measures	Provide information	+++	--	--
	Organize educational supplies	++	+++	+
	...	...	...	...
	Foster dialogue and collaboration	++	+	+++

Additional research is needed to base these assumptions on solid empirical evidence. It is a challenging research task to understand inferences for types of learning on competence dispositions and to prove causal inference for a set of competence development measures on the acquisition or enhancement of action competence. This perspective requires a laboratory research design and methods with a strong focus on psychologically grounded competence assessment instruments, which measure the impact of specific learning interventions on specific competence dispositions of learners across a sufficient period of time.

CONCLUSION

When we think about integrating eLearning in higher education, eCompetence of faculty has an important role to play. Academic teachers have to enhance existing and to acquire new competencies that enable them to know and to judge why, when and how to use ICT in education. The main objective of institutional measures for eCompetence development is to support faculty in this learning process. These measures are part of strategic innovation in those universities which strive to improve the range and quality of their educational services with learning technologies; the faculty development includes a portfolio of formal and informal competence development measures and wider institutional incentives for eLearning. We have defined eCompetence in this chapter as a specific action competence of faculty to master learning technologies; its acquisition requires more than to respectively learn new knowledge, to develop new skills or to take on new attitudes. Action competence is a holistic concept which demands a holistic design of competence development measures.

A comprehensive combination of learning options and stimuli in several dimensions increases the probability to efficiently influence all three dispositional key components of the action competence. Multi-dimensional approaches combine several types of competence development measures within portfolio models. These portfolio models are better suited to serve the learning needs of faculty than one-dimensional approaches, which often rely on traditional training as the only type of measure. The main problem is currently that those types of measures, which are likely to have the strongest impact on competence development, are at the same time the most complex and challenging measures to be put into place. Measures which establish a learner-activating quality development or make innovation mandatory are the types which demand a high degree of eLearning commitment from universities to be taken into practice.

A research area for further exploration is the analysis of different eLearning adopter types in faculty which have different learning motivations and necessities. Not even the more advanced eCompetence practices have developed concise methodologies to assess specific learning needs and interests of different types of faculty members. Measures like communities of practice or faculty networks are rather planned and carried out in experimental designs. The evidence of this study has for example shown that peer exchange among faculty members is a highly efficient stimulus for learning and competence development. Will the readiness of faculty to participate in peer meetings increase if they are offered as tailored learning options within specific science disciplines? Should staff measures take place rather as tailored solutions at departments and study course levels than to be offered as central training for all faculty members within universities? Although some research has been undertaken on the topic of faculty types and motivational backgrounds for eLearning adoption, much remains to be further explored.

This chapter concludes with the insight that it is necessary to win the commitment of faculty in order to exploit the potential of learning technologies in higher education in this period of rapid and disruptive technology-driven innovation. eCompetence measures have to serve the real interests and learning needs of faculty; these interests and needs vary according to different types of eLearning adopters. A holistic perspective on competence development implies that universities have to increase investment into portfolio models. Well-designed portfolio measures have the potential to overcome with the development of eCompetence one innovation fundamental barrier and to get more faculty members on the boat for eLearning in higher education.

REFERENCES

Allen, I. E. and Seaman, J. (2007). *Online Nation - Five Years of Growth in Online Learning*. Needham, MA: Sloan Consortium. http://www.sloan-c.org/publications/survey/pdf/online_nation.pdf.

Barrios, B. and Carstensen, D. (Eds.) (2004). *Campus 2004 - Kommen die digitalen Medien an den Hochschulen in die Jahre?* Münster: Waxmann.

Bates, A.W. (2000). *Managing Technological Change. Strategies for College and University Teachers*. San Francisco: Jossey-Bass.

Becher, T. and Trowler, P.R. (2001). *Academic tribes and Territories. Intellectual enquiry and the culture of disciplines*. Buckingham: Open University Press.

Boezerooij, P. (2006). *E-learning Strategies of Higher Education Institutions*. Thesis, (PhD). University of Twente.

Bremer, C. and Kohl, K. (Eds.) (2004). *E-Learning-Strategien und E-Learning-Kompetenzen an Hochschulen*. Bielefeld: W. Bertelsmann Verlag.

Carraher, D.W. and Schliemann, A. D. (2002). The transfer dilemma. *The Journal of the Learning Sciences, 11*(1), 1-24.

Cattaneo, A. and Boldrini, E. (2006). A quali-quantitative research pattern for the surveying of a competence profile of the teacher using ICTs in a blended learning project. In U.

Bernath and A. Sangra (Eds.), *ASF Series Vol. 13* (pp. 35-47). Oldenburg: Bibliotheks- und Informationssystem der Universität Oldenburg.

Collis, B. and van der Wende, M. (2002). *Models of Technology and Change in Higher Education*. University of Twente.

Cook, R.G., Ley, K. Crawford, C. and Warner, A. (2009). Motivators and Inhibitors for University Faculty in Distance and e-learning. *British Journal of Educational Technology, 40*(1), 149–163.

Dejoux, C. (1996). *Organisation qualifiante et maturité en gestion des compétences. Personnel, 369*, 61-67.

Duderstadt, J., Atkins, D., and Van Houweling, D. (2003). The Development of Institutional Strategies. *Educause Review, 38*(3), 48–58.

Ely, D.P. (1999). Conditions that facilitate the implementation of educational technology innovation. *Educational Technology, 39*(6), 23–27.

Erpenbeck, J. and Heyse, V. (1999). *Die Kompetenzbiographie – Strategien der Kompetenzentwicklung durch selbstorganisiertes Lernen und multimediale Kommunikation*. Münster: Waxmann.

Euler, D. and Hahn, A. (2004). *Wirtschaftsdidaktik*. Bern: Haupt.

Euler, D. and Seufert, S. (2004). *Nachhaltigkeit von eLearning-Innovationen – Ergebnisse einer Delphi-Studie* (Swiss Centre for Innovations in Learning Report 2). University of St.Gallen.

Hagner, P.R. and Schneebeck, C.A. (2001). Engaging the Faculty. In C.A. Barone and P.R. Hagner (Eds.), *Technology Enhanced Teaching and Learning: Leading and Supporting the Transformation on Your Campus* (pp. 1-13). San Francisco: Jossey-Bass.

Johnson, D.F. (2003). Toward a Philosophy of Online Education. In D.G. Brown (Ed.), *Developing Faculty to Use Technology - Programs and Strategies to Enhance Teaching* (pp. 9-12). Bolton: Anker Publishing.

Kerres, M., Euler, D. Seufert, S., Hasanbegovic, J., Voss, B. (2005). *Lehrkompetenz für eLearning-Innovationen in der Hochschule (Swiss Centre for Innovations in Learning Report 6)*. University of St.Gallen.

Kerres, M. and Voß, B. (2006). Kompetenzentwicklung für E-Learning: Support-Dienstleistungen lernförderlich gestalten. In Harald Gapski (Hrsg.), *Entwicklung von Medienkompetenz im Hochschulbereich* (pp. 35-55). Schriftenreihe Medienkompetenz des Landes Nordrhein-Westfalen. Düsseldorf: Kopaed Verlag.

Latchem, C., Jung, I., Aoki, K. and Ozkul, A.E. (2007). The tortoise and the hare enigma in e-transformation in Japanese and Korean higher education. *British Journal of Educational Technology, 39*(4), 610-630.

Lave, J. (1988). *Cognition in practice: Mind, mathematics, and culture in everyday life*. Cambridge University Press.

Light, D., Jr. (1974). Introduction: The structure of the academic professions. *Sociology of Education, 47*(1), 2–28.

Mayring, P. and Gläser-Zikuda, M. (2003). *Die Praxis der Qualitativen Inhaltsanalyse*. Weinheim und Basel: Beltz.

North, K. and Reinhardt, K. (2003). Transparency and Transfer of Individual Competencies – A Concept of Integrative Competence Management. *Journal of Universal Computer Science, 9*(12), 1372-1381.

OECD (2005). *E-learning in tertiary education: where do we stand?* Paris: OECD.

Phelps, R., Hase, S. and Ellis, A. (2005). Competency, capability, complexity and computers: exploring a new model for conceptualising end-user computer education. *British Journal of Educational Technology, 36*(1), 67–84.

Prosser, M. and Trigwell, K. (1999). *Understanding Learning and Teaching: The Experience in Higher Education*. Open University Press.

Rogers, E. M. (2003). *Diffusion of Innovations (5th Ed.)*. New York: Free Press.

Sáiz, F. B. (2006). e-Competence of Online Students of the Humanities at UOC. In U. Bernath and A. Sangra (Eds.), *ASF Series Vol. 13* (pp. 71-90). Oldenburg: Bibliotheks- und Informationssystem der Universität Oldenburg.

Saks, A.M. (1997). Transfer of Training and Self-efficacy: What is the Dilemma? *Applied Psychology, 46*(4), 365-370.

Salmon, G. (2004). *E-moderating: The Key to Teaching and Learning Online (2nd ed.)*. London: Taylor and Francis.

Schneckenberg, D. (2008). *Educating Tomorrow's Knowledge Workers*. Delft: Eburon Academic Publishers.

Van der Blij, M. (2002). *Van competenties naar proeven van bekwaamheid, een orientatie* (Unpublished manuscript). University of Twente.

Viebahn, P. (2004). *Hochschullehrerpsychologie - Theorie - und empiriebasierte Praxisanregungen für die Hochschullehre*. Bielefeld: UVW.

Vom Brocke, J. (2005). Organisationsgestaltung im E-Learning - Konzeption und Anwendung für die integrierte Prozessgestaltung an Großuniversitäten. In K. P. Jantke, K. P. Fähnrich, W. S. Wittig (Eds.), *Marktplatz Internet: von E-Learning bis E-Payment* (pp. 157-164). Bonn : Gesellschaft für Informatik.

Weick, K.E. (1976). Educational Organizations as Loosely Coupled Systems. *Administrative Science Quarterly, 21*(1), pp. 1-19.

Wengraf, T. (2001). *Qualitative Research Interviewing*. London: Sage Publications.

Weinert, F.E. (1999). *Definition and Selection of Competencies - Concepts of Competence*. Munich: Max Planck Institute for Psychological Research.

Weinert, F.E. (2001). Concept of Competence: A Conceptual Clarification. In D. S. Rychen and L. H. Salganik (Eds.), *Defining and Selecting Key Competencies* (pp. 45–66). Seattle: Hogrefe and Huber.

Wildt, J. (2004). Vom Lehren zum Lernen - Perspektivenwechsel im Kontext hochschuldidaktischer Weiterbildung. In M. Kerres and R. Keil-Slawik (Eds.), *Hochschulen im digitalen Zeitalter: Innovationspotentiale und Strukturwandel* (pp. 203-214). Münster: Waxmann.

Winterton, J., Delamare Le Deist, F., and Stringfellow, E. (2005). *Typology of knowledge, skills and competences: clarification of the concept and prototype* (Centre for European Research on Employment and Human Resources Report). Toulouse Business School.

Yin, R.K. (2003). *Case Study Research - Design and Methods (2nd Edition)*. Thousand Oaks London: Sage Publications.

Zemsky, R. and Massy, W.F. (2004). *Thwarted innovation: What happened to e-learning and why?* University of Pennsylvania: The Learning Alliance.

In: Faculty Training for Web Enhanced Learning   ISBN: 978-1-61209-335-2
Editors: Manuela Repetto and Guglielmo Trentin   © 2011 Nova Science Publishers, Inc.

Chapter 9

PEDAGOGY OF THE WEB: IMPROVING PRACTICE TEACHING AND LEARNING ONLINE

David B. Whittier

Boston University School of Education, USA

ABSTRACT

This chapter synthesizes three data streams relating to web enhanced learning: literature on the time it takes to teach online as compared with classroom teaching, the author's original research on faculty methods teaching online and in classrooms (Whittier, 2009), and science emerging from neurobiology describing the features of face-to-face communication that bear on social intelligence (Goleman, 2006). Principle findings are that it takes more time to teach online, that faculty are less satisfied with and less enthusiastic about teaching online as compared to classroom teaching, and that evolutionary biology has conditioned us to make decisions based on trustworthiness in the physical world. Relating these findings develops an argument for distinguishing between asynchronous online and synchronous communications, whether online or face-to-face. A conclusion is reached that learning about and practicing synchronous online communications should be a priority in faculty training to improve web-enhanced learning.

INTRODUCTION

Pedagogy as word and concept is in many ways the essence of education but its meaning has varied throughout history. During the 19th and 20th centuries, pedagogy came to be considered as the art *and* science of teaching, an idea encapsulated by American educator Horace Mann in 1837 when writing, "teaching is the most difficult of all arts and the profoundest of all sciences" (Cremin, 1957). Pedagogy has not, however, always had such a stellar reputation. In ancient Greece, for example, a pedagogue was usually a slave considered "useless for other tasks" and thus employed attending a young boy by carrying his study material (Monroe, 1913). In (1885), Payne and Compayre described three branches of the study of pedagogy: the historical, the theoretical, and the practical, including various methods of teaching and learning. In his powerful (1985) work *Pedagogy of the Oppressed,* Freire established another branch of the concept of pedagogy. His descriptions of cultural and socio-economic contexts that limit resources and expectations in such as way as to limit what people thought they could teach and learn and thereby oppress the poor provided a new way to think about pedagogy. This work continues into the 21st century as the study of critical pedagogy.

Given the growth in the use of technology in education and the industrialization of distance education through use of the systems approach to its development and delivery (Moore and Kearsley, 2005), the case may be made that the threats posed by the industrialization and corporatization of education as just another profit making commodity are a real and present danger. From the analytical perspective of Freire and the subsequent school of thought represented by critical pedagogy, the industrialization of education in the form of a technology-based product suggests the possibility of further undermining the value of education as an instrument for the common good, the public good. Technologizing education also raises the possibility of a kind of technology-based cultural imperialism based not on educational and social values but on the ability to deliver the fastest and newest "product," much like cars or airplane travel (Burge, 2008). However, discussion of this branch of pedagogy will have to be the subject of another version of the Pedagogy of the Web. Rather, this chapter focuses on the methods of teaching that describe what it is that teachers and professors actually do when they are teaching. It focuses on how faculty spend their time when teaching, on what and how much, and then seeks to correlate that to their satisfaction in, and enthusiasm for, teaching. As Ralph Waldo Emerson reminds us "Enthusiasm is the mother of effort, and without it nothing great was ever achieved."

Pedagogy of the Web then, is about the quest for methods that effectively exploit web-based resources in ways that support and improve teaching and learning. This chapter weaves together three lines of inquiry into web-enhanced teaching and learning, while focusing primarily on teaching, and more particularly, on the form, quantity, and quality of the time it takes to teach online. Reviewing other research is the starting point followed by a review of the author's *Time Online* research project findings, designed to build on previous research, which elaborate aspects of previous research. The third strand reviews research on neurobiology that offers explanations for the distinctions between teaching and learning online and face-to-face.

LITERATURE REVIEW OF TEACHING ONLINE

Teaching and learning online has changed education on a scale seen by relatively few innovations in the history of education. However, online education does not exclude face-to-face education and thus the proportions with which they may be combined range over the complete spectrum from 100% online to 100% in the classroom. This survey utilized the standard of the Sloan-C organization that defines online teaching as at least 80% of a course delivered online and "typically" having "no face-to-face meetings"(Allen and Seaman, 2008, p. 4). They define a course where 30 to 79% of content is delivered online as a Blended/Hybrid model blending online and face-to-face delivery and where a "substantial proportion of the content is delivered online, typically uses online discussions, and typically has a reduced number of face-to-face meetings. Allen and Seaman further describe a "Web Facilitated Course" as "essentially a face-to-face course" where 1 to 29% of the content is delivered online and "may use a course management system (CMS) or web pages to post the syllabus and assignments." Although Allen and Seaman provide useful distinction, the combinations of online and face-to-face experiences will most likely continue to differentiate to the point where teachers and learners will move more or less effortlessly between online and face-to-face education. As online education scholar Murray Turoff put it in a 2003 letter from the editors of the Sloan-C View:

> "The sooner that distance learning technologies become commonly used to support face to face classes, the sooner we can leave it up to students whether they want to attend face to face classes or not. Maybe this will still take a decade to accomplish, but it will come, and then the concept of distance learning or distributed learning becomes obsolete and we have ALN (Asynchronous Learning Networks) or LN (Learning Networks) for all courses. No artificial separation between regular students and distance students would be the preferred and simplified administrative operation of a University" (Turoff, 2003).

Put another way, in responding to my question regarding the evolution of education as it incorporates online resources, one of my doctoral students replied

> I think this would be ideal – when distance education technologies and methods are so well paired with face-to-face classrooms that there is literally no difference between attending a class in person or by some other means. . . All classes would be available to qualified learners who might not be able to attend them in person. There would be no such thing as "distance learning" because the varied delivery methods would be used in some way by all students (Vigil, K., Personal Communication, 2009).

Despite rosy predictions of easy movement between online and face-to-face teaching, effectively integrating elements of the two forms adds complexity that presents a challenge to many faculty in deciding what resources will be used and when they should be used to advance learning. Examining several dimensions of this challenge is the subject of pedagogy of the web.

Teaching and learning online brings new emphasis on pedagogical methods, as well one of its more recent progeny, instructional design. A few features stand out as facilitating this new emphasis. For example, any online educational experience may be recorded and examined later for its pedagogical effectiveness. Simply that such examination can now be so easily performed means that it will be more frequently performed. These examinations offer opportunities for pedagogical improvements of recorded online courses. Renewed emphasis on pedagogy on the web also may, in part, be attributed to the ease with which online resources are created, stored, compiled, and distributed. This ease has created a danger of amassing a reservoir of online resources so large that learning becomes an exercise in "sipping from a fire hose." With much of humanity's knowledge or information available online, it is easy to be swamped. Another reason is more subtle but nonetheless important to understanding this emphasis.

In the first edition of *Distance Education: A systems view* (1996) Moore and Kearsley noted that when education is structured in media and technology, "presentations are not teaching" (p.133). This idea discounts the legendary lecture as an acceptable pedagogical method in teaching online and suggests pedagogical change in web-based teaching and learning. The opportunities for lecture capture as well as the construction of "made for the web" video and other presentation resources that may be stored and re-used indefinitely reduces the pedagogical value of the lecture form. The lecture may become a product to be produced and consumed rather than an inspiring learning experience. This raises the question that if faculty are not lecturing, what are they doing? The idea that presentations are not teaching when referring to web-based education creates an emphasis on pedagogical methods, as well as arranging their use through "instructional design."

In analyzing teaching and learning online, pedagogical interventions distinguish one online course from another. More important, if presentations are not teaching then pedagogical interventions must generally be composed of some kind of interaction. Spending time in interaction, rather than lecture, provides a description of a shift in pedagogy for faculty who would teach using online resources. McQuiggan described this movement.

> In rethinking their familiar ways of teaching when moving online, a change that is noted numerous times is a shift from teacher-centered instruction to student-centered instruction (Barker, 2003; Conceicao, 2006; Conrad, 2004; Gallant, 2000; Hinson and La Prairie, 2005; Jaffee, 2003; Tallent-Runnels et al., 2006). As faculty learn about alternatives to the transmission model of teaching, they are able to shift their instructional roles to place a greater amount of responsibility for learning on the students (Barker, 2003; Gallant, 2000) due to the increased opportunity for student participation in the online environment (Jaffee, 2003). In fact, in one survey research study (Ali et al., 2005) faculty ranked redesigning and rethinking faculty roles as the highest priority to be addressed in professional development sessions to prepare to teach in the online environment (McQuiggan, 2007).

Despite thinking that suggests online education diminishes the value of the lecture, the presentation of information cannot be eliminated. Learners must have ideas with which to interact. With this in mind it is not surprising that in their second edition of their text, Moore and Kearsley removed the "presentations are not teaching" critique and identify achieving a balance between presentation and interactivity as a significant challenge in teaching effectively online. They further identify another shift in pedagogical balance in suggesting that online resources such as discussion boards, email, and chat may create an "excess of interaction at the expense of presentation" (2005, p.145).These ideas suggest several questions. How are faculty to achieve the "right" balance in teaching online? What are the actual activities in which instructors are engaged in teaching online? And finally, how does this shift in pedagogical time relate to the satisfactions and rewards of teaching? The *Time Online* research reported here seeks to contribute to understanding the implications of data collected to address these questions.

Thinking about how teaching is evolving leads to many questions. For example, how much time and effort is required to develop quality online courses? Once a course is developed, how do faculty experience teaching online, both in itself and in comparison to traditional norm of teaching in the classroom? Other concerns relate to the human side of teaching. For example, does structuring a course for a Web-based platform mechanize and/or automate the experience of teaching? Does online instruction undermine the human bonds that make up the reason so many go into education in the first place?

Investigations of practical pedagogy are describing the strategies online instructors are using and how much time they take faculty to implement. This raises the principle question of this research: How does the way faculty spend time when teaching online affect their satisfaction with teaching? Of course, satisfaction can be a difficult concept to measure. For example, a colleague who in taking his masters program and teaching online had seen his class size grow to 200 and the need for 10 teaching assistants or facilitators described his evolving role as becoming more of a manager than a professor. Pining for the rewards of teaching he expressed the desire to "put the teaching back in teaching online" by delegating management to the facilitators and returning to meeting with students as his primary responsibility. My colleague's comments were addressing the consequences for the experience of teaching in what Moore and Kearsley (2005) consider as the economic necessity of having large-scale classes when teaching online. Achieving economic viability had changed the way he spent his time.

Literature related to how faculty spend time online (Cavanaugh, 2005; Keeton, 2004; Tomei, 2004) accumulate to the suggestion that teaching online takes more time than teaching in the classroom. Pachnowski and Jurczyk summarize earlier findings in stating that "nearly all communications that discuss the time it takes for faculty to teach in a distance environment report that it requires a great deal of additional time compared to traditional classroom teaching" (Pachnowski and Jurczyk, 2003).

Because of the spectacular growth of online education and the rapid evolution of the technology that supports it, it is easy to wonder if research results from even just a few years ago are credible in relation to this rapidly evolving environment. A 2008 to 2009 survey of more than 10,000 faculty in public institutions in the U. S. address this concern.

> Faculty members overwhelmingly believe that it takes more effort to develop and teach an online course than a comparable face-to-face course. Nearly 64 percent of faculty said it takes "somewhat more" or "a lot more" effort to teach an online course compared to a face-to-face course. The results for online course development are even more striking, where more than 85 percent of all faculty with online course development experience said it takes "somewhat more" or "a lot more" effort. Less than 2 percent of faculty thought that online course development took less effort than developing a face-to-face course, while 12 percent thought that teaching online took less effort than teaching face-to-face (Seaman, 2009, p.32).

These studies point to the extra time and effort associated with developing and teaching online. What then, are the possible causes for these concerns and how might we address them? Collecting data with which to explore possible explanations was the objective of the *Time Online* research study conducted during 2008 to 2009.

THE *TIME ONLINE* RESEARCH PROJECT

The "Time Online" research builds on previous research that teaching online takes more time than classroom teaching as well as distance education theory in examining the potential that teaching online changes the practice of teaching. Respondents were faculty who have taught at least one course online and at least one course in a classroom in higher education. The research was based on a conceptual view that teaching itself is the larger concept and teaching online or in a classroom were smaller, more exclusive concepts, hence, some data was collected on the comparison to teaching in a classroom, where applicable. Respondents were surveyed on their online pedagogies, and their enthusiasm for and satisfaction with teaching online, among other topics. One of the main subjects of inquiry was to learn more about faculty experience of time online. The survey was conducted on paper and online from February 2008 through February 2009.

The survey asked questions related to respondent's pedagogical methods in teaching online and in classrooms, the amount of time they report spending in these teaching methods, ratings of selected teaching outcomes that could offer explanations for any variances found, and their satisfaction in and enthusiasm for teaching. The intent was to probe for correlations between and among the use of different pedagogical methods, certain outcomes in teaching, how faculty spent their time, and satisfaction in, and enthusiasm for, teaching. Basic demographic data was also collected to describe the respondents.

Of the survey respondents (n=102), 84% identified themselves as teaching at a large private university in the Northeastern United States, 15% identified themselves as teaching at the Universidad Nacional de Educación a Distancia (UNED) in Spain, 2% identified themselves as teaching at a community college or a small private in the U. S., and one percent identified him or herself as teaching in higher education in Japan. Seventy eight percent (78%) reported having taught in classrooms for more than eight years whereas 44% had taught 5-8 years online and 37% had taught 2-4 years online. The sample then, was more experienced with classroom teaching than with teaching online. All respondents reported they had taught both in the classroom and online. No other demographic data was collected.

EXAMINING FACULTY METHODS IN TEACHING ONLINE

Two sets of questions in the *Time Online* survey collected data on methods used and the time they took. In the first set, respondents simply indicated the methods they used by checking a box and methods they did not use by not checking a box. Fearing that an open-ended question regarding methods used would result in findings too diverse to summarize, respondents selected from a list given, although both questions on classroom and online methods included a choice for "other" and a request to explain the other if chosen. The "other" category did not yield useful information, however, because of the low number who selected it (20), the even lower number who explained it (8), and the diversity of explanations. In the first set of two questions, respondents were asked to "Please check below the methods you use in teaching face-to-face in a classroom," and then in a separate question, "Please check below the methods you use in teaching online." The ranking resulted from summing the number of selections. These results are reported in Table 1 with the number selecting each one in parentheses.

In a set of questions following from those used to collect data simply ranking methods used, faculty respondents were asked *how much time* they spend in each of the various methods given in the list. Separate questions were asked on the methods used and time spent in them for online and classroom teaching. Table 2 reports methods ranked by the time spent in each one. Methods were chosen from a list provided in the survey.

Table 1. Ranking of methods used by number who use them (N=83)

Classroom	Rank	Online
Lecture or other presentation (82)	1	Email (82)
Discussion in class (78)	2	Discussion board (79)
In class group work (70)	3	Web-based instruction "transmission" (77)
Assessment (61)	4	Assessment of assignments posted online (69)
Student presentations (60)	5	Group work/collaborative learning (44)
In class individual work (46)	6	* Three types synchronous conferencing summed (42)
Mentoring (37)	7	Guided inquiry (33)
		Chat (33)
Guided inquiry (34)	8	
Discussion online (reading and writing) (29)	9	Mentoring (26)
Drill-and-Practice (28)	10	Drill-and- practice (13)
Other (9)	11	Other (11)

* Three types of conferencing summed: Synchronous video conferencing with visual of person(s), Synchronous audio conferencing without any visual, Synchronous audio conferencing with visual source such as Power Point, URL, or Whiteboard but without visual of person(s).

Table 2. Ranking time spent in different teaching methods online versus in classrooms (N=83)

Classroom	Rank	Online
Lecture or other presentation	1	Discussion board
Discussion in class	2	Email
In class group work	3	Web-based instruction "transmission"
Assessment	4	Assessment of assignments posted online
Student presentations	5	Chat
In class individual work	6	Guided inquiry
Mentoring	7	* Three types synchronous conferencing summed
Guided inquiry	8	Group work/collaborative learning
Discussion online (reading and writing)	9	Mentoring
Drill-and-Practice	10	Drill-and- practice
Other	11	Other

* Three types of conferencing summed: Synchronous video conferencing with visual of person(s), Synchronous audio conferencing without any visual, Synchronous audio conferencing with visual source such as Power Point, URL, or Whiteboard but without visual of person(s).

The rankings of methods by time spent describe some similarities and some obvious differences in the way faculty spend their time online as compared to classroom teaching. The rankings of time spent in methods are similar for classroom teaching and online teaching for discussion, for lecture (classroom) and web-based transmission (online), for assessment, for mentoring, and for drill and practice. Differences were recorded between the amount of time spent in group work and student presentations in classroom teaching and the amount of time spent in group work/collaborative learning in teaching online. Respondents reported more time spent in these types of student activities in the classroom than online, suggesting a noticeable shift in how their time is spent. From these rankings it appears that faculty spend less time interacting with students online than in classrooms.

Although the data showed a similar ranking in time spent in discussion online and in the classroom, there are differences within this method that were not investigated. Specifically, judging from my own experience classroom teaching for more than 20 years and teaching online for more than seven years, much of the discussion in online teaching is typed text and much of it in classroom teaching is spoken. Typed text is much more time consuming to prepare than speaking. The survey, however, did not make this distinction although analyzing the results suggests it as an area for further research.

Another prominent result from the data is the report that respondents ranked email as the second most time consuming method in teaching online. This corresponds to respondents ranking email as the most used method online as reported in Table 1. Unfortunately, email was not listed as a possible selection in the question on classroom methods, a limitation of this research that would benefit from further study. Nevertheless, the high ranking of email in teaching online was of particular interest and additional questions were included in the survey to examine it in more detail.

Questions were included in the survey to probe these potential differences in text-based communication should they occur. Thus, respondents were asked to report the average number of hours on email per week. When asked "Overall, in an average week of teaching (online and classroom listed separately), how much time in hours do you spend in the following teaching tasks?", respondents (n=81) reported spending 3.9 hours/week on email related to online teaching and 1.96 hours/week on email related to classroom teaching, almost exactly double the amount of time spent on email when teaching online. When this is viewed from the perspective of a 40-hour workweek, no doubt something most faculty only wish for, faculty spent nearly 10% of their teaching time on email. This raises the question: is email an acceptable, occupational hazard in 21st century teaching or can email be managed better to improve education?

To probe further the issue of communications with students, faculty respondents were asked about the differences in communicating with students when teaching online versus when teaching in the classroom. The results to this question were consistent with previous research reporting that it takes more time to communicate with students online. For example, in responding to the question: "How would you rate the time it takes to communicate with your students online as compared to the time it takes to communicate with your students in a class?" Eighty one percent (n-80) reported that it took "more time." To follow up on the nature of this time, respondents were asked to "Please explain your response to the previous question. What is it that takes more or less time when communicating online versus face-to-face?" Of 51 comments to this question, qualitative analysis suggested eight categories of responses. The most responses (n=13 or 25%) indicated that it takes more time to communicate with students when teaching online because of the need to make sure that "communications are clear." For example, in a statement representative of the others, one respondent wrote, "I take more time writing and revising my communications to online students because I want to be sure my ideas are clear." The second most frequent comment (n=11 or 22%) was that the nature of asynchronous communication takes more time because asynchronous emailing back and forth typically requires waiting for a response. The third most frequent (n=10 or 20%) identified the time it takes emailing individuals online instead of addressing the whole class at once as a reason it takes more time to communicate online than in classrooms. The fourth most frequent response related to the time it takes to physically type (n=6 or 12%) rather than converse in person. These categories, as well as others that occurred less frequently, are presented in Table 3.

Table 3. Ranking explanations for more time communicating with students online than in classrooms. N=51

1	Making sure communications are clear	N=13 - 25%
2	Asynchronous takes more time waiting for a response	N=11 - 22%
3	Emailing individuals instead of whole class	N=10 - 20%
4	Typing rather than speaking	N=6 - 12%
5	Discussion Board	N=3 - 6%
6	Technical problems (a) and More time on assessments (b)	N=2 - 4% (a); N=2 - 4% (b)
7	Schedule requires more immediate, less flexible, and more frequent communication	N=2 - 4%
	Comments indicating online communication same or better than classroom communication	N=2 – 4%

These findings suggest implications for the design of online learning that might increase satisfaction in teaching by reducing the need for text-based communication. Betts (2009) also reports findings consistent with these *Time Online* research results.

In the article 'Egocentrism over e-mail: Can we communicate as well as we think?' Kruger et al. (2005) investigate the difficulty of conveying emotion and tone via email without the 'benefit of paralinguistic cues' (p.1). They conducted five studies to examine overconfidence over email by comparing the perceived and actual ability of participants to communicate via email. The results of the five studies indicated that participants who sent emails overestimated their *ability to communicate* by e-mail and that participants who received emails overestimated their *ability to interpret* e-mail. Furthermore, participants who sent emails predicted about 78% of the time their partners would correctly interpret the tone. However, the data revealed that only 56% of the time the receiver correctly interpreted the tone (Kruger et al., 2005; Winerman, 2006). As further noted by Winerman, the receivers in the study 'guessed that they had correctly interpreted the message's tone 90% of the time' (2006, p. 16) (Betts, 2009, p.26).

To investigate further the differences between how faculty spend their time in teaching online versus teaching in the classroom, respondents were asked to report on three basic methodological functions intended to capture data on shifts in how time is spent when teaching. These included the number of assignments they give over the duration of a particular course, the amount of time students spend in active learning in an online course(s) as compared to a face-to-face course(s), and whether learners gained more control over their learning experience as their online course progressed. Respondents were asked about the number of assignments per course for two reasons. One was because if less time is devoted to lecture when teaching online and the presentation of information becomes structured and prepackaged in technology, it seemed logical to conjecture that there may be more assignments. The second was to anticipate that the need to keep students engaged when teaching online as a method to overcome the isolation of distance education might result in more assignments. Results in response to the question "On average, how many assignments do you give in a semester when teaching a course" showed that 50% of respondents reported giving 10 or more assignments when teaching online as compared to only 40% when teaching in a classroom yielding an average of 20% more assignments when teaching online. In general one can conclude from this that more assignments means more grading.

The question on the amount of time student spend in active learning was devised to collect data in response to ideas such as that reported by McQuiggan (2007) in stating that "In rethinking their familiar ways of teaching when moving online, a change that is noted numerous times is a shift from teacher-centered instruction to student-centered instruction". Data confirmed this by showing that when asked: "How would you rate the amount of time your students spend in active learning in your online course(s) compared to your face-to-face course(s)?" 57% of respondents (n=70) reported more or substantially more, 25% the same, and 18% less or substantially less. This raises the question that when students are more active in their learning what are faculty doing as compared to the traditional models?

A final question in the sequence probing the relationship between teaching methods and how faculty spend their time was designed to capture data related to learner control of their teaching. Learner control, particularly relevant to adult learners who are the most frequent consumers of distance education, generally describes the ability of the learner to set their own objectives, devise their plan of study, and evaluate their own performance. This is not a binary option but a continuum and in general, learners' ability to exercise these attributes grows as they mature, especially over age 25. To capture the notion of learner control, Moore developed the concept of *Learner Autonomy* in 1972 to address the manner in which distance education may allow for active learners as opposed to the behaviorist model of education where learners are expected to react to teacher input (Moore and Kearsley, 2005, p.228). Moore and Kearsley define the concept of LA in stating that it stands for the idea that "learners have different capacities for making decisions regarding their own learning" that is, for deciding "how to study, what to study, when, where, in what ways, and to what extent" to study (Moore and Kearsley, 2005, p.227). If a learner has a greater capacity for making those decisions they have greater learner autonomy and vice versa. In response to the question "As my online course progresses, learners gain more control over their learning experience" 91% of faculty respondents (n=79) either agreed or strongly agreed. If learners are taking more responsibility for their own learning, what are the implications for how faculty are spending their time when teaching online?

OUTCOMES

Despite the high ranking of email in teaching online, that is, despite the report that faculty spend more time on email when teaching online, only 30% of faculty who teach online "strongly agree" they are "able to have productive conversations with my students" as compared to 56% who teach in classrooms. Results also suggest that technology is not responsible for this discrepancy as 58% chose four or five on a five-point Likert scale where five equaled that "technology increases satisfaction" and one equaled "technology deceases satisfaction." This suggests that it is the effort of communicating via email that takes more time but that even when faculty do make that extra effort, it does not result in more productive conversations with students.

Not surprisingly, given previous research on the topic showing that students achieve as well as or better online as compared to the classroom (Moore and Kearsley, 2005), when asked how well students achieve online as opposed to in the classroom, the numbers were very close. Forty five or 55% reporting "good" online and 47 or 59% reporting good in classroom and 25 or 31% reporting very good online and 27 or 34% reporting very good in the classroom. Ten or 12% reported student achievement as "fair" online and only five or 6% reported student achievement as fair in the classroom. One respondent (1%) reported student achievement as "poor" online and zero respondents reported student achievement as "poor" in the classroom. Although these numbers are very close they do show slightly better achievement in the classroom as compared to online, with 86% reporting good or very good achievement online and 93% reporting the same in the classroom.

One of the more intriguing findings of the survey in relation to the future of teaching came from responses to the question: Has teaching online improved any aspect of your classroom teaching? In response, 78% said, "yes" while only 22% reported no (N=78). Important explanations for this finding came in response to the request to respondents to "please explain" their choice of yes or no. Forty-one of the respondents elaborated on how the experience of teaching online has led them to make improvements to their classroom teaching. In analyzing these results, we categorized their comments into four categories suggesting that teaching online improves classroom teaching by helping faculty to:

1. Incorporate new technologies/ideas into classroom teaching
2. Improve materials, instructional design, and instruction
3. Improve assessments and assignments
4. Conduct more personalized, and better communication/discussion (n=41).

The respondents' comments further explain this finding. For example, in the category of online teaching helped improve classroom teaching through helping faculty to: "Incorporate new technologies/ideas into classroom teaching," there were 13 written comments. These included:

- It helps me become more focused and to incorporate online activities (hybrid) into my on campus classes.
- I now ALWAYS weave technology into my face-to-face classes because I use the learning objects and other materials I developed already for the online classes.
- Material is now given via multiple modes (text, video, hands-on learning).

In the category of online teaching helped improve classroom teaching through helping faculty to "improve materials, instructional design, and instruction" samples of responses included:

- "It has made me be aware of instructional design. My classes are better planned out, structured and organized.
- Now I give more clear, precise instructions. I am now more organized.
- Identified additional online resources to bring into classes, forced to be more organized, added clearer learning outcomes".

In the category of online teaching helped improve classroom teaching through helping faculty to "improve assessments and assignments" (14 comments), samples of responses included:

- I am much more thorough in my grading of assignments.
- Creative assignments that were created for online class have been transported to the F2F class.
- I now give a quiz on the syllabus at the start of the semester in my classroom courses.

In the category of online teaching helped improve classroom teaching through helping faculty to have "More personalized, better communication" (7 comments), samples of responses included:

- I communicate much more personally and more frequently with my students in the classroom. Online teaching made me aware of how much my students and I benefit from regular and ongoing dialogue.
- More aware of student learning styles.
- It has moved more discussion based methodology into the classroom.

SATISFACTION IN, AND ENTHUSIASM FOR, TEACHING ONLINE AND IN CLASSROOMS

A series of questions captured data on faculty satisfaction in, and enthusiasm for, teaching online. The first question asked faculty the extent to which faculty agreed with the statement "enthusiasm for your subject is an element of effective teaching," with potential responses "strongly disagree, disagree, agree, or strongly agree." In response, 78% strongly agreed and 98% either agreed or strongly agreed (n=78) with the statement that enthusiasm for your subject is an element of effective teaching. A question then investigated the degree to which faculty respondents experienced enthusiasm teaching either in classroom or online. In response to the question: "To what degree do you experience enthusiasm when teaching in a classroom?" where the potential responses were "none, some, quite a bit, and high," 69% reported high enthusiasm for teaching in a classroom whereas only 26% reported experiencing high satisfaction for teaching online. When combining "quite a bit" and "high" as the ratings for experiencing enthusiasm when teaching in a classroom, 95% of respondents reported these levels of enthusiasm for classroom teaching as compared to 63% for teaching online. In this data sample, faculty respondents rated themselves as being more enthusiastic about classroom teaching versus online teaching at a ratio very close to three to two (n=80).

Continuing the line of inquiry into enthusiasm for teaching, a question asked respondents "How often do you experience enthusiasm when teaching?" Potential responses included "never, occasionally, frequently, always." Results indicated that not only did faculty experience more enthusiasm in classroom teaching, but they also experienced it more frequently with nearly 94% reporting they experienced enthusiasm "frequently" or "always" in classroom teaching whereas 62% reported experiencing enthusiasm "frequently" or "always" in teaching online. Again, faculty report they experience enthusiasm for classroom teaching as compared to teaching online at a near perfect 3:2 ratio (see Figure 1).

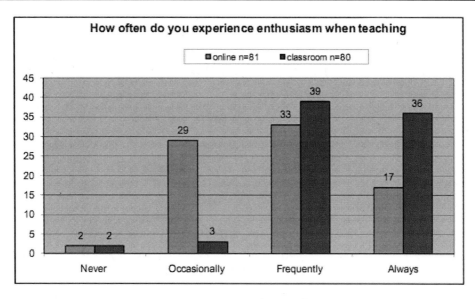

Figure1. Frequency of enthusiasm in either classroom or online teaching.

To probe further faculty attitudes toward classroom teaching compared to online teaching, the survey asked "Overall, how satisfied are you in your classroom teaching?" and, in a separate question, "Overall, how satisfied are you in your classroom teaching?" Potential responses included "very satisfied, satisfied, dissatisfied, very dissatisfied." Findings showed that sixty three (63%) of faculty who were teaching or have taught both online and in classroom(s) (n=80), reported being "very satisfied" with teaching in a classroom whereas only 33% reported being "very satisfied" in teaching online. Combining satisfied and very satisfied shows much more parity between classroom and online teaching with 91% of respondents reporting they were either satisfied or very satisfied teaching online and 97% reporting the same ratings for classroom teaching. Although classroom teaching still ranks higher on this scale, the difference is less significant.

In considering the findings related to enthusiasm for, and satisfaction in, teaching, Moore's theory of transactional distance offers a lens through which to analyze the results. First proposed in English in 1972 and published in 1980 (Moore, 1991), the theory describes the relationship of three key variables in determining the degree to which a distance education experience may be subject to a "potential for misunderstanding" where instructors and learners are physically separate. Moore and Kearsley (2005) emphasize that in distance education, physical separation leads to a "psychological space of potential misunderstandings between the instructors and the learners that has to be bridged by special teaching techniques; this is the Transactional Distance" (p.224). The theory hinges on the relationship between dialogue and structure. Dialogue was initially described the flexibility of student to instructor communication, in general referring to the ease with which a student can ask questions to clarify their understanding. Because technology must always intervene in distance communication, it adds complexities to the ideal dialogue that may occur, for example, between an instructor and a learner physically present in a one on one tutorial. In this sense, computer-based text structures email communication and as such, construct a particular form of dialogue. It is worth noting that scholars have expanded the concept of dialogue in transactional distance theory seeking to understand it better in a contemporary context of online communication. Both Zhang (2003) and Rabinovich (2008) expand the concept to include, in addition to the original student to instructor interaction, student-student, student-content, and student-interface interactions.

Structure as a key variable in transactional distance theory refers to the rigidity of a distance education experience determined largely by course design and the technology in which a distance course is embedded. When these factors are rigidly structured, they tend to suppress dialogue and a learning experience is less responsive to student questions. This leads to greater transactional distance or in other words, a greater potential for misunderstanding.

When seen as a closed system, the variables of dialogue and structure are proportional, as one increases the other decreases and vice versa. A responsive system can increase dialogue and decrease structure in response to student needs. In an unresponsive system, structure is rigid and limits dialogue thus increasing the potential for misunderstanding when students are restricted in their ability to ask questions (Saba and Shearer, 1994).

A key factor mitigating the potential for misunderstanding in any learning experience is the degree to which a learner is capable of learning independently. Moore labeled this variable "learner autonomy" and it describes the learners' ability to manage their own learning. Learner autonomy is a continuum of learner characteristics describing how well one is able to manage and direct their own learning. This includes setting objectives, finding and engaging with appropriate resources, and evaluating one's own performance, among other features. Learner autonomy tends to increase in the course of human development and by age 25, many people have developed the skills to direct and manage their own learning. Developing learner autonomy is increasingly a secondary agenda for many distance education experiences, especially with high school and undergraduate age learners (Rice, 2006).

Finding in the *Time Online* research that email communication takes more time than face-to-face communication and yet yields less productive conversations with students is consistent with the theory of transactional distance. The structure of email communication reduces flexible dialogue and thus increases the potential for misunderstanding. A logical hypothesis then is that the increased transactional distance also leads to less satisfaction in and enthusiasm for teaching online. To further investigate this line of inquiry in the time online survey research, a question was asked about the structure of teaching online. When asked: "Online education through technology adds structure to teaching. Rate the degree to which this additional structure affects your satisfaction with teaching where 1 equals it greatly decreases satisfaction and 5 equals it greatly increases satisfaction", 58% of the respondents (n=77) reported 4 or 5. This suggests a counter-intuitive conclusion that overall, technology does not impair faculty satisfaction in and enthusiasm for teaching online.

SUMMARY OF THE *TIME ONLINE* RESEARCH FINDINGS

Four findings are substantial enough to warrant further research and implementation of recommendations for faculty training and development seeking to optimize the value of web-enhanced learning in teaching. The findings that should be considered as guidance for faculty development flow from findings on teaching online as compared to teaching in the classroom. The highlights of the findings are:

- Faculty are less enthusiastic about teaching online (OL).
- Faculty are less satisfied teaching OL.
- Faculty report they have less productive conversations with students online as compared to classroom teaching.
- Communication OL is more time consuming than communication face-to-face.
- However, faculty report structure of technology does *not* substantially decrease satisfaction in teaching.

A second set of findings suggesting that online teaching may improve classroom teaching. These findings could have implications for both classroom and hybrid or blended educational experiences. The findings are that online teaching:

- Helps incorporate new technologies/ideas into classroom teaching.
- Leads to improved materials, instructional design, that may be useful in the classroom.
- Leads to improved assessments and assignments.
- May lead to more personalized, better communication.

These findings may suggest a course development trajectory in that faculty may benefit from initially developing a classroom course, then adapting it to online, and finally taking the best from both forms to create a hybrid or blended format making the best of both worlds.

MOMENTUM IN TEACHING

In adapting my classroom teaching to my online teaching there was one particular assignment that changed dramatically when presented online. This assignment was a case study report. Students were given a rubric of criteria they were to address in reporting on their case. When I taught this in the classroom, the student presentations of their case studies was always one of the highlights of the semester. Students enjoyed talking about their case studies, the criteria worked well to create an informative, engaging, and manageable assignment for student presentation and discussion. Everyone learned a great deal in a relatively short amount of time. It was good work that was fun and paid strong learning dividends. However, in the online environment I was never able to find a form that was equivalent to the classroom form. Inevitably, the energy of the case studies drained away in the online environment even though the quality of the student work was itself as good as that produced by the students when we were in the classroom. However, online there was no way to duplicate the positive energy that resulted from the classroom presentations. What would explain this loss of energy? In searching for an explanation for this loss I speculated on the physics concept of momentum. Momentum is simply described as mass times velocity. My experience was that there was a certain mass times velocity present in the classroom on which we all would feed that I could not recreate online. To probe this concept in the survey, respondents were first asked if they thought momentum was a legitimate expression in relation to teaching through this question:

"Another way to gauge enthusiasm in teaching is to borrow from the physics concept of momentum that results from mass times velocity. Please rate the degree to which you agree with the statement that momentum is an element of effective teaching."

In response, seventy-eight percent (78%) agreed or strongly agreed that momentum is an element of effective teaching (n=79).

To pursue the idea, respondents were asked if they "experienced momentum when teaching online," and, in a separate question, if they "experienced momentum when teaching in a classroom." The potential responses were: yes, no, or NA for not applicable. In response, 84% reported that yes, they did experience momentum in classroom teaching and 64% said yes, the experienced momentum in teaching online. Fourteen percent (14%) reported it was not applicable online and 10% reported it was not applicable in the classroom.

While the results to the inquiry into momentum in teaching are not conclusive, they did suggest that the flow of energy is different in the two formats and that this could offer some explanation for differences that could inform the design of fully online, fully classroom, and hybrid or blended learning experiences. Although the concept of momentum may be too abstract to accurately capture the explanations for the differences between online and face-to-face communications, it does link to a body of research on non-verbal communication. In examining this issue for guidance in designing faculty development for web-enhanced learning, work by Daniel Goleman offers further explanations for this line of thinking and research that has implications for faculty development in web-enhanced teaching and learning.

FROM MOMENTUM TO SOCIAL INTELLIGENCE IN TEACHING AND LEARNING

In summarizing findings on the evolutionary neurobiology of face-to-face interactions, Goleman (2006) describes research on how humans have evolved to assess the trustworthiness of people in ways of which we are both aware and unaware. Goleman's summary is compelling in this context because it illustrates how online interactions may differ from face-to-face interactions. He frames his account in the context of human social interaction and in the way people have evolved to communicate their emotional responses in non-verbal ways. He also describes the links between head and heart as flowing through our very cells. The neuroanatomy of the thinking brain (cortex) is linked to the emotional trigger center (amygdala) that receives much of the non-verbal communication we have evolved to receive. The connection includes the limbic or "reptilian" brain stem that regulates our automatic responses. As Goleman puts it " this tight connection suggests a rapid and powerful linkage, one that facilitates instantaneous coordination of thought, feeling, and action" (p.64). The online domain is more abstract and more cognitive than the physical world through which humans have evolved. Text, video, and audio delivered online do not carry the social wavelengths to which our neural systems are attuned. As Elinor Ochs, Director of UCLA's Center on Everyday Lives of Families has observed:

Thousands of years of human evolution created human physical communication – facial expressions, body language – that puts broadband to shame in its ability to convey meaning and create bonds. What happens as we replace side-by-side and eye-to-eye connections with quick, disembodied e-exchanges? (cited in (Wallis, 2006, p.52)).

Another example highlights the relatively abstract nature of online communication. If I make an illegal copy of a copyrighted work from the Internet, I am "stealing" it. However, as many children ask, "how can I be stealing when the original work is still there?" In this scenario, I need to be able to think abstractly about how taking the file is depriving the owner of the opportunity to sell or be credited for producing the work. This is a more abstract concept than the physical world where if an object disappears, the owner is deprived of its use. Our biology has evolved in the physical world and it is in that world that we gain what Goleman terms social intelligence.

> The social brain is the sum of the neural mechanisms that orchestrate our interactions as well as our thoughts and feelings about people and our relationships. The social brain represents the only biological system in our bodies that continually attunes us to, and in turn becomes influenced by, the internal state of the people we're with (Goleman, 2006, p.10).

Relating findings that it takes more time to teach online to findings of faculty being less satisfied with teaching online to findings that evolutionary biology has conditioned us to make decisions based on trustworthiness in the physical world, develops an argument for distinguishing between asynchronous online and synchronous communications, whether online or face-to-face. In support of this argument, Wallace (1999), suggests that the psychology of online experience can be overly abstract and cognitive, lacking affective cues and social intelligence. This relates to Goleman's conclusion that "a purely cognitive perspective slights the essential brain-to-brain social glue . . . and so excludes social talents that have been key to human survival" (Goleman, 2006, pp. 100-101)

Goleman goes further in commenting on the growing force of virtual worlds. He suggests that impact of spending unreasonable amounts of time in virtual worlds "deadens" people to "those who are actually nearby. The resulting social autism adds to the ongoing list of unintended human consequences of the continuing invasion of technology into our daily lives" (p.8).

IMPLICATIONS FOR FACULTY DEVELOPMENT TO TEACH AND LEARN ONLINE

The implication of this chapter for faculty training is the suggestion that an emphasis on synchronous online learning as a dimension of web-enhanced learning will increase faculty satisfaction with web enhanced learning. Betts has stated that online, "students may not have the advantage of the many visual and vocal cues inherent in face-to-face courses; however, through advancements in technology, faculty can reach out to students through learning system tools that support text, voice, and video communication" (Betts, 2009). The conclusion is that one way to improve web-enhanced learning is to devote time to synchronous, online communications in faculty training and development. Synchronous online formats include (live e-learning) online meetings, virtual classrooms, web seminars and broadcasts, coaching, instant messaging, conference calls (Singh, 2003). More specifically, these results suggest that online educational providers may benefit from better faculty training in using synchronous online communications. Synchronous conferencing software such as Wimba, Adobe Connect, Saba Centra, Skype, Elluminate Live, WebEx and others provide various tools and features within their software systems. It takes time for faculty to become familiar with the options and comfortable using them when online. Faculty need to learn how to be a presenter but also make students presenters when appropriate, use an online whiteboard, upload files, present files and websites, use the chat feature while maintaining voice communications, use application sharing, use video and audio, provide for and control student hand raising and turn taking, use various polling features, and archive sessions for those who cannot attend to name a few of the ever growing list of features in synchronous conferencing. When synchronously conferencing online, faculty are challenged to synthesize their knowledge of technology, pedagogy, and content in the way Mishra and Koehler (2006) refer to as Technological Pedagogical Content Knowledge or TPACK. TPACK builds on Shulman's (1986) ideas on the synthesis of pedagogy and content required to be a good teacher and raise it to the higher level required of the 21st century faculty, that is, synthesizing TPCK. Recognizing the sophistication that this level of expertise requires suggests its importance to faculty development.

CONCLUSION

The research cited in this chapter suggests that both teaching and learning online can be improved through devoting time and resources for online faculty to gain competency in using synchronous conferencing. Teaching online translates into different work for faculty. This research inquired into the nature of this work finding that responding faculty think it takes more time to teach online and that it is less satisfying than teaching in a classroom. The use of technology in distance education, especially text-based asynchronous communication, means that it takes more time to avoid miscommunication, miscommunication humans have evolved to more readily clarify face-to-face. Online, however, the potential for misunderstanding in text-based communication may very easily mutate into an independent study with everyone in the class. This research suggests a rationale for faculty who teach online to integrate more synchronous communication into their online teaching. More synchronous communication may help faculty to benefit from both collective and conversational interactions that link together the emotional and the cognitive that combine to make education both instructive and satisfying. This can be balanced with the narrower bandwidth of the text-based asynchronous online environment that brings with it expectations of instant access, 24/7 availability, and highly structured communications that can be excessively time consuming to prepare.

Explaining web-enhanced teaching and learning in a reliably actionable way is an exercise in probability assessment. Because technology evolves continuously and because educators are constantly gaining experience in and adapting to, the special requirements for and practice of, teaching and learning online, faculty development will be a continuously moving target. However, by combining research that teaching online takes more time than and is less satisfying than classroom teaching with research on the neurobiology of social intelligence, it is possible to build a case for making synchronous online communications a priority in web-enhanced learning. Through this analysis, the rewards of conversing with students in ways that reflect the nature of social intelligence, suggest that both face-to-face and synchronous online communication may contribute to faculty enjoyment of teaching and enthusiasm for the job. Thus, education can benefit from facilitating these interactions in programs for faculty development.

REFERENCES

Allen, I. E., and Seaman, J. (2008). *Staying the course: Online education in the United States.* Needham, MA: The Sloan Consortium (Sloan-C). http://www.sloan-c.org/.

Betts, K. (2009). Lost in translation: Importance of effective communication in online education. *Online Journal of Distance Learning Administration, 12*(2), Summer 2009. University of West Georgia, Distance Education Center. http://www.westga.edu/~distance/ojdla/summer122/betts122.html.

Burge, E. (2008). Online issues carrying ethical implications. *Notes for the 14th Annual Sloan-C International Conference on Online Learning.* November 5-7, 2008. Orlando, FL.

Cavanaugh, J. (2005). Teaching Online - A Time Comparison. *Online Journal of Distance Learning Administration, 3*(1),Spring 2005. State University of West Georgia, Distance Education Center. http://www.westga.edu/~distance/ojdla/spring81/cavanaugh81.htm

Compayre, G. (2002/1902). *Abelard: The origin and early history of universities.* Honolulu, Hawaii: University Press of the Pacific.

Cremin, L. (1957). *The republic and the school: Horace Mann on the education of free men*: *No. 1. Lawrence A.Cremin ed. Classics in education.* New York: Bureau of Publications, Teachers College, Columbia University.

Freire, P. (1985). *Pedagogy of the oppressed.* New York: Herder and Herder.

Goleman, D. (2006). *Social intelligence: The new science of human relationships.* New York: Bantam Dell

Keeton, M. (2004). Best online instructional practices: Report of phase one of an ongoing study. *Journal of Asynchronous Learning Networks, 8*(2), April 2004. Needham, MA: The Sloan Consortium (Sloan-C).

Kruger, J., Epley, N., Parker, J., and Ng, Z. (2005). Egocentrism over email: Can we communicate as well as we think? *Journal of Personality and Social Psychology, 89,* 925-936.

McQuiggan, C. (2007). The role of faculty development in online teaching's potential to question teaching beliefs and assumptions. *Online Journal of Distance Learning Administration, 10*(3), Fall 2007. University of West Georgia, Distance Education Center. http://www.westga.edu/~distance/ojdla/fall103/mcquiggan103.htm

Mishra, P., and Koehler, M. J. (2006). Technological Pedagogical Content Knowledge: A new framework for teacher knowledge. *Teachers College Record, 108*(6), 1017-1054.

Monroe, P. (1913). *Cyclopedia of education*: *Vol. 4.* New York: MacMillan.

Moore, M., and Kearsley, G. (2005). *Distance education: A systems view* (2nd ed.). Belmont, CA: Wadsworth.

Moore, M., and Kearsley, G. (1996). *Distance education: A systems view.* Belmont, CA: Wadsworth.

Moore, M. G. (1991). Editorial: Distance education theory. *The American Journal of Distance Education, 5*(3), 1-6. http://www.ajde.com/Contents/vol5_3.htm#editorial.

Pachnowski, L., and Jurczyk, J. (2003). Perceptions of Faculty on the Effect of Distance Learning Technology on Faculty Preparation Time. *Online Journal of Distance Learning Administration, 6(3),* Fall 2003. State University of West Georgia, Distance Education Center. http://www.westga.edu/%7Edistance/ojdla/fall63/pachnowski64.html.

Rabinovich, T. (2008). Transactional distance in a synchronous Web-extended classroom learning environment. *Unpublished doctoral dissertation,* Boston University.

Rice, K. L. (2006). A comprehensive look at distance education in the K-12 context. *Journal of Research on Technology in Education, 38*(4), 425-448.

Saba, F., and Shearer, R. (1994). Verifying key theoretical concepts in a dynamic model of distance education. *American Journal of Distance Education, 8*(1), 36-59.

Seaman, J. (2009). *Online Learning as a Strategic Asset Volume II: The Paradox of Faculty Voices*: Views and Experiences with Online Learning. Washington, DC: Association of Public and Land-grant Universities (APLU).

Singh, H. (2003). Building effective blended learning programs. *Educational Technology, 43*(6).

Shulman, L. (1986). Those who understand: Knowledge growth in teaching. *Educational Researcher, 15*(2), 4-14.

Tomei, L. (2004). The impact of online teaching on faculty load: Computing the ideal class size for online courses. *International Journal of Instructional Technology and Distance Learning* (Online serial), *1*(1). January 2004.

Turoff, M. (2003). Coming to Terms: ALN. *Sloan-C View: Perspectives in quality online education.* Sloan Consortium. http://www.aln.org/publications/view/v2n4/coverv2n4.htm

Wallace, P. (1999). *The psychology of the Internet.* Cambridge, UK: Cambridge University Press.

Wallis, C. (2006). The Multitasking Generation. *Time Magazine.* March 27, 2006.

Whittier, D. (2009). Time online: Faculty methods and satisfaction teaching online and in classrooms. *Proceedings, Ed-Media 2009 World conference on educational multimedia, hypermedia, and telecommunications.* Chesapeake, VA: Association for the Advancement of Computing in Education (AACE).

Winerman, L. (2006). Emails and egos. *American Psychological Association Online, 37*(2), 16. http://www.apa.org/monitor/feb06/egos.html.

Zhang, A. (2003). Transactional distance in Web-based college learning environments: Toward measurement and theory construction. *Unpublished doctoral dissertation,* Virginia Commonwealth University.

In: Faculty Training for Web Enhanced Learning
Editors: Manuela Repetto and Guglielmo Trentin

ISBN: 978-1-61209-335-2
© 2011 Nova Science Publishers, Inc.

Chapter 10

FROM PEDAGOGIC RESEARCH TO EMBEDDED E-LEARNING

Harvey Mellar and Magdalena Jara

London Knowledge Lab, Institute of Education, University of London, UK

ABSTRACT

This chapter describes an approach to faculty training and course redesign in the area of Technology Enhanced Learning (TEL) which tried to build bridges between the TEL research expertise of a research intensive university in the UK and its pedagogic practice. It describes the origins of the PREEL project (From Pedagogic Research to Embedded E-Learning) within the context of UK national initiatives of which this specific project was a part. The issues around the research-teaching divide in universities are described through a review of the literature, and the design approaches to faculty training and course redesign adopted in the PREEL project are described in relation to ways of tackling this divide suggested in the literature. An account is given of evaluations of the project at the end of the first year and then again two years later. The chapter concludes by reaffirming the value of connecting research to teaching practice as a method of faculty training and course redesign and reflecting on the limitations of the specific approach adopted and suggesting how it might be improved.

INTRODUCTION

This chapter describes an approach to faculty training and course redesign in the area of Technology Enhanced Learning (TEL)[1] that tried to build bridges between the TEL research expertise of a UK research intensive university and its pedagogic practice. It examines the issues around the research-teaching divide in universities, how this impacts on the implementation of TEL, and how the issues about the relationship between the two might be addressed. It then describes the PREEL project (From Pedagogic Research to Embedded E-

---

[1] In this paper we will treat the terms Technology Enhanced Learning, e-learning and on-line courses as synonyms.

Learning) which attempted to implement these ideas as an approach to faculty training and course redesign.

The primary purpose behind the study was to support the integration of technology into teaching and learning in universities, most particularly in 'research-led' universities where the strong emphasis on research can sometimes lead to teaching having a lower priority. One way of ensuring that Technology Enhanced Learning remains high on the agenda in these universities is through more explicit linking of research and teaching. A secondary objective of the study was to ensure greater utilization of existing research. There is a great deal of research in the area of TEL but university teachers are often not aware of it, and as a consequence there is much repetition of similar experimentation uninformed by what has gone before.

In order to set the scene for this project it will be useful to describe a little of the UK context at the time that the project was carried out. In 2000 the UK had invested some £50 million of public money in the UK eUniversity in order to market and deliver UK university degrees via the internet, a move that was intended to transform UK higher education provision. The collapse of the project in 2004 was a painful experience for UK universities, and left them distrustful of central initiatives. The Benchmarking of e-Learning and Pathfinder Programme was launched shortly after the collapse of the UK eUniversity. The Programme was a major initiative led by the UK's Higher Education Academy in partnership with the Joint Information Systems Committee (JISC) and funded by the Higher Education Funding Council for England (HEFCE) with the aim of helping English universities assess where they were up to, and where they wanted to go in the area of Technology Enhanced Learning. Importantly this was a turning away from nationally driven initiatives such as the UK eUniversity, to an approach that handed over responsibility for development to the institutions themselves. By the end of the programme 77 higher education institutions had taken part in the Benchmarking part of the programme, and 37 of these had also taken part in the Pathfinder initiative (Mayes et al., 2009).

The PREEL project was one of these Pathfinder projects, and was carried out at the Institute of Education, University of London (IOE). The IOE is a specialist research intensive higher education institution specializing in education and social science. It has some 500 academic staff, and 6,000 students. Almost all of its teaching is postgraduate, and the Doctoral School comprises some 800 research students. During the summer of 2006 the IOE took part in an e-Learning Benchmarking exercise in which it examined its TEL provision in collaboration with five other universities, and with the support of the Observatory for Borderless Higher Education. This pointed up the existence of several TEL research communities as well as pockets of outstanding TEL practice within the institution, but found that these groups were only minimally co-ordinated, and that this limited the deployment of research and good practice. The PREEL project was set up with the aim of connecting TEL research with TEL practice at the IoE. It sought to use a variety of strategies to link research and practice in e-learning, in particular building collaborations between researchers and practitioners and supporting course teams in a process of reflective redesign of their courses informed by research. Before describing this process in detail we will look at the literature about the relationship between research and teaching in universities more generally, and review the approaches which have been suggested for tackling this divide.

THE RELATIONSHIP BETWEEN RESEARCH AND TEACHING

In the public statements of research-led universities the idea that there is a strong link between research and practice is either taken as axiomatic or, at the very least, as a desirable goal to be achieved. However, there are those who argue that there is less connection between research and teaching than might be thought, or that the relationship may even be antagonistic, or who point to the range of kinds of research with different forms of relationship to teaching in the complex modern university. As a consequence there is no single view of what the relationship between research and practice should be (see for example: (Barnett, 2003; Barnett, 2005; Dempster, 2003; Jenkins and Healey, 2005; Jenkins, Healey and Zetter, 2007; Kezar and Eckel, 2000; Roach, Blackmore and Dempster, 2001)). It is often assumed that the relationship between research and teaching is that the results of research should inform teaching (either in relation to content or pedagogy), and so teaching is seen as a way to disseminate research findings, but alternative perspectives include seeing teaching as research, teachers as researchers, students as researchers and learning as research. Keller (1998) distinguishes between scholarship (research that is meaningful, important and insightful) and research in general. Hughes (2005) argues for the importance of defining the contextual factors that can influence the development of research and teaching relationships: the type, level of research and academic discipline; the mode delivery of teaching; the learning philosophy; the individual's teaching, scholarship and research role; the students' ability and level of study; the type of university and its strategy; and national culture and politics. In practical everyday terms there have long been those who have pointed to the difficulty faced by academics in trying to maintain commitment to both teaching and research, seeing them as competitors for time and resource rather than as complementary aspects of scholarly endeavor (Fox, 1992).

Some of the reasons suggested for tensions between research and practice in higher education, and for the difficulties found by practitioners in applying research are:

- There is a conflict between the cultural values of research and teaching, arising from the reward systems, socialization of faculty, and disciplinary orientations (Kezar, 2000).

- Practitioners do not appreciate what constitutes sound research knowledge, and they lack interest in theory because it doesn't apply directly to them (Hirschkorn et al., 2008).

- Practitioners perceive research as providing too much detail, or conflicting evidence, and as not addressing the immediate issues that concern practice (Hirschkorn et al., 2008; Hargreaves, 1996).

- Research dissemination is often by presentation of conference papers and research reports, but researchers and practitioners have very different expectations from research reports (Kezar and Exkel, 2000).

- The specialized vocabulary used by researchers makes interpretation of disseminated research findings difficult for practitioners. Interestingly many researchers begin as practitioners in an area and as they become researchers in that area they have to develop specialized vocabularies and ways of writing precisely to differentiate themselves from practitioners (Kezar and Exkel, 2000).

- Practitioners are often expected to do the hard work of interpreting the research in their own terms, as researchers argue that they are not funded to do this (Kezar and Exkel, 2000).

A number of influences external to the university system have impacted upon universities in recent years bringing changes to academics' work that have contributed to further widening the gap between research and practice:

- There has been an increased demand for university education as a result of the globalization of higher education and the increase in education of women (Carnoy, 2005). The emergence of a large global market where the demand for education exceeds the capabilities of the institutions to deliver, has resulted in a position where academics are sometimes employed on a temporary basis, and where their role has changed from that of an academic professional to that of a knowledge-worker (Stromquist et al., 2007).
- The increase in the numbers of students has led to demands for greater accountability, but the different processes of quality assessment and assurance for teaching and for research (in the UK - institutional audit by the Quality Assurance Agency on the one hand, and the Research Assessment Exercise on the other) and then separately calculating and identifying resources for teaching and research have led to widening the gap between research and teaching (Watson et al., 2007; Harland and Staniforth, 2000).
- Universities have come to be conceptualized as agents of economic productivity (Carnoy, 2005), and there has been a "shift from activities … aiming at the acquisition of scientific and academic capital to activities intended for income generation" (Naidoo, 2005, p.29). In his case studies of two English and two Swedish universities, Taylor (2007) describes the perception of university staff that the growing impact of market forces and competition was leading to difficulty in maintaining a commitment to both teaching and research, and to a growing specialization in the separate areas of teaching, research, technology transfer etc., and how international and global competition has led to research excellence being seen as the badge of international status.
- There have been changes in the nature of university education. There is an increasing focus on preparing graduates with skills immediately applicable in the marketplace (Taylor, 2007). The move towards mass higher education, Dearing's influential report into teaching in higher education (National Committee of Enquiry into Higher Education, 1997) and the introduction of tuition fees have all impacted on attitudes towards university teaching in the UK leading to a greater emphasis on the value of teaching within universities (Harland and Staniforth, 2000).

Kezar and Exkel (2000) seek to identify some possible techniques to address this divide, and they focus on the development of communities of researchers and practitioners through reading groups and reflective action research. Their conception of the relationship between research and practice, however, remains one of viewing teaching as essentially a way to disseminate research findings, whilst we have argued that there are other ways to conceptualize the relationship: teaching as research, teachers as researchers, students as researchers and learning as research. We will now turn to a description of the PREEL project 'From Pedagogic Research to Embedded E-Learning' in which we attempted to use approaches informed by these perspectives in order to bridge the research-practice divide in the area of TEL.

THE PREEL PROJECT (FROM PEDAGOGIC RESEARCH TO EMBEDDED E-LEARNING)

Before looking in detail at the PREEL project it is worth while looking briefly at the place that the concept of research had within the reports from the other 18 Pathfinder Projects in the Benchmarking of e-Learning and Pathfinder Programme[2]. Three-quarters of the reports referred to research in one way or another, some of the most common approaches were:

- Project teams saw their work as being informed by research, as building on previous research, or as identifying pieces of research that they needed to carry out before they could implement their Pathfinder project.
- Project teams saw their role as to inform teaching staff about research in the field of e-learning, so that staff could incorporate this research in their teaching. This was sometimes conceptualized as the construction of evidence-based practice in the area of Technology Enhanced Learning.
- Action research was sometimes developed by project teams as an aspect of professional development, and as the basis of the development of TEL communities of practice.

The PREEL project (From Pedagogic Research To Embedded E-Learning) had a specific focus on relating research and practice that was informed by our position as a research intensive university and that was prompted by the benchmarking exercise which had pointed up the lack of connection between our leading edge TEL research and our everyday practice. Module leaders were invited to submit proposals for the redesign of MA modules to incorporate greater use of TEL, to take the proposed redesigns through the course validation process and to deliver the redesigned courses. Eleven academic teams redesigning 14 modules between them were selected. Staff were given some funding which could be used to buy them out of some of their teaching responsibilities, or support their work in other ways (of the order of seven days work per member of staff). We implemented four strategies to support these staff in the redesign of their courses:

1. The development of a scoping study to identify research carried out at the IOE most likely to impact on TEL teaching practice in universities, and the production of a report on the work of these projects. This study identified some 24 researchers and 43 research projects at the IOE that offered findings, approaches and issues that could support and improve the work of university practitioners when designing,

[2] These reports are available at: http://www.heacademy.ac.uk/ourwork/teachingandlearning/learningandtechnology/completedprogrammes?tabIndex=2&#tab3.

delivering, assessing and evaluating courses using TEL (there were also many other projects involving the use of TEL with children, or adults in other contexts than university which were not included in the review). The summary report written about these projects tried to draw out the lessons for university practice and to express these in terms that would be relevant to practitioners rather than researchers. The selection of 'local' projects was further intended to make interaction between researchers and teachers possible.

2. The delivery of a staff development programme, consisting of sessions during which TEL researchers and practitioners met to discuss research and its implications for practice. The core programme consisted of six workshops during which a selection of the projects and initiatives identified in the scoping study were presented and discussed by their primary investigators. This was intended again to try to draw out the lessons for university practice and to express these in terms that would be relevant to practitioners rather than researchers, and also to get researchers and practitioners in the area actually working together.

3. The redesign of modules to embed TEL. The process of redesign was carried out by the course teams with the support of the project research officer who used this role to mediate the research findings identified in the scoping study (Elton, 2001). The intention here is that the course teams would be actually applying the research, and that this research (and other research information) would be mediated by an individual through discussion and joint working. Course teams were also asked to report back to the other course teams about the process of their course redesign in a number of workshops during the process of the project. In this way it was intended to bring about something of a rethinking about the nature of the relationship between research and teaching, as well as to support the development of a community of practice.

4. The publication by course teams of research articles thus completing the circle, with the course teams reflecting on their own course development work, written up and published in a special issue of the online journal Reflecting Education[3]. In this way practitioners were involved in the research process, which then also opened up possibilities of other ways of thinking about the research-practice relationship.

After this redesign process course teams were then supported by the project staff in their production of proposals for the Validation Committee and then the delivery of the first run of the course.

EVALUATION

An evaluation was carried out by an evaluator external to the project at the end of the first year. The evaluator attended some of the staff development workshops and course team workshops and carried out interviews with a selection of the course teams and project staff. The evaluation paid specific regard to the link between research and practice, the ways that practitioners accounted for this relationship, and the implications for research-based practice.

---

[3] http://www.reflectingeducation.net/index.php/reflecting.

The results indicated that the research-practice link was not always established in the ways planned, but that links were established, sometimes in ways we had not foreseen. In reporting on this evaluation Pelletier and Jara (2008) described the outcomes of the project in the following way:

> The PREEL project was designed to connect e-learning research and practice more effectively. Practitioners' accounts suggest that this connection did not work in quite the way it had been planned to. Research from the staff development workshops and the research report was used pragmatically, strategically, as a legitimating device, rather than primarily, it seems, to shape the re-design of the modules. The evaluation interviews raise important questions about the distinctions, values and hierarchies implied in the notion of 'connecting research and practice' in higher education, given how research and teaching are organized in relation to each other. This article has explored reluctance, resistance perhaps, towards 'importing' research 'into' teaching practice, and a more favorable perception, in contrast, towards 'researching teaching practice', with such research occasioned in this instance by a specific kind of interaction.

> This is one of the positive outcomes of PREEL. Although the connection between research and practice was not made in quite the way it had been planned for, it seems, the project has generated reflection and research on practice, an outcome which is likely to benefit the design as well as the delivery of the new modules. According to the accounts presented in this article, e-learning research shaped the re-design process, including its validation, in significant ways; notably in generating confidence in the re-design process, as well as in facilitating and informing the externalization, examination and development of practitioners' assumptions and knowledge.

It is clear that whilst the project had made some progress in linking research to practice that many of the problems in connecting research and practice that had been identified in the literature still remained. We will now discuss in a little more detail the staff development workshops, the course design process and the place of research and teaching within the institution in order to illustrate the nature of the successes and the problems that remained.

There was generally positive feedback about the staff development researcher-practitioner workshops, indicating that they were found to be enjoyable and useful for generating ideas. However, most of the tutors who were interviewed also stated that the sessions did not significantly impact on the course redesign process, and they identified a number of problems in establishing links between research and practice. The research that was presented was sometimes felt not to match the realities of practitioners' own approach to teaching, and it was argued that this made it difficult to translate the research into effective practice. The timing of input about research was another crucial aspect, if the input was to be effective then it was very important to match it both to the practitioner's stage of development in thinking about the use of e-learning, and also to the stage of development of the course redesign, so it might happen that research on approaches to planning an e-learning course might be given too late after the course design was well under way, or that accounts of research about students' experience of e-learning might be presented while a team were still working on the outline of the course and had not really got to the stage of thinking about how the students would react to the course activities.

Interestingly the researchers who made presentations at the workshops (even those who also teach) also had their reservations about the workshops. They found it a challenge to present their research in such a way as to make it applicable. This difficulty often arose from the stance they adopted as researchers, pursuing generalizable knowledge, in contrast with the practitioners' particular needs for applicable teaching guidance. As a result the research was generally presented in terms of problematics rather than solutions or 'how-to' formulae, and so could be seen as addressing the researcher's concerns rather than the practitioner's. Whilst from the practitioner's point of view the research was often seen as too specialized, covering a relatively marginal aspect of practice, this was a choice that from the researcher's point of view was often motivated by a desire for methodological rigor.

The impact of the project on the course redesign process was more positive and more in line with our intentions. Firstly, practitioners were enabled to call on different conceptualizations of the research-practice link and this led them to reflect as researchers rather than as practitioners on their own modules (essentially their development process became for them an action-research project). Secondly, the practitioners' interaction with the research officer whilst she was providing support for the redesign generated opportunities for the timely mediation of e-learning research, so, for example, the research officer was able to call on research on task design, on embedded evaluation and on tutor peer observation while working with practitioners on those specific aspects of their courses. The research officer was therefore not perceived to have 'conveyed' her knowledge, but rather to have facilitated a process of reflection and exploration informed by research.

In terms of institutional culture, many of the practitioners felt that the formulation of the PREEL project in terms of putting research into practice linked to professional and institutional hierarchies between research and teaching practice, and hence reproduced those hierarchies. However interviews also provide evidence that one effect of linking research and practice in the way that it was done in the PREEL projects was that participation in the project gave the project team's teaching, and their redesigned modules, a certain level of credibility, increasing their status in their department and their own confidence in the module's future delivery.

FOLLOW UP EVALUATION

We carried out a follow up evaluation two years after the initial evaluation in order to look at the enduring legacy of the project. This was carried out through a series of interviews with a selection of those who had taken part in the project, and with other teaching staff whose work might have been impacted by the project as well as with Heads of Departments in order to examine any possible wider impact within the institution.

Tutors said that involvement in the PREEL project had given them confidence in designing on-line courses, allowed them time to think about their course designs, enabled them to be more creative in their designs, and given them a more explicit basis for design in order to organize and structure their on-line teaching. Tutors who had redesigned courses reported that the redesigned modules had continued to be used, with further improvements made as time went on. Many tutors had gone on to use similar approaches in the design of new courses. Student evaluations show that the module designs were successful, with the exception of two blended modules which have shown uneven levels of student engagement and the tutors were now redesigning the online activities to integrate them better into the module.

Turning to the issue of the connection between research and practice, many of the tutors looking back did not perceive this as having been for them a core aspect of the project. Some of those for whom it was a core activity talked about the way it had fed into the publication of a paper as part of the project, and the papers they had written after the project and the way in which this had forced them to engage with the literature in the field in a way they had not done before. Others saw research as a core activity in that they saw the project as researching their own practice through the process of analyzing and redesigning their modules.

The tutors did not perceived the report on ongoing IOE research that we prepared at the start of the project as a result of the scoping study as having been particularly significant, some didn't remember it existed! (This does not mean, however, that it was not a worthwhile exercise since the production of this report was crucial in informing the work of the research officer on the project.) The staff development workshops were generally welcomed, but they were felt to have been too much concerned with reporting research projects, and also to be too didactic (interestingly it was particularly those tutors who already had some experience in TEL who felt this the most). The tutors felt that these sessions should have been organized as expert facilitated discussions around problems, or issues for design (e.g. how to design on-line activities, evaluation).

Tutors welcomed the opportunities to share their experiences with other course teams in the project workshops. Some felt that there should have been more requirements on participants to share in a structured way, perhaps within small groups working on similar things. However, there was also a feeling that the tutors had quite different levels of experience of TEL, and that it would have been more useful to organize these group discussions by level of experience.

For most participants the process of course redesign and the support provided by the research officer were the key elements of the project, and they felt that this process of supported design was the most important element in enabling them to apply the new concepts in their practice.

Those staff who had participated in the project as researchers, sharing their research through the staff development activities saw PREEL as having been a positive experience for them, and believed that the project had contributed to the development of TEL in the IOE. They also felt that the project had impacted on their own work as teachers – particularly in opening up new areas of interest.

The impact of the work of the course teams in the project on the wider teaching context was another area of interest for us, and whilst the PREEL participants said that they had reported back their activities to wider groups within their departments, the information given to others seems to have been limited and only in a few instances did this sharing generate changes in courses outside the project.

Moving now to look at the institutional level impact, head of departments were aware that TEL was moving higher up the institutional agenda but they were unclear as to the developments within the IOE that had brought this about, and were only aware of PREEL in a general way. However their overall impressions of PREEL were positive as they had heard members of their own departments who were involved in the project discussing it in positive terms. The project had two direct influences at the organizational level: firstly, the appearance of 14 modules with significant TEL elements before the Validation Committee added a significant push to the quality assurance process for on-line learning and as a result new criteria for the validation of on-line courses were developed and applied, and secondly the need for additional guidance on the course development process for staff in general became apparent and a group was set up to devise guidelines to support tutors in the course development process, including the use of TEL.

CONCLUSION

We remain convinced that there is real value in trying to connect institutional research and practice in the area of TEL as one form of faculty development. That is not to reject other forms of faculty development – we also run a variety of training courses in aspects of Technology Enhanced Learning, organize seminars, produce on-line training materials and support the development of on-line communities of TEL practitioners, but we think that exploring this relationship between research and practice in TEL is part of our responsibility towards both research and practice.

At the start of this chapter we argued that there was a need to go beyond Kezar and Exkel's (2000) conceptualization of the relationship between teaching and research as teaching being a way in which research findings could be disseminated, and we proposed additional ways to conceptualize this relationship: teaching as research, teachers as researchers, students as researchers and learning as research.

Within the PREEL project we saw 'teaching as research' emerging as a strong element. The process of course design led staff to look critically at their own knowledge area, reflecting on its structure, purpose, and relevance. Tutors were also enabled to explore students' learning in their area more deeply as the use of technology often made this learning more visible to inspection.

We also saw examples of 'teachers as researchers'. Some teachers took an approach from the research literature and tested it in new contexts and under different conditions. Some adopted a more investigative approach to new technologies: exploring new approaches, testing them in their courses, and then looking for new applications. For many the re-design of the course was seen as a form of research and development, which was then reported in an academic publication.

There are aspects of the PREEL approach to faculty development that worked well, and other aspects that worked less well. The tutors did engage with some aspects of the research-practice connection that we were promoting, and something of a community of practice was developed, but this community did not fully encompass both researchers and practitioners. Some aspects of the changes that the tutors would have liked us to make might have pushed us towards a more standard form of training delivery, and this sidelined some of the research elements that we wished to stress. Reflecting on each of the four elements of our approach in turn:

1. The report based on a scoping study of research being carried out locally that was most likely to impact on TEL teaching practice in universities.
   This was important in terms of informing the project of the wide range of research available, and acting as a resource to be called on as necessary, but it was of little

direct use to the practitioners as despite our best efforts to make this accessible, the difference in goals of research and teaching meant that practitioners could not derive what they needed from this directly themselves.

2. The staff development programme, consisting of sessions during which TEL researchers and practitioners met to discuss research and its implications for practice. It was clear that this was important, but the tutors made it clear that it needed to be organized around problems and issues rather than research findings. However, it is not easy to keep the balance and to maintain the research voice if the programme is only presented in terms of the tutors' short term design needs.

3. The supported redesign of modules to embed TEL.

   This was clearly the most helpful element of the approach, though a greater element of sharing designs in a structured and organized way would have further supported this element. Whilst this is highly effective, the big downside is that it is very labor intensive, and the development of on-line tools to support the work of the innovation leader would be a useful way to make this approach sustainable; more radical would be to design tools that would provide this sort of support directly to the teachers (for examples of this approach see (Laurillard and Masterman, 2009)).

4. The involvement by course teams in research publications relating to their course designs.

   For some (though a minority of the total group) the publication of research papers based around their work in redesigning the course provided a useful means of linking their teaching work to research.

The feedback from the tutors would indicate a preference for the use of an action research methodology, which is a valuable and useful approach which we have used in other contexts, but in order to address the issue of the research-practice divide our approach in this project called to some degree on the approach of 'design based research' (Sandoval and Bell, 2004), an approach to research in which researchers work together with educators to develop their theories through a process of designing, studying, and refining theory-based innovations in realistic teaching contexts.

REFERENCES

Barnett, R. (2003). *Beyond all reason: Living with ideology in the university*. Buckingham: SRHE and Open University Press.

Barnett, R. (2005). *Reshaping the university: New relationships between research, scholarship and teaching*. Maidenhead: SRHE and Open University Press.

Carnoy, M. (2005). Globalization, educational trends and the open society (Paper presented at the Open Society Institute Education Conference 2005).
http://soros.multeam.hu/initiatives/esp/conference/index.php?id=0204

Dempster, J.A. (2003). Developing and supporting research-based learning and teaching through technology. In C. Ghaoui (Ed.), *Usability Evaluation of Online Learning Programs* (pp.128-58). USA: Information Science Publishing, Idea Group Inc.

Elton, L. (2001). Research and teaching: Conditions for a positive link. *Teaching in Higher Education, 6,* 43-56.

Fox, M.F. (1992). Research, teaching, and publication productivity: Mutuality versus competition in Academia. *Sociology of Education, 65,* 293-305.

Hargreaves, D.H. (1996). *Teaching as a Research-based Profession: Possibilities and prospects.* London: Teacher Training Agency.

Harland, T., and Staniforth, D. (2000). Action research: A culturally acceptable path to professional learning for university teachers. *Educational Action Research, 8,* 499-514.

Hirschkorn, M., and Geelan, D. (2008). Bridging the research-practice gap: Research translation and/or research transformation. *The Alberta Journal of Educational Research, 54,* 1-13.

Hughes, M. (2005). The mythology of research and teaching relationships in universities. In R. Barnett (Ed.), *Reshaping the University: New relationships between research, scholarship and teaching* (pp. 14-26). Maidenhead: SRHE and Open University Press.

Jenkins, A., and Healey, M. (2005). *Institutional strategies to link teaching and research.* York: The Higher Education Academy.

Jenkins, A., Healey, M. and Zetter, R. (2007). *Linking teaching and research in disciplines and departments.* York: Higher Education Academy.

Keller, G. (1998). Does Higher Education research need revisions? *Review of Higher Education, 21,* 267-278.

Kezar, A. (2000). Understanding the research-to-practice gap: a national study of researchers' and practitioners' perspectives. In A. Kezar, and P. Eckel (Eds.), *Moving beyond the gap between research and practice in higher education* (pp.9-19). San Francisco: Jossey Bass.

Kezar, A., and Eckel, P. (Eds.) (2000). *Moving beyond the gap between research and practice in higher education.* San Francisco: Jossey Bass.

Laurillard, D., and Masterman, E. (2009). Online collaborative TPD for learning design. In J. O. Lindberg and A. D. Olofsson (Eds.), *Online Learning Communities and Teacher Professional Development: Methods for Improved Education Delivery* (pp. 230-246). Hershey, Pennsylvania: IGI Global.

Mayes, T., Morrison, D., Mellar, H., Bullen, P., and Oliver, M. (Eds.) (2009). *Transforming Higher Education through Technology-Enhanced Learning.* York: Higher Education Academy.

Naidoo, R. (2005). Universities for sale: Transforming relations between teaching and research. In R. Barnett (Ed.), *Reshaping the university: New relationships between research, scholarship and teaching* (pp. 27-36). Maidenhead: SRHE and Open University Press.

National Committee of Inquiry into Higher Education (1997). *Higher Education in the Learning Society.* London: Her Majesty's Stationery Office.

Pelletier, P., and Jara, M. (2008). Linking e-learning research and teaching practice – lessons from PREEL. *Reflecting Education, 4,* 42-50.

Roach, M., Blackmore, P., and Dempster, J. (2001). Supporting high level learning through research-based methods: A framework for course development. *Innovations in Education and Training International, 38,* 369-82.

Sandoval, W. A., and Bell, P. L. (2004). Design-Based Research Methods for Studying Learning in Context: Introduction. *Educational Psychologist, 39,* 199-201.

Stromquist, N.P., Gil-Anton, M., Balbachevsky, E., Mabokela, R., Smolentseva, A., and Colatrella, C. (2007). The Academic Profession in the Globalization Age: Key Trends, Challenges and Possibilities. In: P.G. Altbach, and P.M. Peterson (Eds.), *Higher Education in the New Century: Global Challenges and Innovative Ideas* (pp. 1-31). Rotterdam: Sense Publishers.

Taylor, J. (2007). The teaching: research nexus: a model for institutional management. *Higher Education, 54*, 867-84.

Watson, D., and Amoah, M. (Eds.) (2007). *The Dearing Report: Ten years on.* London: Institute of Education Bedford Way Papers.

In: Faculty Training for Web Enhanced Learning
Editors: Manuela Repetto and Guglielmo Trentin

ISBN: 978-1-61209-335-2
© 2011 Nova Science Publishers, Inc.

Chapter 11

CULTURAL IMPACT ON ONLINE EDUCATION: HOW TO BUILD SELF-AWARENESS FOR ONLINE TEACHERS

Manuela Milani

Laboratoire EMA, Education Mutation Apprentissage
Université de Cergy-Pontoise, France

ABSTRACT

The purpose of this chapter is - at a first level - to analyze the concept of "Web-Enhanced Learning" in online education within the European Online Academic Education's context, how this concept takes shape, and how it becomes part of teaching practices within the instruction of a specific course. Subsequently, the chapter will present tools and strategies to help teachers develop self-awareness about the way they teach online and about how the cultures they belong to also have an impact on their teaching. Not only there is an increasing need of teaching methodologies able to address individuals and groups while reckoning with cultural differences, there is also a need to learn about culture itself in order to identify its rich and multi-faceted variability.

The theory discussed hereof is part of the results of a research aimed at exploring the impact of cultural differences on the design of online courses offered by several universities throughout Europe.

INTRODUCTION

In the last years the globalization and internationalization of higher education has been a topic of interest and discussion. These two words seem to be key terms in the educational trend of the most recent years (Castells, 1996; Bonk and Graham, 2006; Evans, 2007).

There are many eminent voices that support the idea of a borderless educational context, a concept that denotes forms of education that cut across traditional boundaries. Such boundaries include (Middlehurst, 2002):

- levels and types of education, such as further and higher education, vocational and academic education, adult and continuing education; in some cases this represents a genuine effort to create seamless, lifelong learning opportunities;
- private and public, for-profit and non-profit education: combining 'public good' and 'private gain' organizational structures and forms of provision;
- state and country boundaries, for example, between the private and the public sectors and higher education, creating new corporate universities, transnational consortia as well as joint ventures and strategic alliances;
- boundaries of time and space in the creation of virtual learning environments, online learning programs and e-universities.

Academic mobility, though, whether physical or virtual, almost uniquely seems to concern students. Faculty mobility is rare and partnerships between teachers of different universities focusing on academics rather than research are even rarer. While teachers are known to collaborate with colleagues when it comes to scientific research, the same cannot be said regarding teaching methodologies, and in the rare circumstances in which a partnership exists, there is no structured procedural support. But, as Moore suggests, behind educational traditions lie philosophical ideas. "These can vary significantly from one culture to another, and it is in these variations that lies the root of problems in cross-cultural understanding – and misunderstanding (Moore et al., 2006)".

Such remarks can best apply to Virtual Campuses, not solely but most significantly, given that such institutes have been largely promoted by European Community policies of the last decade. Although the expression 'Virtual Campus' is nowadays an important concept in the field of education, there is no theoretical framework for it. As a matter of fact, there are plenty of variables involved in defining the concept of the Virtual Campus. Depending on the context, the target group, the different goals and the technology involved a definition of 'Virtual Campus' can be formulated.

In this chapter we will use the term Virtual Campus as defined by the European Commission in 2007: "Cooperation between higher education institutions in the field of e-learning, regarding: design of joint curricula development by several universities, including agreements for the evaluation, validation and recognition of acquired competences, subject to national procedures; large–scale experiments of virtual mobility in addition to physical mobility and development of innovative dual mode curricula, based on both traditional and on-line learning methods. This broad definition involves many issues from partnerships between traditional and/or distance universities and HEI (Higher Education Institutions) with a view to offering joint certifications (for undergraduate and/or postgraduate levels) and cooperation with learning support services. This might also include collaborative activities in strategic areas of education or research through cooperation involving researchers, academics, students, management, administrative and technical personnel. 'Virtual campuses' should not be confused with e-learning platforms" (Source: http://ec.europa.eu/education/ programm es/llp/guide/glossary_en.html).

One of the projects financed by the European Commission, Re.Vi.Ca project (http://revica.europace.org), is very useful in thoroughly analyzing such phenomenon, for its objective is to provide an inventory and to carry out a systematic review of cross-institutional

Virtual Campus initiatives of the past decade, within higher education, at European, national and regional levels.

It is fairly easy to identify the different phenomena and policies that have contributed to promoting this trend in Europe: the impact of the Bologna Process (the process aims at creating the European higher education area by harmonizing academic degree and quality assurance standards throughout Europe for each faculty, as declared in the official document "The Bologna Declaration of 19 June 1999", source: http://ec.europa.eu/education/higher-education/doc1290_en.htm), the role of the European Union, and the impact of national initiatives. The Re.Vi.Ca project's general conclusion is that while certain regional conditions do have an impact and can be important when analyzing Virtual Campuses, no clear picture of a distinctly 'European' Virtual Campus has emerged and Virtual Campuses in Europe appear to be subject to many of the same constraints and opportunities as those in other parts of the world.

As a result of promotional efforts conducted to this day (2010), 167 Virtual Campuses exist in Europe while the Re.Vi.Ca project records 360 campuses in the rest of the world.

The context of Virtual Campuses, in Europe and the world, is therefore very broad and involves a very large number of students and faculties a number which is meant to grow, and offers the opportunity to examine the different models of online education. In fact, Virtual Campuses allow us to understand the existing cultural differences and their impact on online education through the study of concrete artifacts like online courses in lieu of the necessary physical presence in the classroom during a lecture in a traditional setting.

This is also particularly important due to the frequent failure of this type of experience. As Burgi affirms (2009) the relatively low involvement of faculty could explain the difficulties, and sometimes the complete failure, of these enterprises. The bottom-up approach means that mainly technology innovators participate, and collaboration between project partners occurs mostly in the production phase (during which grants are allocated), with little sharing of courses afterwards. Improving this situation would require top-down incentives to develop consortia and produce new e-modules, which in most cases puts a financial strain on the host institutions.

CULTURAL DIFFERENCES IN ONLINE TEACHING AND LEARNING

An analysis of literature, as well as an analysis of the projects financed by different organizations, allows us to recognize how cultural factors, such as student/teacher cultural background, and the influence of such backgrounds on the choice of underlying teaching methodologies, have not been extensively taken into consideration in the conception of tools and eLearning systems so far (Milani, 2008). Developing cultural awareness could therefore contribute to lessening the potential for misunderstanding student or teacher behavior.

Students and teachers involved in online learning and teaching, not only have different cultural backgrounds, but are surrounded by more than one culture. The simplest definition of culture includes values, beliefs and practices shared by a group of people. Going deeper, culture is recognized as an attribute of individuals, of small groups, of organizations, and of nations (even if the latter tends to be considered the most relevant aspect of culture, as affirmed by Hofstede's work) (2001, 2005).

Our starting point is that each individual (teacher, tutor, or student) can belong to a multiplicity of cultures, each one important at any given time (Brislin, 1993).

Different "categories of culture" can be identified. Margaryan, and Littlejohn (2007) recognized how organizational culture can be reflected in the ethos of higher education or corporate training; professional culture includes for example that of teachers or of learning technologists; disciplinary culture embodies both humanistic or scientific knowledge; and national cultures reflect ethnic diversity. It is difficult to detect and reveal cultural impact because each facet of culture can simultaneously influence a range of processes. For example, the ways in which learning resources might be shared and reused will be influenced by a range of organizational, professional, disciplinary and ethnic factors, such as community size, member proximity, roles, and the types of tasks for which resources are used.

Teaching practices, as human actions, are based on cultural values, but how can we let the awareness of this influence emerge? And how could we promote virtual mobility of teachers and students without a policy about understanding cultural differences and their impact on learning and teaching practices?

Furthermore, in a world in which interactions between culturally diverse people and groups are becoming common, developing models for cultural interpretation is a valuable undertaking. Not only is there an increasing need of teaching methodologies to address individuals and groups with respect to culture, there is also a need to learn about culture itself in order to identify its rich and multi-faceted variability.

Literature on this topic (Blanchard, Razaki and Frasson, 2005) suggests observations denoted by the following key words: borderless, cross-cultural, transnational, intercultural education and/or communication .

The vast production of the past years is confirmed by the numerous debates, studies and publications regarding cultural diversity (Collins, 1999; Gunawardena and Wilson, 2003; Dunn and Marinetti, 2007), although often one deals only with analysis that accentuate the concept of culture as ethnic culture.

Most literature regarding this topic describes this phenomenon focusing on the student (Gunawardena, 1996; Dillon and Greene, 2003) and very rarely does the attention on the cultural diversity shift to the faculty, and in such case the phenomenon may become prosaic: "Teachers speaking the same language and living in the same country are likelier to collaborate, which can inhibit cross-border projects. Culture also can affect teaching methods. In Europe, for example, people in southern countries seem to favour synchronous interactions and working with computers in small groups, while people in northern countries stress individual work" (Burgi, 2009).

Obviously, when presented with such statements, the following questions may arise spontaneously: What data can sustain such statements? Which faculty does it encompass? How was this trend detected? In summary: how can such a delicate topic be approached adequately?

TRAIN TO DEVELOP CULTURAL AWARENESS

From our point of view, it is relevant to focus the attention on tools and strategies aimed at supporting a growing awareness in teachers involved in online courses. This awareness should be able to reveal to teachers themselves, their own idea of what an online course is, when this course is "good" and why it is good. How do they develop their own idea of Web-Enhanced Learning? How do they "apply" this idea in their day-by-day teaching activities?

To reach this objective, this research proposes to test and evaluate different methodologies and tools to achieve two different kinds of aims: to observe and analyse online courses and to support teachers training and specifically to promote teachers' awareness on how their way of teaching is developed and implemented.

The first tool proposed to teachers is composed by a "grids of description" to help the trainer (this chapter will also take into account also the profile and role of the trainer in relation to the training objectives proposed) and the teachers collect all the different variables that could be involved in the description of a course. The grids are to identify the variables able to describe the courses: that means investigating how a variable is identified and then used. In other words: what variables do teachers use to describe an online course? And what are their relative weights (if and when provided)?

The second tool proposed is based on concept maps or ontologies: teachers will be asked to develop their own concept map of what an online course is and provide definitions and examples for each lemma and each relation they identify in the map.

Some partial results about the use of the tools are available, thanks to the comments and observations provided by teachers who tested them and explained which tool helped them more to develop self awareness of their day-by-day teaching activity.

These tools could be used to reach this aim at an individual level but also with a group of teachers (of the same department or faculty) to develop a common vision and a common language on online teaching.

WHO MANAGES THE TRAINING

A crucial aspect in university teachers training, and thus in the thesis proposed in this chapter, involves who plans, manages and delivers it. Furthermore, the question is who owns the necessary authoritative manner to deal with teachers in order to make training effective.

This is a general problem in teachers training, that has a considerable impact on online training too. Unfortunately, it often happens that the university centres (the eLearning Centres) in charge of delivering the training about online teaching and learning, just have a specific technological characterization lacking in pedagogical features.

This is one of the reasons of some misunderstandings about the pedagogical or technological meaning of training in Web-Enhanced Learning contexts.

It is interesting to note that, even in this case, we are dealing with "cultural" matters. Teaching and Learning Centres which are typical in British, Australian and North American universities do not exist in Italy as well as in other Southern European countries.

These centres have as main objectives to explore, promote, and support excellence in teaching and learning with diverse technologies, to enrich the professional growth of faculty, instructional staff, and teaching assistants through programs, services, and resources that promote significant learning experiences for students. Or, as declared – for example - on the webpage of the Centre for Teaching and Learning supporting teaching at the University of Pennsylvania (http://www.sas.upenn.edu/ctl/): "the Centre works to help standing faculty, adjunct faculty and teaching assistants develop and improve their teaching; to promote valuable conversations about teaching among those groups; and to enhance the quality of education at Penn. (…) CTL is committed to helping instructors at Penn achieve excellence in the classroom and other venues where learning takes place. By fostering discussions about teaching, CTL encourages instructors to reflect on their own practices, to gain new insights, and to learn new ideas and strategies from each other".

Summarizing, the Centre for Teaching and Learning main aim seems to be to help instructors at all levels develop the skills necessary to implement powerful pedagogies – and not technologies - in their teaching.

This attention to both pedagogical and technological aspects in online teaching is not common in Southern European Countries and particularly not in Italy. For this reason, there is not an institution in charge of monitoring learning aspects of online training, while technological aspects are normally monitored by specific eLearning Centres, that have been working in almost all universities since the 90s. These eLearning Centres focus their activity especially on technological aspects, but had to take into account also learning aspects in order to deal with a long-lasting lack of attention on this point.

As a consequence, it often happens that teachers have to discuss and clear their teaching choices for the first time introducing technology in their every-day teaching practice and re-designing their activity. This is even more clear in the case of the teachers involved in experiences such as virtual campuses or of virtual mobility.

Thus, in general, but especially in a careful consideration of one own teaching practice, as the one described and proposed here, it is important for the trainer interacting with teachers to be considered authoritative from the pedagogical point of view.

TRAINING TOOLS: GRIDS AND MAPS

In this chapter, two training strategies are proposed, both referring to two different kinds of teaching tools: grids of description and concept maps.

The built grid was thought as an analysis and observation tool of online courses in an European university context.

The main function of this tool is that of collecting more information as possible about a course, and putting some focus points to evaluate the internal coherence of the course design (for example between the learning objectives and the assessing tools).

The construction of a grid of description is identified as the first step of the methodology here presented, to help collect all the different variables that could be involved in the description of a course.

In this work the "training octagon", developed by Albert Raasch (1989), is assumed as main theoretical reference. The octagon identifies the following categories: learner, teacher, methods, content, media, objectives, evaluation, institution.

Raasch affirms that every didactic event can be described by defining eight poles and their relation among each other, as represented in Figure 1.

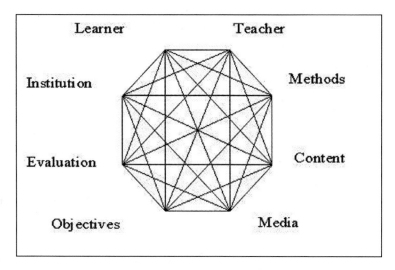

Figure 1. The Training Octagon (Raasch, 1989).

Starting from the eight poles of the octagon, a grid of description of a course was developed.

Into the grid it is necessary to "deepen" each pole identifying the variables that defined it and the ones connected to it. A first grid has been developed, defined as "the theoretical grid".

The theoretical grid is organized on different levels: the first indicates the poles of the octagon, the second a first level of variables related to the poles and then some important connected references with deeper levels of details.

Starting from what is included in the theoretical grid, a second grid was created and defined as "practical".

In this second grid, the poles and the first level of variables are included (first column of the grid: "Variables related"), adding practical suggestions, in the form of questions, to observe and evaluate the course (second column of the grid: "Practical questions"). After the questions some "cross check alerts" were added (third column of the grid: "Coherence check alert"): this labels usually point the link among poles and/or variables that are indicators of coherence, and represent also the real focus proving whether a course is coherently designed or not.

An extract from the grid, related to the pole "Evaluation" (pole 4) is represented in Table 1. In this table some variables related to the pole are analyzed, in appendix the entire description of Pole 4 – Evaluation is provided.

In relation to the learning objectives and to the kind of users, conceptual maps can be used together with - or as an alternative to - grids, which are predetermined tools.

The use of a map to describe an online course, permits to start from the perception of every teacher of their own course and of the different items of it, their importance and the relations among them.

The activity begins by asking teachers to describe their online course using the mind mapping software they prefer. The product requested is a conceptual map to describe all variables the teachers think are important in the course description and design.

Table 1. Extract from the Practical Grid: Pole Evaluation

Variables related to pole 4: evaluation	Practical questions	Coherence check alert
4.1 Monitoring	4.1.1 Are tracking tools used? 4.1.1.1 If yes, Which tracking data are available? 4.1.1.2 Which indicators are used? 4.1.1.3 Are assignments' results used as indicators for the monitoring system? 4.1.1.4 Are learner records sufficient, accurately maintained and up to date?	*4.1.1.3 Institution* *For which kind of evaluation the data available are used?*
4.2 Learning assessment	4.2.1 Which assessment methods are used? 4.2.1.1 Referring to the assessment approach described: which tools are used? 4.2.2 Who is going to make the assessment: the students, their peers, or the instructor and/or tutor? 4.2.2.1 How teachers/ tutors carry out the assessment? 4.2.3 Is there any kind of formative assessment (providing feedback during learning)? 4.2.3.1 If yes, which kind of feedback is provided? 4.2.4 Which kind of summative assessment is used (measuring learning at the end of the process)? 4.2.5 Which perspectives of learning are going to be assessed, cognitive (acquisition of knowledge), behavioral (skill development), or humanistic (values and attitudes)? 4.2.6 Is the appropriateness of the approach evaluated? 4.2.7 Is there an amount of assessable work required? 4.2.8 Are information about assessment criteria available? 4.2.8.1 If yes, how will assessment criteria be determined? 4.2.8.2 Does the weighting of an item reflect its importance in terms of subject objectives? 4.2.8.2.1 Is it clear? 4.2.9 When will assessment be undertaken? 4.2.10 Is information about assessment submission available? 4.2.10.1 If yes, what will assessment submission procedures be? 4.2.11. Is feedback provided? 4.2.11.1 If yes, when and how? 4.2.12 Will students be advised of assessment ground rules on deadlines, academic integrity, citation styles etc.? 4.2.12.1 If yes, how?	*4.2.1 Methods* *Are assessment methods put in relation with methods?* *4.2.1 Objectives* *Are assessment methods coherent with the objectives of the course?* *4.2.1 Institution* *Are assessment procedures defined at an institutional level?*

In Figure 2 an example of this kind of map is provided: here follows a map referred to a course of Computer Graphics in the College of Energetics and Electronics at Technical University of Sofia.

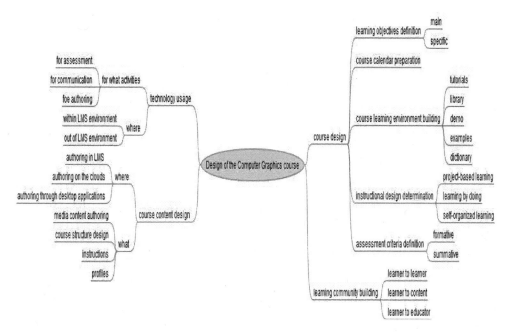

Figure 2. Example of a Computer Graphics course map.

Once teachers are ready with their maps, the given information is analyzed together with the teacher to verify whether each piece of information has been put in a hierarchical order or not, and whether all relations among items have been cleared.

Then, key information is requested to completely understand the type of course, the teachers themselves are responsible for adding any missing information. In this second step, some predefined forms (such as CDM, Course Description Metadata) can be used.

Using the example presented in Figure 2, the teacher will be asked (referring to the learning community cited into the map) to explain who are the learners/students, their background, their number, how the learning community is created and managed, if and how the learning community activities are assessed, if this information is clear to the students, and so on.

The first feedback about the introduction to teachers of this teaching proposal is given by the fact that all of them found themselves, for the first time in occasion of this kind of request (to fill in the grid or design the map), in the position of thinking about and explicating part or all the items that compose their own way of teaching online. Occasionally, in map designing teachers tend to repeat the course syllabus or the items of the assessment grids of the course in use at their University.

The grid seems to be more suitable to collect comparable data and, as a consequence, to point out recurrences that can be useful to analyse possible typical features of the courses.

The use of the grid in its first case studies revealed to be time-demanding for the compilers, who most of the time were not able to fill it in completely.

The map, instead, permits the user to design a thorough teaching plan, starting from the perception of the individual of their own course and, above all, of what characterizes it, what variables they consider relevant to describe it, how they define it and what examples they make.

Being the objective to uniform the online teaching practice with the proposal of a consciously shared model, a model based on the use of the grid is undoubtedly the most suitable to uniform the language and the knowledge of all the teachers involved.

Being, instead, the objective of the teaching practice to work for a sharing of knowledge and different practice, pointing out emerging differences and keeping them, to start from the use of maps might be more effective.

The study of maps permits above all to analyse the variables included by the teachers, evaluating the possible recurrences for each subject area (disciplinary culture), belonging university (institutional culture) but also, why not, for nationality (national culture).

An example of emerging data given by the analysis of maps and grids is related to a national culture factor: in Italy academic career is due to research results and not to the quality of teaching. Furthermore, it is not even clear how to asses teaching quality and on the basis of this national culture factor a common culture of how to do research has been developed, while no hints are given and shared about how to teach.

The unfortunate cultural element, proves how didactics is not the starting point for teachers who, when asked to describe their courses through a map, will start and focus on the content of them, while they have considerable difficulties in filling in the grid especially when they are asked to describe specific pedagogical items.

Another example: the belonging institutional culture is clearly visible when explicating the technological feature of the designing process of the online course.

The variable "platform" or "Learning Management System" is, in fact, often perceived as an independent variable. In almost all cases, the choice of the technological platform to be used to deliver the course is not made by teachers, but by the technology experts of the university, with the consequence that the relevant items in the decision are chosen without comparing classroom and online didactics.

The training activity, managed via grids or via maps, should finally focus on developing self-awareness about what culture means, that it means not only "to be Italian, or to be French, or to be Scottish". An online course is an artifact influenced not only by conscious decision of the teacher but also by the impact of the cultures he or she belongs to. To be aware of this process could lead the teacher to a better management of course design and also – most important of all – of the interactions with students, when involved in virtual mobility as in traditional online teaching.

CONCLUSION

Traditional and virtual campuses are experiencing pressure to become more competitive all over the world.

Traditional institutions are still playing a dominant role in providing higher education to meet the aforementioned needs (Sanyal and Martin, 2007); they are also changing their roles as follows: becoming partners in regional and international consortia, being engaged in different forms of transnational education, joining virtual university initiatives, building partnerships with industries. At the same time a number of e-learning projects, not always with good results, along with the accountability movement in higher education are responsible for a growing interest on quality. One of the more relevant dimensions of quality is strongly connected with the teachers' self-awareness.

This chapter describes a specific training offer to teachers involved in teaching experiences in virtual campuses, specifically in an international partnership context or dealing with international students with different learning experiences.

The proposal has the objective of increasing the teachers' awareness of what is "implicit" in their way of teaching online, and what are the "cultures" that influenced and shaped their way of teaching.

The main aim is supporting teachers who are involved in delivering online classes, in particular – but not only - within Virtual Campuses, identifying design criteria and way of teaching, and how their teaching developed and took shape.

Which "cultures" have the biggest impact in influencing online pedagogies? The training activities proposed in this chapter suggest to answer this question taking into account the national culture, in which also the law and rules influencing directly didactics must be included -how teachers are assessed, under which criteria, what are career terms; the institutional culture, related to the belonging university, and here the constraints imposed by the institution are included too, as for example in the choice of the platform to be used to deliver the course and the disciplinary culture, that means the culture of the belonging department or the group of teachers one cooperates more often.

Identifying the "cultures" influencing each teacher does not mean to cancel them, but to make the teacher more aware in order to design the course and to interact with students and other teachers belonging to "other" cultures in an effective and meaningful way.

The training activities and teaching practices proposed have been designed to help reaching this objective.

APPENDIX 1

Variables related to pole 4: evaluation	Practical questions	*Coherence check alert*
4.1 Monitoring	4.1.1 Are tracking tools used? 4.1.1.1 If yes, Which tracking data are available? 4.1.1.2 Which indicators are used? 4.1.1.3 Are assignments' results used as indicators for the monitoring system? 4.1.1.4 Are learner records sufficient, accurately maintained and up to date?	*4.1.1.3 Institution* *For which kind of evaluation the data available are used?*

4.2 Learning assessment	4.2.1 Which assessment methods are used?	*4.2.1 Methods*
	4.2.1.1 Referring to the assessment approach described: which tools are used?	*Are assessment methods put in relation with methods?*
	4.2.2 Who is going to make the assessment: the students, their peers, or the instructor and/or tutor?	*4.2.1 Objectives* *Are assessment methods coherent with the objectives of the course?*
	4.2.2.1 How teachers/ tutors carry out the assessment?	*4.2.1 Institution*
	4.2.3 Is there any kind of formative assessment (providing feedback during learning)?	*Are assessment procedures defined at an institutional level?*
	4.2.3.1 If yes, which kind of feedback is provided?	
	4.2.4 Which kind of summative assessment is used (measuring learning at the end of the process)?	
	4.2.5 Which perspectives of learning are going to be assessed, cognitive (acquisition of knowledge), behavioral (skill development), or humanistic (values and attitudes)?	
	4.2.6 Is the appropriateness of the approach evaluated?	
	4.2.7 Is there an amount of assessable work required?	
	4.2.8 Are information about assessment criteria available?	
	4.2.8.1 If yes, how will assessment criteria be determined?	
	4.2.8.2 Does the weighting of an item reflect its importance in terms of subject objectives?	
	4.2.8.2.1 Is it clear?	
	4.2.9 When will assessment be undertaken?	
	4.2.10 Is information about assessment submission available?	
	4.2.10.1 If yes, what will assessment submission procedures be?	
	4.2.11. Is feedback provided? 4.2.11.1 If yes, when and how?	
	4.2.12 Will students be advised of assessment ground rules on deadlines, academic integrity, citation styles etc.?	
	4.2.12.1 If yes, how?	

4.3 Validity, reliability, flexibility and fairness	4.3.1 Does the assessment methods measure what is intended? 4.3.2 Does it consistently produce the same information? 4.3.3 Are a variety of methods of assessment used to accommodate different needs? 4.3.4 Is assessment authentic, related to real life situations? 4.3.5 Are judgments of performance to be made against peer standards (norm referenced) or established criteria (criterion referenced)?	
4.4 Grading rubrics	4.4.1 Is there a standard defined at the start of the term for what the teacher consider to be average work? 4.4.1.1 If yes, is it publicized to the students? 4.4.2 Is an appropriate grading rubric clear and published so that students know what the standards will be and how the teacher will evaluate their assignments grade it?	
4.5 Quality evaluation	4.5.1 Is a clear approach to quality adopted? 4.5.1.1 If yes, which one? (Quality audits, Quality assessment, Accreditation) 4.5.1.2 If an approach to quality is not cited, are criteria declared? 4.5.2 Is the course's educational effectiveness measured? 4.5.2.1 If yes, which method is used?	*4.5.1 Institution* *Is this choice taken at an Institutional level?*
4.6 Satisfaction	4.6.1 Are satisfaction levels measured? 4.6.1.1 If yes, how? 4.6.1.2 Who is going to use the data?	*4.6.1 Learner* *Are students informed about the results?* *4.6.1 Teacher* *Are teachers informed about the results?* *4.6.1.2 Institution* *How the results will be used at an institutional level?*

REFERENCES

Blanchard, E., Razaki, R. and Frasson, C. (2005). *Cross-cultural adaptation of e-learning contents: A methodology.* Paper presented at the World Conference on E-Learning in Corporate, Government, Healthcare, and Higher Education, Chesapeake, Virginia, USA.

Bonk, C. J., and Graham, C. R. (2006). *The handbook of blended learning: Global perspectives, local designs* (1st ed.). CA: Pfeiffer.

Brislin, R. (1993). *Understanding culture's influence on behavior.* New York: Harcourt Brace.

Burgi, P. Y. (2009). Challenges in Setting Up Cross-Institutional Virtual Campuses, *EDUCAUSE Quarterly Magazine*, 32(2). www.educause.edu/eq

Castells, M. (1996). *The rise of the network society.* Oxford, UK: Blackwell.

Collins, B. (1999). Designing for differences: Cultural issues in the design of www based course-support sites. *British Journal of Educational Technology 30*(3), 201-215.

Dillon, C., and Greene, B. (2003). Learner differences in distance Learning: Finding differences that matter. In M. G. Moore and W. G. Anderson (Eds.), *Handbook of distance education* (pp. 235-244). Mahwah, NJ: Lawrence Erlbaum Associates.

Dunn, P., and Marinetti, A. (2007). Beyond localization: Effective learning strategies for cross-cultural e-learning. In A. Edmundson (Ed.), *Globalized e-learning cultural challenges* (pp. 255-266). Hershey, PA: Information Science Pub.

Evans, T. and Nation, D., (2007). Globalization and emerging technologies, in Moore, M. G. (Eds.), *Handbook of distance education*, pp. 649-660, Mahwah, N.J: Lawrence Erlbaum.

Gunawardena, C. N. (1996). *Designing learner support for media-based distance education.* Paper presented at the Turkey First International Distance Education Symposium, Turkey: Ankara.

Gunawardena, C. N., and Wilson, P. L. (2003). Culture and online education. In M. G. Moore, W. Anderson and A. C. Nolla (Eds.), *Handbook of distance education* (pp. 754-775). Mahwah, NJ: Lawrence Erlbaum Associates.

Hofstede, G. (2001). *Culture's Consequences – Comparing Values, Behaviours, Institutions, and Organization Across Nations.* USA: Sage Publications.

Hofstede, G. and Hofstede, G. J. (2005). *Cultures and organizations: software of the mind* (Revised and expanded 2nd ed.). New York: McGraw-Hill.

Margaryan, A. and Littlejohn, A. (2007). Cultural dimensions of learning object repositories. *Proceedings of Ed-Media Conference 2007.* www.aace.org

Middlehurst, R. (2002). Variations on a theme: Complexity and choice in a world of borderless education. *Journal of Studies in International Education*, 6(2), 134-155.

Milani, M. (2008). Cultural Impact on Online Education Quality Perception. *The Electronic Journal of e-Learning.* www.ejel.org, 6(2), pp. 149-160.

Moore, M., Shattuck, K., and Al-Harthi, A. (2006). Cultures meeting cultures in online distance education. *Journal of E-Learning and Knowledge Society*, 2(1). www.je-lks.it

Raasch, A., Burkhardt, L., and Sick, C. (1989). *Fremdsprachen für Erwachsene - Bibliographische Hinweise.* Saarbrücken: Universität des Saarlandes.

Sanyal, B. C., and Martin, M. (2007). Quality Assurance and the Role of Accreditation: An overview. In Higher Education in the World 2007, 2nd Edition, *Accreditation For Quality Assurance: What Is At Stake?,* Palgrave Macmillan.

In: Faculty Training for Web Enhanced Learning   ISBN: 978-1-61209-335-2
Editors: Manuela Repetto and Guglielmo Trentin   © 2011 Nova Science Publishers, Inc.

Chapter 12

FACULTY LEARNING COMMUNITIES FOR WEB-ENHANCED LEARNING

Anne H. Moore, Shelli B. Fowler
and Jennifer L.V. Sparrow
Virginia Tech, USA

ABSTRACT

This chapter discusses a model for faculty development for the integration of web-enhanced learning tools to increase student engagement and active learning. Web-enhanced learning environments allow students opportunities to increase critical and creative thinking, problem solving, and inquiry and analysis (Churches, 2008). A challenge before modern colleges and universities is to facilitate widespread pedagogical shifts away from simple lecture/examination models of teaching and toward learning environments that motivate students to become actively involved in the learning process (Bonwell and Eison, 1991; Land and Hannafin, 2000). This chapter presents an emerging case study on the use of a faculty learning community (FLC) as an impetus for pedagogical change. The FLC provides opportunities for faculty groups to address web-enhanced active learning strategies for large enrollment courses. The discussion focuses on a rationale and implementation process for facilitating adoption of technology- and web-enhanced active learning across disciplines to increase student engagement and fluency with information technology (FITness) in ways that allow undergraduates to succeed as 21st-century professionals and citizens. Further, we examine best practices for faculty learning communities, institutional support for creating effective faculty learning communities, and provide a brief overview of several web-based tools that faculty may use.

INTRODUCTION

There is a critical need to actively engage 21st-century learners in higher education (Association of American Colleges and Universities - AACandU, 2007; Churches, 2008). In light of this observation, the AACandU (2007) recommended that colleges and universities adopt essential learning outcomes to prepare students for 21st century challenges. These outcomes include having students demonstrate achieving such abilities as critical and creative thinking, information literacy, inquiry and analysis, and teamwork and problem solving. Unfortunately, widespread pedagogical change aimed at realizing such outcomes remains an ongoing struggle within higher education.

Web-enhanced learning (WEL) environments can aid faculty in addressing the AACandU essential learning outcomes. Web-enhanced learning is defined as the "use of the web purposefully and intentionally" (Grabowski, Koszalka, and McCarthy, n.d., p.3) to engage learners in inquiry and analysis, and inherently, to increase information literacy skills. In addition, WEL environments can be employed to enhance teamwork through the use of web-mediated communication tools like wikis, blogs, social bookmarking and tagging, Google Docs, Google Wave, Twitter and other Web 2.0 tools. Critical and creative thinking and problem solving skills can advance through the use of web-based tools for information searches, web collaboration tools, and data analysis tools. Technology tools, such as tablet PCs, digital slates, digital note-taking tools and mobile devices, can also further interaction between learners.

In recent years, colleges and universities have increased class size and decreased faculty development opportunities in the face of severe economic constraints (Graham, Heiman, and Williams, 2007). Continuously growing class sizes combined with the lack of funds for faculty development has exacerbated the challenges for universities seeking to substantially enhance active, engaged learning across disciplines. In particular, providing students with learning experiences beyond a simple lecture/examination model is increasingly difficult. Fortunately, web-enhanced learning tools can facilitate active and engaged learning even in large enrollment courses that typically are viewed as not conducive to group work, collaboration, active participation, and problem solving. Yet, for such tools to benefit learning and be well used, faculty need opportunities to experiment with appropriate pedagogy and tool applications.

Bonwell and Eison (1991) reported that while active learning increases both student skills and perceptions, faculty are often reluctant to change from a lecture/examination model of teaching since they may perceive active learning as a risky undertaking and may be anxious about using new learning technologies. Faculty may "feel a loss of control, lack the necessary skills, or be criticized for teaching in unorthodox ways" (Bonwell and Eison, 1991, p. vi). To lower faculty learning anxiety and encourage experimentation, institutions need to provide faculty development opportunities that allow for enhancing faculty knowledge of and adequate planning time for changing teaching strategies and for incorporating modern learning technologies appropriately. The shift from lecture format to web-enhanced active learning is a significant one for many faculty, who often have very little structured training in teaching methods. Nevertheless, faculty learning communities can effect change by addressing faculty concerns, developing a cooperative dialogue among faculty, and allowing for exploration of web-enhanced tools in a collaborative and constructive environment. As such, these learning communities may prove to be modern, yet time-honored and trusted, instruments of substantive pedagogical change.

STUDENT TECHNOLOGY ABILITIES AND LEARNING NEEDS

In contrast to faculty technology integration issues and modern teaching challenges, today's students arrive at colleges and universities familiar with many aspects of technology. As a result, students are not anxious about using technology. At the same time, students need content-based knowledge and skill development through contemporary approaches to learning that will help them flourish over a life span, enabling roles that higher education has assumed historically. But to continue to perform this role in ways that help to meet today's complex challenges, higher education must address its enabling roles and aims anew in light of pervasive technology use and the attendant possibilities for technology-assisted learning. In other words, despite the fact that students use technology readily and easily today, it has become all the more important to understand what students need to know and be able to do in technology-assisted learning environments across areas of study.

The trends in students' use of information technology are clear. Since 2004 when the Educause Center for Applied Research (ECAR) began its annual study of undergraduate students and information technology, the dominance of technology in students' personal and academic lives continues to rise (Caruso and Smith, 2009). In the 39-institution survey sample, student computer ownership was almost ubiquitous, with a shift from desktop ownership (45.8%) to laptop ownership (87.8%), and 34.5% owning both. Virtually all students surveyed indicated that they used library websites (94.6%) and presentation software like PowerPoint (93.8%), while spreadsheets (86.8%) and course or learning management systems (86.0%) followed closely in prevalence of use. This survey also showed increased use of social networking sites (90.3%), as well as heavy use of text messaging (89.8%) and downloading web-based music or videos (84.2%).

Students participating in ECAR's survey (2009) also consider themselves to be mainstream adopters of technology, as they attempt to stay in step with peers. Average student use approximates 21.3 hours per week in internet-based activities, with early adopters spending more hours per week than most. Also, a student's degree program influenced hours of use indicated, with quantitative-intensive majors like engineering reporting more hours than other majors.

These data follow a similar pattern to other studies looking at K-12 students' technology-based activities. Project Tomorrow's surveys of K-12 students note that students tend to more readily embrace using technology than their parents, teachers or principals. The near ubiquitous access to technology both inside and outside of schools makes students more self-reliant in using their skills in Internet-based activities to find data and information (*Learning in the 21st Century: 2009 Trends Update*, 2009). As a result, in *Disrupting Class* (2008) Christensen et al. suggest that since more than a million K-12 students took online courses in 2007-08, by 2019 as many as 50% of high schools students may be learning online. Whether this prediction holds true or not, it seems clear that many technologies are available and being used to assist social interaction and learning, technologies that are likely to continue developing and remain present in a broad spectrum of the population.

With growing technology use in K-12, today's students arrive at higher education's doorsteps with many skills. By the time students reach college they consider themselves to be skilled in using many technologies: fairly or very skilled in using presentation software, college or university websites, learning management systems, and spreadsheets; very positive about using online information; and very skilled or expert at using the Internet to effectively and efficiently search for information if early adopters (Caruso and Smith, 2009).

Despite students' new ease and abilities with technology, being skilled in using various technologies and being fluent with information technology are not the same achievement or level of accomplishment: to be fluent with information technology, one must acquire and engage a complex repertoire of knowledge and skills. In this particular aspect of learning, both faculty and students can become learners together – albeit at different places in the learning process – in acquiring knowledge and skills to negotiate modern technology-assisted learning environments in beneficial ways.

For example, computers make it possible to use many applications, from spreadsheets to databases, without knowing how the hardware or software works. Sherry Turkle (1995) says that today's college students are so used to thinking about things at "interface" value, clicking on icons to accomplish their work and play, that the only transparency they require is *seeing* how something works rather than *knowing* how it works. This proclivity of today's students has profound effects for their potential to engage in learning activities that are rooted in rote practice as a potential path to deep understanding and making meaning. Furthermore, today's students cut their teeth on computer games and simulations. Fortunately for faculty interested in course redesign, games and simulations of complex and simple phenomena can be used to provide truly beneficial insights, even as they are rule-bound and safe. Yet, since life tends not to play out solely through the logic or binary rules of games and simulations, other pressing considerations ought to accompany even the best simulacra so as to appropriately inform students' learning today. With contemporary student behaviors in mind, faculty need to remain ever vigilant to the question of what they think students should know and be able to do; what new technologies mean to themselves, to their students, and to life-long learning habits of mind and heart; and what the new, emerging, and converging literacies are in a digital millennium (Turkle, 1995).

For at least ten years, colleges and universities have attempted practical, though difficult, change interventions aimed at integrating technology into teaching and learning activities. Faculty in many places have found recognizable reasons for learning basic, contemporary computer skills and for keeping those skills current. Just as important, some faculty have become catalytic agents for change within their institutions and also advocates for change in their professional organizations and personal lives. Many early adopter faculty and staff set out to engage their colleagues in the give-and-take of change for themselves and for their students by inviting others to join in broadening and deepening the development, support, and communication efforts necessary to diffuse change across academic community sectors and institutional boundaries - all within time-honored, if slowly paced, academic processes.

Fluency with Information Technology

There has been a modicum of success in realizing two of the three knowledge and skill-development areas listed below that the National Research Council (NRC) says are required for fluency with information technology in higher education. In (1999), the NRC published results of a two-year study of information technology literacy. The National Science Foundation (NSF) had requested the study because the ubiquity of computing, information, and communications technologies in modern life called for better articulation of what everyone needs to know to be productive citizens. Entitled "Being Fluent with Information Technology," the report acknowledged tendencies to focus on skills when approaching technology literacy. The report explained that literacy today requires a complement of knowledge and related abilities to be fluent with information technology (FIT). According to the report, FITness is a long-term process of self-expression, reformulation, and synthesis of knowledge in three realms:

- *Contemporary skills*, the ability to use today's computer applications, enable people to apply information technology immediately…are an essential component of job readiness…(and) provide…practical experience on which to build new competence.
- *Foundational concepts*, the principles and ideas of computers, networks, and information, underpin the technology…explain the how and why of information technology…give insight into its limitations and opportunities…(and) are the raw material for understanding new information technology as it evolves.
- *Intellectual capabilities,* the ability to apply information technology in complex and sustained situations, encapsulate higher-level thinking in the context of information technology…empowers people to manipulate media to their advantage and to handle unintended and unexpected problems when they arise…(and) foster more abstract thinking about information and its manipulation. (NRC, 1999, pp. 1-5)

The report offers an intellectual framework that can help distinguish between achievements (those of a particular time) and learning outcomes (results over time) when assessing what competencies students need to have. The proposed framework might also help differentiate among research (of teaching and learning theories), evaluation (of learning programs and processes), and assessment (of learning outcomes) as scholars and their audiences seek to show what students know and are able to do. Although the specific skills for each area will change with the technology and learning needs, the concepts are rooted in the basic information and abilities required to function in technology-enabled environments.

The NRC report suggests new goals for instruction today that involve the educated use of modern information technology. It places intellectual capabilities at the top of a list of what students need to be FIT. The report suggests that students should be able to "engage in sustained reasoning; manage complexity; test a solution; manage problems in faulty solutions; organize and navigate information structures and evaluate information; collaborate; communicate to other audiences; expect the unexpected; anticipate changing technologies; and think about information technology abstractly" (NRC, 1999, p. 4).

Being FIT means being fluent with information technology; but FITness is more than just knowing how to use learning technologies – more than mere technique. FITness also involves a range of activities connected to process and program excellence, to effective learning and discovery efforts, to demonstrated outcomes where indispensible skills and abilities are evident in educational settings, but more important, in daily life – in short, to behaviors that benefit citizens and society.

Many of the broad goals for intellectual capabilities related to information technology fluency apply across other content domains. In order to use domain-specific digital information in beneficial ways, students must simultaneously demonstrate FITness and information literacy related to domain competencies. To determine whether students have acquired the intellectual capabilities for FITness in the context of other technology-enabled domains, one needs, for example, to ask what achievements look like in sustained reasoning while considering what kind of technological fluency(s) might be brought to bear to demonstrate sustained reasoning in that domain. In this interdisciplinary iteration of FITness, content-specific information, and technology tools are obviously joined. They come together as interacting variables in the same teaching and learning plane, and students must have information literacy in a domain and be FIT to use information technology effectively (NRC, 1999).

The current challenge to FITness involves understanding whether we are discovering, developing, and institutionalizing good pedagogy today – pedagogies right for our contemporary age. Are colleges and universities consciously deciding what students need to know and be able to do to be productive citizens in the world today? Are institutions organizing learning activities based on applied knowledge of how students actually learn? Then, are they appropriately integrating modern, learning technologies across a spectrum of learning activities?

Today, rich, research-validated, pedagogical models are possible – models based on how students learn, effective teaching and learning practices, and general outcomes that have broad support (e.g., critical thinking, problem posing and problem solving, communication, collaboration, and more). As important, these models must include powerful contemporary tools that average citizens will use in learning activities and in their daily lives and work. These new technologies allow for more individualized approaches to learning as well as for solving problems about the complex, highly interactive systems that describe the world today. (For fuller discussion and a taxonomy of learning theory, instructional design, and technology application, see (Cheal and Rajagopalan, 2007)).

FITness involves more than technical prowess. FITness involves generalized, deep understandings of how to apply technology in ways that not only promote student learning, but also benefit learning over a lifetime of challenges to be met and overcome. FITness involves training, discipline, and skill development that prepares learners to make highly informed choices aimed at functional practices and flourishing societies. By applying modern technologies appropriately with an understanding of its relevance to learning, excellence may surface and be realized in daily activities of one and many learners.

To embrace FITness concepts and practices moves toward seeing new instructional possibilities; toward becoming adept at technology-assisted teaching, learning, and research; toward developing generalized, transferable aptitudes in using and applying modern technologies; and toward functional independence for learners of all stripes. As with any other kind of physical and mental fitness regimen, developing and exercising FITness must be grounded in individual and local activity if new learning is to surface and flourish. Faculty learning communities may provide a familiar approach to launching and sustaining local activities on behalf of such learning.

FACULTY LEARNING COMMUNITIES

A faculty learning community (FLC) is "a cross-disciplinary faculty and staff group of six to fifteen members who engage in an active, collaborative, yearlong program with a curriculum about enhancing teaching and learning" (Cox, 2004, p. 8). An FLC should have frequent activities that allow for faculty to learn, reflect, and build a community that is focused on the scholarship of teaching and learning (ibid.). The existing, continuously developing FLC discussed in this chapter has had a primary focus on increasing faculty knowledge of web-enhanced teaching and learning tools that would provide students with more opportunities for active and engaged learning, particularly in large-enrollment courses. The FLC provides faculty with opportunities to (re)consider their pedagogy and explore technology tools best suited to effect active engagement in their specific courses. This multidisciplinary, topic-based FLC is encouraging cross-discipline, cross-rank interactions and collaborations among tenured faculty, instructors, and graduate teaching assistants to provide diverse perspectives and feedback.

Theoretical Framework for Faculty Learning Communities

Faculty learning communities have their roots in student learning communities (SLC) (Cox, 2004). Tinto (1995) reports that students participating in an SLC have deeper, more integrated, and more complex learning. The theoretical model for both faculty and student learning communities is based in research that supports experience-based learning, socialization about the topic, engagement in the learning process, and reflection on the process of learning as critical pieces for effective learning. Faculty learning communities allow for experiential learning as outlined by Dewey (1913) by providing a safe place to explore and test new teaching and learning practices. Vygotsky (1978) framed learning within the socio-cultural context in which people interact and share experiences. The very nature of an FLC creates a context for faculty to discuss and interact on specific topics. Using an FLC for creating web-enhanced learning also allows participants to develop ideas for implementing new teaching and learning modules, test new technologies, and discuss challenges, limitations, and successes throughout the change process. Further, Kolb's (1984) experiential learning cycle is embodied in the FLC since faculty may obtain hands-on experience with web-enhanced technologies. In addition, FLC facilitators may use web-enhanced technologies to provide an immersive model for faculty. Kolb identified engagement in complex problems and the empowerment of the learner as critical aspects of the learning process.

The FLC provides an atmosphere that can empower participants to make changes based on the knowledge of what technologies are available and of the potential impact of those technologies on transforming learning. In other words, FLC facilitators may intentionally model the creation of an interactive, web-enhanced learning environment to allow faculty participants to experience the kind of learning methods they are encouraged to implement in their own learning spaces. Bloom's taxonomy and Churches' (2008) revisions of Bloom for digital and web-enhanced learning addressed the importance of developing higher-order thinking skills in learning. Churches added action verbs to Bloom's taxonomy to include creation (blogs, wikis, videos, podcasts) of web-based materials, evaluating using technology tools (commenting, blogging, moderating) and analyzing of materials (tagging, linking, mashing). The FLC allows participants hands-on learning and testing of various web-enhanced technology tools.

Faculty Learning Community Components: A Developing Case

An FLC requires several components to be effective: a mission and purpose, a specific curriculum, support of the administration, effective facilitators, meetings/activities, a scholarly framework, assessment, and a reward system (Cox, 2004). Cox suggests that the degree to which each of these components is emphasized will depend on the unique situation; each component is likely to include several contributing pieces; and the specific pieces may evolve as an FLC develops.

The mission and purpose of an FLC can be to facilitate significant pedagogical change. In the context of this discussion that is based upon an existing, developing FLC, the aims of change were focused on increasing active and engaged learning with the use of web-enhanced technology tools. The mission and purpose should also be aligned with institutional goals, as was the case here. The focus of our FLC was aligned with the guiding mission of the general education courses at our institution, and by the recognition that there should be more active and web-enhanced learning (WEL) integration in large sections of those courses, since they impact a large percentage of undergraduate students. An FLC is best structured as a colloquium with emphasis on dialogue among participants. We designed our FLC structure to model the kind of learning community we intended FLC participants to build in their own specific courses. FLCs should have a topic-based curriculum, and our primary focus was on the use of technology- and web-enhanced tools to facilitate greater student engagement.

The Mechanics of the FLC

The FLC facilitators represented an intentional partnership between Learning Technologies (a division of the Office of Information Technology) and the Center for Instructional Design and Educational Research (housed in the Provost's Office). This collaboration brought together experts in WEL and pedagogy on our campus. Discussions about who would be invited to participate in the year-long FLC were collective, as were decisions to emphasize learner-centered teaching, and encouraging participants to shape the discussions to meet their needs. FLC meetings were scheduled approximately every three weeks in the fall semester, and in addition to a topic focus, each session was also organic and dynamic, as specific emphases and discussions were driven by the participants. Invited participants were selected on several criteria: current and planned teaching of large-enrollment courses; an openness to curricular and pedagogical redesign and a willingness to discuss the process of change; and diversity of rank and discipline.

The FLC began with an initial overview and informational session. Participants were invited to join the FLC by the Vice President and Dean of Undergraduate Education in order to convey clear administrative support of the program. FLC participants were provided with copies of Weimer's (2002) *Learner-Centered Teaching* and the NRC's (1999) *Being Fluent with Information Technology*. Readings were assigned prior to the next meeting to establish a common vocabulary for further discussions.

Meetings throughout the fall semester were designed to foster discussion, build community, demonstrate technology, and address issues and concerns about course redesign as they arose. Faculty participants shaped a good portion of the FLC curriculum because they came to the table with a variety of needs and desired outcomes. Similar to a learner-centered classroom, the developing FLC described here began with a general analysis of the pedagogical and WEL knowledge bases of the faculty participants. FLC participants and facilitators collaborated in addressing the following questions:

a) What is my current pedagogical approach?
b) Does it include active and engaged learning (how and to what extent)?
c) Why is active and engaged learning important to 21st century students?
d) Are there barriers to active learning in my classes (both physical and pedagogical)?
e) What are the learning objectives of each course?
f) What are the web-enhanced technology tools available?
g) Which technology tools integrate best with my pedagogical approach and which tools will best meet the learning objectives of the courses?
h) How am I assessing student-learning outcomes? Am I addressing web-enhanced learning in my assessments?
i) What are the training and support needs of each individual FLC participant? How can we best ensure successful implementation of the technology tools?

Participants discussed Weimer (2002) in order to begin evaluating the learner-centered aspects of their own teaching. Participants also discussed related topics, including technology-enhanced active learning, problem-based learning, and constructivism. These two-hour sessions featured hands-on demonstrations of potential WEL and other technology solutions. As the fall semester progressed, participants composed and presented their course redesign plans to their FLC colleagues: they explained the pedagogical rationale behind their choice of WEL, developed potential project deliverables, proposed a timeline for implementation, and discussed potential challenges. By mid-point of year-long FLC meetings, each participant had outlined a plan for pedagogical/curricular revision with specific deliverables for their individual course redesign. During the second semester, FLC meetings focused on the implementation of proposed changes. These sessions were intended to place more emphasis on the mechanics of change, the technology tools needed to implement change, and participant support and training needs. Second-semester sessions were driven increasingly by participants, as they supported each other through individual challenges faced during the change process.

Assessment of the FLC itself is emerging and continuous with FLC developments. As FLC participants are scheduled to teach their redesigned courses, facilitators will continue to track measurable change in course delivery/structure and redesigned course objectives and learning outcomes. Early indicators via informal feedback and emerging redesign activities suggest that the FLC is providing the environment, expanded knowledge base, and support to allow participants to make significant change in their approach to teaching and learning.

Finally, Cox (2004) has suggested that a reward system should be implemented that recognizes the efforts of FLC participants. Each participant in this case study received a stipend for participation and a materials supplement that could be used for purchasing technology tools. Also, student technology support is available as FLC participants implement new technologies and web-enhanced learning in their redesigned courses. Cox indicated that rewards could include release time and recognition by the university or department administration. Although funds were not available for faculty release time, FLC stipends were provided by the Provost's office, and each participant will be recognized as an ambassador for pedagogical change in their departments and colleges as a result of committing to the FLC.

Using Community to Facilitate Pedagogical Change

Making significant changes in approaches to teaching and learning is often a difficult task for experienced faculty. Few faculty outside of areas of study which are focused on teaching and learning foundations and processes have developed a theoretical framework which grounds their teaching practice; and most simply follow models they had as students. Perhaps the most common, observable pedagogical approach in many disciplines is for an instructor to develop 50- or 75-minute lectures with PowerPoint slides, and to use traditional exams, asking students to show "mastery" of information delivered via lecture and textbook. Although lecturing is still a very common practice in many large-enrollment public institutions of higher education in the United States, such 'stand and deliver' teaching is not the most effective way to facilitate active learning. Current research indicates that active, rather than passive, learning helps students understand and apply complex material toward problem solving in other contexts (Bransford, Brown and Cocking, 2000; Fink, 2003). Further, and as we have suggested earlier, contemporary learners need to be able to use a range of technologies as they engage with and struggle to solve increasingly sophisticated 21st-century domestic and global problems.

Fostering pedagogical change among individual instructors begins with the self-reflexive awareness that overreliance on lecture formats occurs often because it is a teaching strategy with which faculty are familiar and comfortable (McManus, 2005). Prior to decisions about integrating different technology/web tools, faculty need to begin their own learning process by reflecting on and understanding their particular pedagogical approach(es) and biases. Too often technology workshops assume faculty familiarity with pedagogy, and move quickly into the adoption of a specific technology or web 2.0 tool. It is important to begin with pedagogy, rather than technology: an individual's pedagogical approach to guiding their students toward what they need to know and be able to do should inform the kind of technology integration chosen to achieve the desired learning outcomes for specific activities. Placing pedagogy before technology is, in fact, viewed as a critical indicator of the overall success of a technology-enhanced learning environment (Ziegenfuss, 2005).

Faculty learning communities create a collaborative working time and space that allow participants to reflect on their teaching, explore a topic in-depth, and experiment with new teaching strategies (Petrone and Ortquist-Ahrens, 2004). Communities of practice, such as an FLC, enable participant interaction and reflection that can instill an increased sense of professional identity as a teacher and increased innovation (Hammerness, Darling-Hammond, Bransford, et al., 2005). In the instance described, FLC facilitators were intent upon creating a learning climate that foregrounded collegial interaction and community building. Community is established through (a) safety and trust; (b) openness; (c) respect; (d) responsiveness; (e) collaboration, (f) enjoyment, and (g) empowerment (Cox, 2004). In turn, the community focus offers faculty an essential ingredient—a friendly, supportive environment for exploring change.

For the purposes of encouraging a transition to technology- and web-enhanced active learning, FLC facilitators remain focused on learner-centered pedagogy (Weimer, 2002) that could easily incorporate problem-based learning (Duch, Groh, and Allen, 2001) and/or team-based learning (Michaelsen, Knight, and Fink, 2004), depending on the specific disciplinary context. In a learner-centered teaching practice, "the purpose is not to transfer knowledge, but to create environments and experiences that bring students to discover and construct knowledge for themselves, to make students members of communities of learners that make discoveries and solve problems" (Barr and Tagg, 1995, p. 699). Participants in this developing FLC began the first session by discussing their reading of Weimer. For example, initial FLC conversations centered on debunking common misperceptions of a learner-centered pedagogical praxis (*e.g.,* 'teachers don't teach anything and students don't learn'; 'teachers lose control of the curriculum and the classroom'). Discussions became more nuanced, as participants addressed the shift from placing the teacher at the center of a course to emphasizing the learners' engagement and ability to apply knowledge. Finally, the dialogue moved to the topic of how to make a learner-centered praxis effective in a variety of disciplinary and course-size contexts.

A learner-centered approach strives to build upon the knowledge base that students bring to a learning environment (Bransford, Brown, and Cocking, 2000). A learner-centered pedagogy emphasizes "what the student is learning, how the student is learning, the conditions under which the student is learning, and how current learning positions the student for future learning" (Weimer, 2002, p. xvi). Such an approach also focuses on student responsibility for learning, and that aspect more than any other seems to help many participants understand that effective student-centered, technology-enhanced, active learning environments require all of their best practices as teachers to engage, challenge, and mentor the students they teach without relying on 'stand and deliver' lecturing as their primary pedagogical approach.

Throughout FLC meetings, participants continued to be encouraged to articulate and begin to address the challenges they perceived as they conceived of, developed, and implemented their course redesigns. The community-building component of an FLC created a supportive environment in which participants remarked that they had the opportunity to learn from each other in ways that our institutional structure does not usually support. The participant-driven curriculum was focused on topics such as a) overcoming perceived barriers to learner-centered teaching; b) dealing with the challenges of the physical layout/design of classrooms and other learning spaces for WEL; c) staying current with emerging technology tools; d) developing measurable learning objectives that reflect active learning; e) having pedagogical decisions drive technology implementation. These FLC discussions balanced the theoretical framework for change with hands-on experience of different web-enhanced technology tools. Participants were encouraged to think beyond traditional uses of the technology as they considered innovative ways to foster technology-enriched collaboration in their learning environments.

Changes Implemented

To date, the FLC participants have planned for a fall implementation of the following WEL technologies to increase engagement and active learning in their classes:

1. Student-created video podcasts that require small groups to develop a position on a topic, articulate, and defend that position. Additionally, students will provide a "director's commentary" to demonstrate in-depth knowledge of a topic, use of valid sources, and analytic reasoning skills.
2. Student-developed content websites that are housed on a cloud-based wiki. The websites include stand-alone materials for a debate topic, multimedia resources, annotated bibliography, and the articulation and defense of a position.
3. Twitter feeds to support student interaction during in-class debates and beyond the classroom as issues arise.
4. Problem-based learning activities that include web-based resources to support ethics case studies.
5. Cloud-based wikis that allow for student collaboration on problem scenarios.
6. Faculty-created, informational Youtube-style videos that present pre-lab curriculum to students.
7. Youtube-style videos that present real-world scenarios by engineers to bring "experts in the field" to students.
8. Interactive, web-based, reusable learning objects (RLOs) that engage students in self-paced curricula that focuses on understanding the process of group dynamics in problem-based learning, exploring their own individual communication strengths, and self-awareness of preferred learning styles prior to participating in group work for the course (these RLOs can be tailored to several disciplines).

Flc Participant Reflections

Throughout this pilot FLC faculty were encouraged to reflect on the process of change, their growth as teachers, and the challenges to implementing curricular and pedagogical change. Participant reflections will be used to garner support for generating other FLCs for course redesign, and to improve institutional support for transforming teaching and learning across the institution. To date, faculty have reported the following:

1. The FLC "is helping me implement innovative teaching technologies to increase the size of the class without sacrificing student interaction or quality of learning."
2. "The means changed the ends. We moved the class to a public forum and made student material available to a broader community. Students are thinking about how they engage and shape the public debate. The class has the potential to provide a service to others and may eventually help students feel empowered to influence public debate—their opinion and research matters."
3. "I typically feel completely overwhelmed at the magnitude (perhaps the PERCEIVED magnitude) of the task at hand when the task involves improving the educational experience for undergrads on (our) campus. This (FLC) has encouraged me to START SOMETHING . . ."
4. "Getting together in the same room with FLC members helps me to appreciate the variety of teaching efforts on campus and the difficulties presented to different programs, gives me ideas and ways to think about my own teaching questions from

different perspectives, and inspires me to think of this project as a first step . . . (and) that I can and should think bigger than I currently do."

Reflections will continue to be encouraged throughout the implementation of the course redesigns.

CONCLUSION

It is no accident that successes accruing to faculty learning communities are similar to those found in student learning communities: both approaches to engaging communities of learners lend themselves to more integrated, complex learning and change because of the learning environment in which faculty or students actively participate. Indeed, participants in such communities are, in a manner of speaking, the creators, organizers, and implementers of their own learning and the resulting products of their learning. Facilitators of such learning activities work closely to gently guide and support an emerging process, but not to over take or lead it. Indeed, leadership must reside with engaged, empowered participants who retain responsibility for their own active learning in order to realize aims for substantive shifts or learning with long-term benefits.

Close observation of this developing case study suggests that faculty learning community members can be continuously and effectively encouraged to employ active and engaged learning through web-enhanced technologies as a vehicle for pedagogical change. Some participants have approached this challenge with an entire course redesign that includes re-examining their pedagogy, their learning objectives, and developing web-enhanced learning activities that increase not only the acquisition but also the actual application of domain knowledge, skills and specific competencies for 21st century learners. Other participants are continuing to examine their pedagogical praxis and to develop several smaller individual- or team-based activities that integrate web-enhanced technology active learning into the existing structure of their course.

Research suggests that the pedagogical practices that faculty employ, regardless of specific discipline or curriculum, will be most effective if they create learning environments in which students actively and critically engage with the content material as they apply the knowledge they are learning. As important, learning environments should offer and enable faculty and students to use technology tools – tools that are ever more pervasive in modern society – in creative and sophisticated ways that help them analyze and solve the complex challenges of today and tomorrow. As replication and dissemination of emerging effective practices occurs, FLC participants can encourage their home departments and colleges to sustain and broaden the adoption of technology-enriched active learning across disciplines. Faculty learning communities provide one model for contributing effectively to meeting the much-discussed need for substantive shifts in teaching and learning facing modern higher education.

ACKNOWLEDGMENTS

We gratefully acknowledge the ongoing contributions of the facilitation team, which, in addition to the authors, includes Peter Doolittle and C. Edward Watson.

REFERENCES

Association of American Colleges and Universities (AACandU) (2007). *College learning for the new global century: Executive summary.* Washington, DC: Association of American Colleges and Universities. http://www.aacu.org/leap/documents/Global Century_ExecSum_3.pdf.

Barr, R., and Tagg, J. (1995). From teaching to learning: A new paradigm for undergraduate education. *Change, 27*(6), 697-710.

Bonwell, C. E., and Eison, J.A. (1991). *Active learning: Creating excitement in the classroom.* Washington, DC: ERIC Clearinghouse on Higher Education.

Bransford, J.D., Brown, A.L., and Cocking R.R. (2000). *How people learn: Brain, mind, experience, and school.* Washington, DC: National Academy Press.

Caruso, J.B. and Smith, S.D. (2009). *The ECAR study of undergraduate students and information technology, 2009.* Boulder, CO: Educause Center for Applied Research.

Cheal, C. and Rajagopalan, B. (2007). A taxonomy showing relationship between digital learning objects and instructional design. In Koohang, A. and Harmon, K. (Eds.), *Learning Objects and Instructional Design.* Santa Rosa, CA: Informing Science Press.

Christensen, C.M., Horn, M.B. and Johnson, C.W. (2008). *Disrupting class: how disruptive innovation will change the way the world learns.* New York, NY: McGraw Hill.

Churches, A. (2008). *Bloom's Taxonomy Blooms Digitally. Tech. and Learning.* http://www.techlearning.com/article/8670

Cox, M.D. (2004). Introduction to faculty learning communities. *New Directions for Teaching and Learning, 97,* 5-23.

Dewey, J. (1913). *Interest and effort in education.* Boston, MA: Riverside Press.

Duch, B.J., Groh, S.E., and Allen, D.E. (2001). *The power of problem-based learning: A practical "how to" for teaching undergraduate courses in any discipline.* Sterling, VA: Stylus Publishing, Inc.

Fink, L.D. (2003). *Creating significant learning experiences: An integrated approach to designing college courses.* San Francisco, CA: Jossey-Bass.

Grabowski, B., Koszalka, T., and McCarthy, M. (n.d.). *Web-enhanced learning environment strategies for classroom teachers.* Web-enhanced learning environment strategies for classroom teachers. http://www.classkey.com/info/WELES.pdf.

Graham, S. W., Heiman, S., and Williams, R. (2007). Budget Woes in Higher Education: A Call for Leadership. *Academic Leadership , 2*(4).

Hammerness, K., Darling-Hammond, L., Bransford, J., Berliner, D., Cochran-Smith, M., McDonald, M. and Zeichner, K. (2005). How teachers learn and develop. In L. Darling-Hammond and J. Bransford (Eds.), *Preparing teachers for a changing world: What teachers should learn and be able to do* (pp. 358-389). San Francisco, CA: Jossey-Bass.

Kolb, D. (1984). *Experiential learning.* Englewood Cliffs, NJ: Prentice Hall.

Land, S.M. and Hannafin, M.J. (2000). Student-centered learning environments. In D.H. Jonassen and S.M. Land (Eds.), *Theoretical foundations of learning environments* (pp. 1-24). Mahwah, NJ: Lawrence Erlbaum Associates, Inc.

McManus, D.A. (2005). *Leaving the lecturn: Cooperative learning and the critical first days of students working in groups*. San Francisco, CA: Anchor/Jossey-Bass.

Michaelsen, L.K., Knight, A.B., and Fink, L.D. (2004). *Team-based learning: A transfor mative use of small groups in college teaching*. Sterling, VA: Stylus Publishing, Inc.

National Research Council, Committee on Information Technology Literacy (1999). *Being fluent with information technology*. Washington, DC: National Academy Press.

Petrone, M.C. and Ortquist-Ahrens, L. (2004). Faculty learning communities: A compact guide to creating change and inspiring community. *New Directions for Teaching and Learning, 97*, 63-69.

Project Tomorrow (2009). *Learning in the 21st century: 2009 trends update*. Irvine, CA: Project Tomorrow.

Tinto, V. (1995). Learning communities, collaborative learning, and the pedagogy of educational citizenship. *AAHE Bulletin, 47*(7), 11-13.

Turkle, S. (1995). *Life on the screen: identity in the age of the Internet*. New York, NY: Touchstone.

Vygotsky, L.S. (1978). *Mind and society: The development of higher mental processes*. Cambridge, MA: Harvard University Press.

Weimer, M. (2002). *Learner-centered teaching: Five key changes to practice*. San Francisco, CA: Jossey-Bass.

Ziegenfuss, D.H. (2005). By instructional design: Facilitating effective teaching and learning with technology. In M.O. Thirunarayanan and A. Perez-Prado (Eds.), *Integrating Technology in Higher Education* (pp. 19-45). Lanham, MD: University Press of America.

In: Faculty Training for Web Enhanced Learning
Editors: Manuela Repetto and Guglielmo Trentin

ISBN: 978-1-61209-335-2
© 2011 Nova Science Publishers, Inc.

Chapter 13

THE WEL PROJECT AT THE UNIVERSITY OF GENOA: EFFECTS ON FACULTY ATTITUDES AND TEACHING PRACTICES

Manuela Repetto

Institute for Educational Technology, National Research Council, Italy

ABSTRACT

This chapter analyses the results of an innovative initiative of faculty member training in Web-Enhanced Learning (WEL). After an overview of the context, a brief review of the literature and a description of the methodology and structure of the initiative, this chapter reports qualitative findings from a survey which investigated academic staff perceptions of the use of WEL approaches at different phases of the training process.

The study explores which organizational, contextual and subjective factors affected faculty members in the choice of the WEL approaches at three key phases: at the beginning of the training, during the design process and close to delivery of their academic course.

Furthermore, focusing on the question as to whether this action has affected lecturers' teaching and learning practices and enhanced students' learning processes, the chapter reports the problems, potentialities, and benefits of the courses delivered at the end of the WEL intervention.

INTRODUCTION

The WEL (Web-Enhanced Learning) Project was promoted by the computing service of the University of Genoa (CSITA), in collaboration with the Institute of Educational Technology of the Italian National Research Council (ITD-CNR). This action was mainly aimed at experimenting and consolidating a model of Instructional Design already tested in other Italian universities (Trentin, 2006; Trentin and Alvino, Chapter 1). The model should encourage faculty members to adopt strategies and create activities WEL-based.

The complementary expertise of the two institutions leading the action ensured continuous and integrated support for the faculty members involved: the CSITA was responsible for the hosting and overall administration of the Learning Management System (a Moodle open-source platform), for the tool-related training and for permanent technical support; ITD-CNR was responsible for provision of methodological and pedagogical advice, offered via periodical one-to-one consultations and in-depth workshops.

The strategy adopted for the training process is strictly hands-on, since it is focused on the design of online academic courses according to the principles of Project-Based Learning (Howard, 2002). Hence faculty members were trained to develop design and methodological skills. They were involved in a series of periodical collective and individual meetings led by a team of experts on design methodologies and online course development; this team trained lecturers to acquire ID basics as applied to online learning, and supported them in properly nurturing their embryonic ideas.

During the plenaries, lecturers were provided with an overview on how ICT can be used to enhance learning and on the strategic choices necessary for the subsequent operative phases.

The individual meetings were functional to the design of online courses and to the experimentation of the selected methodological approaches. In this phase, faculty members shaped their course structure and its modularization, planned content and online activities starting from the definition of learning objectives, and developed the necessary resources. The progress of each educational project was monitored by the experts with a view to its implementation and delivery.

In addition to the design meetings, a series of techno-methodological workshops were arranged with the purpose of connecting methodological issues with supporting technologies. The University LMS was used for the whole communication flow within WEL and for implementation and delivery of the online courses.

The aim of this chapter is to analyse the results of this experience through identification of faculty members' attitudes to WEL approaches. Their expectations and orientations were investigated through surveys and systematic observation carried out at three key moments of the training action:

- At the beginning of the training, to profile faculty members and their expectations about the initiative and their initial orientations regarding the various approaches to WEL design;
- After a first training session, to analyse their more settled attitudes and any reconsiderations to WEL approaches;
- At the end of the training and after the implementation of their web-enhanced course, to investigate their final orientations to WEL approaches and perceptions of the overall experience.

Before analyzing the results of this enquiry, it is worth reviewing current research on faculty members' attitudes toward the educational use of technologies, and illustrating the approach to and structure of the WEL action.

FACULTY ATTITUDES TOWARD WEL

Many studies of faculty members' attitudes deal with ICT use in present teaching and learning practices and point to a high demand for training in the educational use of technology (Jankowska, 2004; Hammoud et al, 2008; García-Valcárcel and Tejedor, 2009). Some research analyses the disruption of learning practices induced by the adoption of virtual learning environments (VLE) and other systems or tools (Bongalos et al, 2006; Blin and Munro, 2008; Guasch Pascual et al, 2006; Salajan et al, 2010; Hammoud et al, 2008), whereas lack of change in teaching practices is often ascribed to inadequate technical knowledge of the system and its related tools. Other research (Waycott et al, 2010) suggests that, despite poor technical knowledge, academic staff choose to integrate technology into their practice if they see educational value in doing so, at the same time resisting attempts to integrate it for the mere sake of technology.

Current uses of VLEs in most higher education institutions are focused on improving administrative tasks and replicating behaviorist and transmissive models that have no significant impact on teaching and learning practices (Blin and Munro, 2008). As shown by several studies (Woods et al, 2004; García-Valcárcel and Tejedor, 2009; Laurillard, 2007; Waycott et al, 2010), faculty members use a VLE or an LMS mainly to make course documents, lecture notes and other resources available for students, to manage course grades, or at most to communicate with students. Few use these systems for educational or assessment purposes; the creation of environments for collaborative learning or for student assessment is limited or totally missing. Thus technology is used mainly to support and empower traditional teaching strategies (Laurillard, 2007) and does not transform the internal structure of the learning activities (Blin and Munro, 2008).

Even though academic institutions wish to promote innovative uses of learning technologies, their aspirations are commonly limited to the deployment of an open-source VLE, without taking into account that its successful implementation depends on the quality of the learning activities and on the promotion of training actions targeted at the development of task-related and meta-functional competencies in addition to the tool-related skills (ibid). Availability of technological equipment and supporting staff is considered crucial to getting faculty members to integrate technology into their teaching, but these are not the sole factors (Dusick and Yildirim, 2000; Puddu et al, 2008). Lecturers' previous practices and training experiences affect the instructional strategies adopted by them in the use of a web-based system; in the same way, self-confidence, anxiety levels and perceived relevance are highlighted as crucial (Bongalos et al, 2006; Dusick and Yildirim, 2000). Not to mention that faculty members' attitudes towards the use of technology have a significant impact on students' performance and satisfaction (Hammoud et al, 2008).

To innovate lecturers' practice and promote alternative teaching strategies, a learning initiative should be focused on methodological and educational aspects of ICT use, and be aimed at establishing interdisciplinary connections among university teachers, who are usually subject-oriented, thus breaking down the isolation that characterizes them (Margalef García and Pareja Roblin, 2008; Trentin, 2006). In the WEL methodological approach, one of the key ideas is supporting faculty members in planning the most effective instructional strategy for each learning objective to be attained with the support of technology (Trentin, 2006; Trentin and Alvino, Chapter 1).

APPROACH AND STRUCTURE OF WEL ACTION

As mentioned in the introduction, the approach adopted in the WEL project is based on project-based learning and on the assumption that, for a real ICT-enhanced educational innovation, faculty members must achieve mastery in ID methodologies.

The strategy of the WEL training process was distinguished by a highly hands-on approach (Puddu et al, 2008), focused on supporting lecturers in the development of their academic online courses, considered as educational projects. Methodological and technological support was ensured by a team of researchers who are expert in design methodologies and on development of online learning environments. They led a series of alternately collective and individual meetings:

- two start-up plenaries, aimed at providing ID principles applied to online learning and at showing how ICT can enhance learning in higher education;
- three one-to-one design meetings between each lecturer and his/her assigned co-designer (an ITD researcher), aimed at designing the academic courses based on the WEL approaches.

The first one-to-one "macro-design meeting" served: to outline the course structure in a methodologically correct way; for its modularization; to draw up the first section of the course guide; and to define the course schedule.

The second "micro-design meeting" served: to plan the online activities (case studies, problem-solving, assignments, role-play, etc.) which were necessary for attaining the learning objectives; to establish the assessment procedures; to define the resources; and to organize the logical architecture of the communication.

The third and final design meeting was aimed at monitoring project progress with a view to its delivery.

Besides the individual meetings, two series of techno-methodological workshops provided in-depth study of the technologies used in the development of online learning activities:

- a first series to present the main functions of the University LMS used for course delivery;
- a second series of thematic workshops for the development of online learning material such as e-content and video lectures, or for the organization of the envisaged collaborative online activities.

Before implementing the designed course into the university LMS, an analogous online space was made available, encouraging the lecturers to experiment with the learning modules developed during the design phase. In this web space they could create an online environment mirroring the course modularization, manage learning resources, and simulate formation of groups, start-up of activities and online assessment.

One of the main and indefeasible peculiarities of this action was the way in which the methodological skills of the instructional designers from ITD were integrated with the technological ones of the CSITA computer scientists, thus ensuring qualified assistance to teachers in the design and delivery of their university courses.

PROFILES OF FACULTY MEMBERS AND THEIR ATTITUDES TOWARDS WEL

The faculty members engaged in the WEL initiative were recruited through advertisement via email and formal communication on the University platform. No prerequisite was required for adhering to the training action; thus participation was voluntary.

The profiling questionnaire administered to participants (Puddu et al, 2008) was structured into three sections which aimed at: obtaining personal data on teachers and their courses; recognizing teachers' level of knowledge of ICT and its use in education; and acquiring information about the WEL approach selected for the course to be designed and for the development of learning activities. The faculty members who adhered to the WEL action on a voluntary basis were 52; 80 percent of them were tenured, while the remaining 20 percent had temporary contracts as graduate assistants. They came from all 11 faculties of the University of Genoa. The faculties most represented (Figure 1) were the scientific ones (Medicine, Mathematics, Physics and Natural Sciences); nevertheless, there was also a good number of teachers from the faculties of Language and Humanities, which are traditionally less keen on the integration of ICT into education.

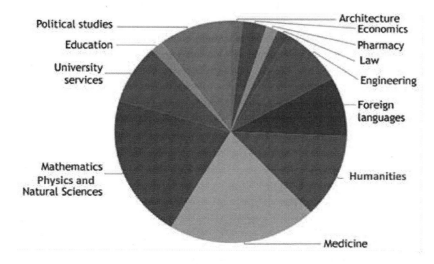

Figure 1. Lecturers involved grouped by faculty.

64% of lecturers perceived the level of their ICT skills as medium, 22% of them considered it as high, while only 13% believed that their skills level in this field was low. Previous experience of teaching through ICT was instead widespread among lecturers, 82% of them reporting that they had already used ICT for educational purposes. In the questionnaire, lecturers could also express their needs and expectations. They mainly stressed the need to develop skills for creating innovative tools for web-enhanced learning, and above all to learn the basics of ID in order to identify:

- which strategies are most effective for each educational objective to be attained;
- which learning activities can acquire added value if achieved online.

Several lecturers expected that acquisition of ID basics could help them to simplify the preparation of learning material and the planning of learning activities, as well as improve students' involvement and motivation. Some staff declared they were simply curious about the contents of the initiative or that they wished to increase their familiarity with ICT.

Concerning lecturers' initial attitudes towards course type, about three-quarters were willing to adopt a blended solution, combining face-to-face lectures with online learning activities. Only 9% expressed a preference for the online modality, in which the course is run entirely at a distance and students' participation is considered as an indefeasible part of the learning path. The integrated approach, based on enrichment of traditional face-to-face lectures with online distribution of learning material not necessarily created for that course and with generic online assistance (Trentin, 2006), was chosen by 15% of lecturers.

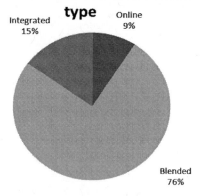

Initial attitudes towards course type

Integrated 15%
Online 9%
Blended 76%

Figure 2. Initial attitudes towards course type.

Regarding attitudes towards online activities, in about 50% of cases an initial orientation towards the content-driven approach was detected (based on delivery of online learning materials, i.e. lecture notes, slides, video and podcasts), while 20% of lecturers opted for the Networked Collaborative Learning approach (NCL, based on online collaborative learning). A mixed approach, combining the delivery of learning materials with the organization of online collaborative activities, was preferred by about 30%.

ATTITUDES DURING THE DESIGN PROCESS

A further analysis was carried out after the first individual design meeting, when faculty members would already have made a decision about the WEL approach to adopt. Co-designers could infer lecturers' orientations from project reports drawn up during the individual meetings, where they noted faculty choices of course type and WEL approach, as well as the main course features.

Comparison of initial profiling data with those gathered through the project reports allowed identification of tendencies and changes in lecturers' attitudes (Puddu et al, 2008).

The tendencies which emerged were compared with: faculty members' previous ICT knowledge and level of experience; the discipline taught; student numbers; and the need for further training as expressed by lecturers.

Co-designers detected a general shift in lecturers' inclination towards online and blended courses, 43% and 57% opting for them respectively, to the detriment of the integrated course, which was completely dismissed (ibid). Concerning learning activities, in almost half the cases (44%), the orientation expressed in the initial survey was confirmed, while it was no longer the same in 56% of cases, 36% of which shifted towards the NCL approach. Taken as a whole, the NCL approach was preferred in 50% of cases, while the other half was equally subdivided between content-driven and mixed approaches.

If the change in approach is compared with the previous ICT knowledge declared in the initial survey, it appears that 60% of lecturers with high-level knowledge stuck to their initial orientation, while the others shifted to the NCL approach. This percentage is reversed among teachers with medium knowledge (60% of them changed approach), whilst the number of persons with low skills who changed learning approach shot up to two-thirds of the total. Hence a significant correlation was detected between ICT knowledge level and propensity for change. An analogous correlation was discovered between approach change and experience in the educational use of ICT.

The relationship between the chosen approach and the lecturer's discipline disproves the belief that a collaborative approach is perceived as more suitable for the humanities, since it featured for 60% of courses on scientific subjects.

Changes in initial orientations were in part induced by co-designers, since during the design meetings they invited lecturers to consider the feasibility of the chosen approach in relation to student numbers. If at the beginning many faculty members preferred a content-driven approach regardless of this factor, later on they maintained their initial orientation only if student numbers were very high. Whereas if the number of students was small, many lecturers switched to the NCL or mixed approach. As shown in Figure 3, the tendency to select collaborative and mixed approaches increases with the numerical range of students.

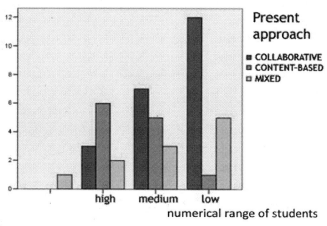

(Puddu et al, 2008)

Figure 3. Orientations and student numbers.

As to the further training needs expressed by lecturers, a significant interest was detected in topics related to the selected approach, even if in some cases they also manifested curiosity for ICT tools and other issues not specifically related to the approach.

FACULTY MEMBERS' ATTITUDES AT THE END OF THE WEL ACTION

The final survey administered to the lecturers engaged in WEL was aimed at analyzing the results of the training phase and at detecting their attitudes to said training, as well as to the design process of their course, and to the management and outcomes of learning activities. Their attitudes were measured on a 30-item five-point Likert scale.

One-quarter of delivered web-enhanced courses had a number of students exceeding 100 units, one-third had between 50 and 100 students, and 42% had less than 50. In three-quarters of the courses all the students adhered to the activities designed by the lecturers, while in the remaining quarter about 50 % of students participated in the activities, either voluntarily or by designation of their lecturer.

40% of courses were launched on the University LMS for the first time, one third had been started up in the two previous academic years, and one quarter had been launched even before that. Although in the previous years the university LMS had already been in use, no methodological support was available and ID principles for preparing learning activities and material were totally unknown.

Participation in the Training Process

Two-thirds of the lecturers participated in both the plenaries and the three individual meetings with the co-designer. One third attended one plenary and two meetings at least. The techno-methodological workshops were attended by three-quarters of the lecturers. Each of the eight workshops was attended by at least 50% of lecturers. The co-designer who supported each lecturer was perceived as being "completely effective" by 50% and "very effective" or "adequately effective" by the other 50%. The co-designer influence on the choice of the WEL approach was considered "high" by 58%, "adequate" by 25% and "poor" or "null" by about 16%.

As a continuation of the basic ID experience of WEL, all the participants considered it would be useful to be involved in a possible second phase of this initiative, a "WEL 2" edition, in which e-pedagogy issues would be dealt with more in depth.

Effectiveness of the Proposed ID Model

All the envisaged activities of ID training were judged to be from "useful" to "completely useful"; the estimations of the efficacy of the general training approach proposed within WEL, based on the development of an educational project, achieved the top score (Figure 4).

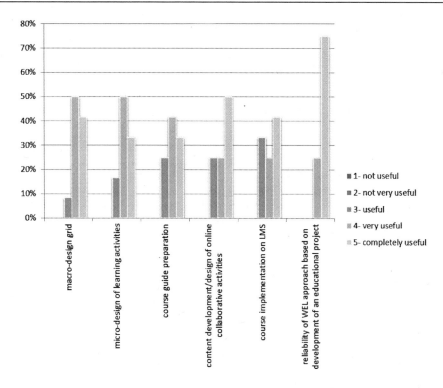

Figure 4. Lecturers' attitudes toward the WEL ID model.

Two-thirds of the courses were blended, with at least one online learning module (Figure 5); the remaining one-third was subdivided among completely online courses and courses based on the integrated approach (entirely face-to-face with web used only as support). Thus, comparing lecturers' final orientations toward course type with those expressed initially (Figure 2), there are no significant differences.

The reasons expressed for online or blended courses were:

- organizational/operational (course supplied in various academic centers, students physically distant, shortness of courses, heaviness of traditional course, less effort for both teachers and students);
- educational (online activities and material considered more interesting and attractive for students, academic course can be integrated and enriched online, traditional lectures should be alternated with online collaborative work);
- the encouraging results of previous experiences.

Those lecturers who during the design process abandoned their previous choice (blended or online course) for the integrated approach were concerned about adding to students' workload with extra tasks and considered this approach easier to apply. Others were compelled to revise the chosen approach during the design process as soon as they discovered the actual number of students enrolled in their course, which was too high to manage.

The same reasons induced many lecturers to abandon the NCL approach. In two-thirds of courses the approach adopted for learning activities was mixed, in one-quarter it was content-driven, while the collaborative approach was chosen for only 8% of courses (Figure 5).

Those who selected the content-driven approach underlined the clearness and self-consistency of a course shaped in such a way. Lecturers who preferred the NCL or the mixed approach pointed to the opportunity for increasing teacher/student interactivity and improving the learning process; others underlined that with this approach students do not feel isolated, since they are aware of taking part in a common learning process.

Final approach

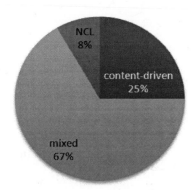

Figure 5. Final orientations on learning approaches.

Analyzing the trend of the orientations, the choice of the purely collaborative approach is seen to have dramatically decreased after an intermediate peak, while the choice of the content-driven approach, which halved at the intermediate verification, has remained stable; instead the choice of the mixed approach has prominently increased. This means that at the end of the design process almost 70% of lecturers were able to include in their courses both learning content specifically created for it and online collaborative activities.

The technologies most used by lecturers for course delivery were features of the university LMS (100% of lecturers), later on Wiki (40%), and some authoring tools.

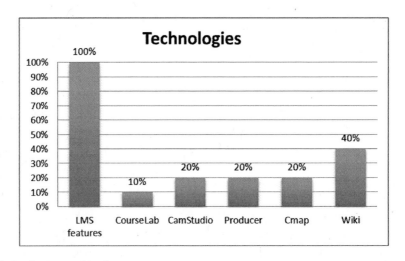

Figure 6. Technologies used by lecturers.

Overall Evaluation of WEL

The assessment of the large majority of faculty members tends toward medium to high scores. Concerning topics treated in the training actions, they would:

- add advanced learning sessions on technical issues of the platform, on the adopted authoring tools and on specific software subject-oriented simulations for the delivery of digital content; instances and case studies of subject-oriented online courses with related approaches and modalities from which to draw inspiration; criteria for assessing individuals and groups and reliability of web resources; techno-methodological information concerning connectivism; the basics of communication and interaction analysis theories; an advanced course for expert elearning users.
- eliminate learning sessions on ICT tools and authoring systems since the university LMS include the same or similar tools among its functionalities.
- improve ease of material retrieval on the LMS; interaction with experts and co-designers with further meetings; treatment of pedagogical issues; organization of workshops and other events which should be separated according to participants' skills levels.

The large majority of participants perceived as "very" to "completely" useful the institution of a permanent service for techno-methodological support during the design and implementation of their web-enhanced courses.

Outcomes of the Courses Designed within WEL

72% of faculty members succeeded in implementing their web-enhanced course. In all respects, the obstacles encountered by the majority of lecturers in implementing the course designed within WEL were minimal or easily surmountable.

On being asked to clarify the difficulties encountered, lecturers highlighted the following:

Technological issues:

- difficulty in uploading resources onto the university LMS;
- need for further details on an authoring software for video lectures (MS Producer);
- the university LMS itself, seen as not very user-friendly;

Organizational aspects:

- difficult accreditation of online learning activities;
- lack of adequate labs and human resources at the faculties (i.e. assistants or tutors);
- problems with time and monitoring management;

Educational issues:

- students' initial concern or skepticism about the innovative course setting;
- difficulties for assessment of individual contribution within online collaborative activities.

With regard to spillover effects on teaching and learning practices, lecturers' attitudes towards educational, relational and motivational aspects were very positive, as shown in the figure below (Figure 7). Undoubtedly, the innovation introduced into the courses has affected all these issues.

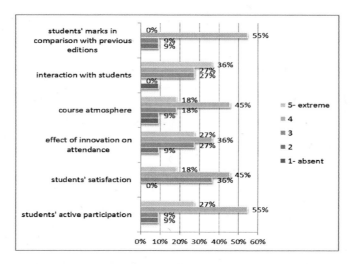

Figure 7. Spillover effects of WEL on teaching and learning practices.

With regard to the general exercise of their profession, lecturers were asked to what extent the approach adopted by them would innovate their assessment practices, preparation of learning material, design of learning activities; and to what extent it would improve their educational strategies. It seems that the adopted approach has significantly influenced all these aspects, most noticeably learning activity design and material preparation (see Figure 8).

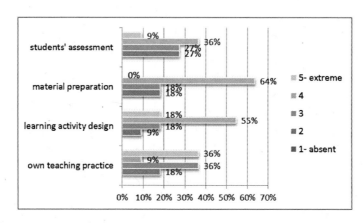

Figure 8. WEL effects on lecturers' professionalism.

Undoubtedly, faculty members' attitudes toward the effects of WEL on their teaching and learning practices and professionalism prove its considerable innovative extent.

Concerning the effects of the innovative aspects introduced with course delivery on colleagues, students and at an institutional level, the majority of lecturers noticed a positive impact on their colleagues and students, while no result emerged at an institutional level. In fact many participants declared that, at this level, although the individual commitment is appreciated, at present there is no official acknowledgement.

Participants' colleagues manifested their interest in several ways: through the request to be included in a subsequent replication of the WEL initiative; through their involvement in events related to WEL; or by showing interest in future common projects.

Concerning the impact on their students, participants particularly pointed out:

- a good level of satisfaction expressed by students at the end of courses, in spite of initial perplexity;
- students' appreciation of improvement in communication and new interaction strategies;
- greater student involvement and the chance to reflect on upon subject-oriented methodological issues that would not have emerged within a traditional learning activity.

CONCLUSION

This chapter describes an innovative experiment carried out in higher education, based on training faculty members in WEL methodologies. The main focus is on participants' expectations and perceptions of the WEL approaches adopted, and on the outcomes of the courses designed during the training phase and delivered in the same academic year.

The reference Instruction Design (ID) model adopted in WEL is only apparently prescriptive as, starting from his/her own situation, each lecturer added a personal touch to the development of his/her educational project, emphasizing some pedagogical aspects, using some ICT tools more than others, and tailoring the selected approach and learning activities to his/her personal teaching style, to the educational objectives and to the characteristics of the taught subject. Starting from the ID model proposed within the WEL action, teachers had the chance to reflect on their common practices, beliefs and methods and to reconstruct them without excessively upsetting their habits. An attitude that instructional designers tried to generate among lecturers in the selection of the WEL approach was to choose the best strategy for attaining a given learning objective, rather than simply selecting a specific technology which is not necessary suitable for managing that particular learning content or activity.

Considering the expectations initially expressed, lecturers appear to be aligned with the objectives and rationale of the WEL initiative, while their initial orientations towards WEL approaches changed various times during the course design process.

Examining factors and conditions that could have affected their choices, previous training appears to be a significant predictor of whether a faculty member adopts and maintains a specific WEL approach in his/her teaching; also previous experience in the educational use of

ICT. The particular subject taught does not on the other hand seem to be an influential factor in the choice of WEL approaches.

Experienced teachers tend to choose a specific WEL approach during the design process and maintain it for the course delivery. Co-designers had a significant role for the less experienced lecturers in the choice of the WEL approach, but a limited influence on the more expert of them, although their support was perceived as important by them as by almost all the participants. Structural constraints (Trentin and Alvino, Chapter 1), such as student numbers, made the choice of the WEL approach almost compulsory, albeit teachers needed to be adequately trained to recognize such a constraint and to adopt the best solution.

Analyzing lecturers' attitudes expressed at the end of the WEL initiative, further training needs come to light. Most of them perceived the necessity of establishing a structure offering permanent support for the development of web-enhanced courses. They noticed a few difficulties in the use of some technologies and encountered some obstacles in online module accreditation and in the lack of equipment and human resources at faculties. Most had problems with time management, though they were aware that time invested in acquisition of methodological skills, preparation of learning content and design of learning activities should be considered as a worthwhile investment for future editions of the course. After all, the amount of time taken to prepare a WEL course as noted by our lecturers is likewise perceived as the most common problem in many other studies (Bongalos et al, 2006; García-Valcárcel and Tejedor, 2009; Trentin, 2006, Waycott et al, 2010).

Nevertheless, faculty members who participated in the WEL initiative were effectively empowered to design WEL courses and succeeded in innovating their own teaching practices. They themselves declare that the newly-adopted approaches have improved their preparation of learning material, design of learning activities, assessment procedures and educational strategies. Furthermore, WEL courses delivered after the design phase had a significant impact on both students and colleagues.

Further research through long-term monitoring of courses is required. Analyses of student drop-out rates, average marks in intermediate tests and exams could be additional objective data for evaluating the impact of the WEL initiative, as could also a qualitative enquiry for detecting whether WEL approaches, content and learning activities are maintained in subsequent editions of those same academic courses.

REFERENCES

Blin, F., and Munro, M. (2008). Why hasn't technology disrupted academics' teaching practices? Understanding resistance to change through the lens of activity theory. *Computers and Education, 50*(2), 475-490.

Bongalos, Y.Q., Bulaon, D.D.R., Caledonio, L.P., de Guzman, A.B., and Ogarte, C.J.F. (2006). University teachers' experiences in courseware development. *British journal of Educational Technology, 37*(5), 695-704.

Dusick, D. M., and Yildirim, S. (2000). Faculty Computer Use and Training: Identifying Distinct Needs for Different Populations. *Community College Review, 27*(4), 33-47.

García-Valcárcel, A., and Tejedor, F.J. (2009). Training demands of the lecturers related to the use of ICT. *Procedia - Social and Behavioral Sciences, 1*(1), 178-183.

Guasch Pascual, T., Álvarez Valdivia, I., and Espasa Roca, A. (2006). Criteria for ICT-supported Higher Education Teachers Training (Research paper). http://openaccess. uoc.edu/webapps/o2/handle/10609/1663.

Hammoud, L., Love, S., and Brinkman, W. (2008). The effect of lecturers' attitude on students' use of an online learning environment. *Proceedings of the 15th European conference on Cognitive ergonomics: the ergonomics of cool interaction.* Funchal, Portugal.

Howard, J. (2002*).* Technology-Enhanced Project-Based Learning in Teacher Education: Addressing the Goals of Transfer. *Journal of Technology and Teacher Education, 10*(3), 343-364. Norfolk, VA: AACE.

Jankowska, M. A. (2004). Identifying University Professors' Information Needs in the Challenging Environment of Information and Communication Technologies. *The Journal of Academic Librarianship, 30*(1), 51-66.

Laurillard, D. (2007). Preface. In Beetham, H., and Sharpe, R. (Eds.), *Rethinking pedagogy for a digital age: designing and delivering e-learning.* London: Routledge.

Margalef García, L., and Pareja Roblin, N. (2008). Innovation, research and professional development in higher education: Learning from our own experience. *Teaching and Teacher Education, 24*(1), 104-116.

Puddu, F., Repetto, M., and Vallarino, E. (2008). The WEL initiative: a model of web enhanced learning for faculty members. *Je-LKS – Applications, 4*(3), 213-221.

Salajan, F.D., Schönwetter, D. J., and Cleghorn, B. M. (2010). Student and faculty inter-generational digital divide: Fact or fiction? *Computers and Education, 55*(3), 1393-1403.

Trentin, G. (2006). The Xanadu project: training faculty in the use of information and communication technology for university teaching. *Journal of Computer Assisted Learning, 22,* 182-196.

Trentin, G., and Alvino, S. (2011). Faculty training as a key factor for Web Enhanced Learning sustainability. *Faculty training for Web-Enhanced Learning.* New York: Nova Science (this book).

Waycott, J., Bennett, S., Kennedy, G., Dalgarno, B., and Gray, K. (2010). Digital divides? Student and staff perceptions of information and communication technologies. *Computers and Education, 54*(4), 1202-1211.

Woods, R., Baker, J. D., and Hopper, D. (2004). Hybrid structures: Faculty use and perception of web-based courseware as a supplement to face-to-face instruction. *The Internet and Higher Education, 7*(4), 281-297.

BIOGRAPHIES

SERENA ALVINO

Consulting Professor in the Educational Sciences Faculty of the University of Genoa for the "E-learning for adults and organizations" course, Serena Alvino has been collaborating with the Institute for Educational Technologies of the Italian National Research Council since 2002 on a number of projects about Computer Supported Collaborative Learning (CSCL) and online learning instructional design. She received a PhD in "Languages, Cultures and ICTs" from the University of Genoa in 2008, discussing the thesis "Computer Supported Collaborative Learning and reusability: an approach to the integration of reusable resources in collaborative learning processes". Her interests and activities mainly focus on learning objects and design models, educational metadata models, ontologies and folksonomies supporting online learning and resource sharing and Instructional Design for CSCL.

KIM FLOYD

Kim Floyd is currently an Assistant Professor at West Virginia University in the Special Education Department. Prior to her appointment at WVU, she was a faculty member at East Carolina University for over twenty years where she was the Director of Revolving Education Around Partnerships, an inclusive developmental preschool program. She has published many articles, chapters, and given numerous state and national presentations in the areas of preschool special education, assistive and emerging technologies, autism, and online instruction.

SHELLI B. FOWLER

Shelli B. Fowler is the Executive Director of Graduate Development Programs and New Pedagogies in Learning Technologies, a division of the Office of Information Technology, at Virginia Tech. One of her primary responsibilities is to help foster wider adoption of technology-enhanced active learning across all departments and colleges. Her research areas and publications focus on critical pedagogy and the integration of teaching, learning, and technologies. Shelli is also an Associate Professor in the Department of English. She earned her doctorate from The University of Texas at Austin.

CATHY GALYON KERAMIDAS

Cathy Galyon Keramidas is currently an Assistant Professor at West Virginia University in the Special Education Department, where she teaches Masters level online courses in Autism and Early Childhood Special Education. She was a research assistant to the National Assistive Technology Research Institute (NATRI) at the University of Kentucky and served on the Tots and Tech board of directors. She has published many articles, chapters, and given many national presentations about best practices in teaching in an online environment.

LAURI GRACE

Lauri Grace is a Senior Lecturer in Education at Deakin University Australia. Lauri has substantial experience in developing, facilitating and evaluating professional development programs for educators. Drawing on her extensive background working with adults and young people in workplace, vocational and higher education, Lauri has particular expertise in developing innovative approaches to education that engage disengaged learners. Lauri's expertise and research interests include varied applications of situated or workplace learning, innovative and engaging uses of educational technology in blended and online learning, and the use of strategies to support learners with particular individual needs. She currently teaches in an innovative blended learning pre-service teacher education program, and also teaches in and is Course Director of a wholly online postgraduate professional development program for adult educators.

SARAH GURI-ROSENBLIT

Sarah Guri-Rosenblit is the Director of International Academic Outreach and the Head of Graduate Studies in Education at the Open University of Israel. She got her PhD from Stanford University in 1984 in education and political science. Her areas of expertise are focused on comparative research of higher education systems, distance education and e-learning. She published books and dozens of articles in these fields. She has participated in the last decade in many international and national forums on various aspects of higher education. She was selected in 2005/6 as one of the 30 New Century Scholars in the Fulbright Program on: 'Higher Education in the 21st Century: Global Challenge and National Response'. Since 2003 she has been a member of the Scientific Committee of Europe and North America in the UNESCO Forum of Higher Education, Research and Knowledge. She is also a member in expert evaluations panels of HESC (Higher Education and Social Change) under the auspices of the European Science Foundation, and the Bellagio Conference Center of the Rockefeller Foundation. Her recent book on Digital Technologies in

Higher Education: Sweeping Expectations and Actual Effects was published in March 2009 by Nova Science in New York.

MAGDALENA JARA

Magdalena Jara recently joined the University Diego Portales, in Santiago, Chile as Director of Undergraduate Teaching and Learning and Academic Quality, where she is also participating in the Research Programme in Policies in Higher Education. In her previous role as Learning Technologies Fellow at the Learning Technologies Unit at the Institute of Education, University of London her professional work focused on the pedagogical design of e-learning courses, the evaluation of e-learning, and her research was concerned with quality assurance for distance and online courses.

TARA JEFFS

Tara Jeffs is currently an assistive technology specialist for Loudoun County Public Schools, Ashburn, Virginia. Her career experiences bring a wealth of expertise focusing on the infusion of assistive and emerging technologies in the classroom. Tara has written more than 25 articles and book chapters and has disseminated knowledge and research in the area of assistive and emerging technologies and online learning through more than 100 presentations at state and national conferences over the past 10 years.

SHARON JUDGE

Sharon Judge is the Associate Dean of the Darden College of Education. Prior to this appointment, she was a professor and coordinator of the doctoral program in Special Education in the College. Before coming to Old Dominion University in 2006, she was Professor of Special Education at the University of Tennessee for 12 years. She has been a consistent recipient of external grants; the most recent include a U.S. Department of Education Teacher Quality Partnership grant. She has published numerous articles, chapters, and a book in the areas of assistive technology, professional development, and children with special needs.

JANE E. KLOBAS

Jane E. Klobas is Alberto Dondena Fellow in the Carlo F. Dondena Centre for Research on Social Dynamics at Università Bocconi in Milan, Italy and Professor at the University of Western Australia Business School in Perth, Australia. She is a teacher, researcher, editor and author. Her research spans the areas of social/collaborative online learning; online scholarly collaboration; human issues in e-learning; research methodology; life course decision making; and organizational psychology for social and economic development. She supervises research students in these areas, and teaches research and data analysis; research strategy; research methods; and multivariate statistics. Her publications include *Wikis: Tools for Information Work and Collaboration* (Chandos, 2006; published in Italy as Oltre Wikipedia, Sperling and Kupfer/EGEA), several book chapters, and articles in journals such as *Decision Support Systems, Organizational Behaviour, Library and Information Science Research, Internet Research, Educational Technology and Society, Computers and Education*, and *Behaviour and Information Technology*.

HARVEY MELLAR

Harvey Mellar is a Reader in Technology Enhanced Learning at the Institute of Education and Head of the Learning Technologies Unit which supports staff in the implementation of e-learning both in on-campus courses and in fully on-line courses. The Learning Technologies Unit is situated within the London Knowledge Lab, a multi-disciplinary research centre of the University of London. He has directed a large number of research projects in the field of e-learning including recently From Pedagogic Research to Embedded E-Learning (PREEL) and Quality Assurance and Quality Enhancement in e-learning. Besides quality enhancement his present research interests include the use of e-learning for Skills for Life learners and formative e-assessment.

MANUELA MILANI

Manuela Milani is an instructional designer, teachers trainer and researcher. She has more than 15 years of distance and online education experience in different roles: online facilitator, instructional technology specialist, learning technology coordinator, and transnational European projects local coordinator. Currently she works as an instructional designer at the CTU, the eLearning Center of the Università degli Studi di Milano, Italy.

She delivers many training and professional development activities for university staff and faculty members in Italian Universities. She collaborates as a researcher with "Laboratoire EMA", Education Mutation Apprentissage, Université de Cergy-Pontoise, France.

Her research aims at exploring the impact of cultural differences on the design of online courses offered by universities throughout Europe. Her publications include several papers on use of technology in higher education, the concept of quality within the eLearning field.

ANNE H. MOORE

Anne H. Moore is associate vice president for learning technologies at Virginia Tech in Blacksburg, VA, USA. She coordinates award winning programs in faculty and graduate student development for technology-assisted learning; in services for testing, assistive technologies, and technology-integrated learning spaces; and in e-portfolio, repository, and learning management systems design and development. In addition to teaching and advising graduate students in policy, planning, and governance arenas, she assists underserved rural and urban communities with technology integration initiatives.

Moore is founding chair of the Electronic Campus of Virginia, a member of the commonwealth's Learning Technologies Advisory Committee, and has served as staff director for two commissioned reports on the future of Virginia higher education. She sits on national advisory boards for such organizations as the Research Channel, the Redesign Alliance, and Pearson; holds three degrees from William and Mary; and has authored numerous articles, book chapters, and policy papers.

STEFANO RENZI

Stefano Renzi is Researcher in Informatics/Computing Systems in the Department of Decision Sciences at "Bocconi" University in Milan, Italy and Research Fellow in the Carlo F. Dondena Centre for Research on Social Dynamics at "Bocconi" University. He has over 25 years of experience in higher education teaching and has taught Internet technologies and related applications using teaching strategies based on collaborative learning for several years. His research interests are related to adoption and diffusion of new information technologies in online collaboration and online education and training, e-learning, and educational technology. He has worked on development of infrastructure for online communication in education and research for many years and has been involved in several university projects to integrate online educational activities in traditional courses. His publications include several technical and evaluative papers and book chapters on use of technology in education, students' psychological response to online education, and factors influencing online collaborative learning adoption by teachers at university.

MANUELA REPETTO

Manuela Repetto is junior researcher at the Institute for Educational Technology (ITD) of the Italian National Research Council (CNR). She earned her master degree in Adult Education at the University of Genoa and her Doctorate in Education and Cognition at the University of Venice. She has been involved in a number of projects in the field of elearning, teacher training, lifelong learning and special education. Her research interests include the definition of models and methods for studying virtual learning communities, and the use of web-based approaches to innovate learning and professional practices.

DIRK SCHNECKENBERG

Dirk Schneckenberg is Assistant Professor for Strategic Management at the ESC Rennes School of Business in France. His research interests are organizational learning, knowledge management and innovation strategies, as well as the necessity to rethink higher education.

JENNIFER LV SPARROW

Jennifer LV Sparrow is the Director of Emerging Technologies and New Ventures at Virginia Tech. She works with a great team of students and professional staff in the Innovation Space, a New Media Center. She has a passion for working with faculty to explore new technologies to increase active and engaged learning. Her areas of research include emerging technologies, collaborative learning, and fostering collaboration with Web 2.0 technologies. Jennifer received her bachelor's degree from Smith College, her master's degree from Florida Gulf Coast University, and doctorate from the University of Central Florida. She currently serves on the EDUCAUSE Learning Initiative Advisory Board and the EDUCAUSE Evolving Technologies Committee.

ELIZABETH STACEY

Associate Professor Elizabeth Stacey (retired) has researched and supervised research students and taught about topics covering a range of interactive communication technologies including blended learning, online learning via the Internet, computer conferencing, collaborative learning in a virtual environment, interactive television, flexible, open and distance education and cyberbullying. She has co-edited two books and published 8 book chapters, 20 refereed journal articles, and 39 conference papers about these areas of research.

KAREN STARR

Karen Starr is the Foundation Chair, School Leadership and Development at Deakin University. Prior to this she was a school Principal for fifteen years in three very different schools in South Australia and Victoria. She was Chief Writer of South Australia's Curriculum, Standards and Accountability Framework (SACSA) and in 2004 won the Victorian and Australian Telstra Business Women's Awards for the not-for-profit sector. She is a Fellow of the Australian Institute of Company Directors and the Australian Council for Educational Leaders. Her research interests lie in educational leadership, change, school renewal, curriculum, professional learning, governance, educational policy, gender and equity.

GUGLIELMO TRENTIN

Guglielmo Trentin is senior researcher and project manager at the Institute for Educational Technology (ITD) of the Italian National Research Council (CNR). His studies have largely focused on the use of network technology informal and informal learning. In this field he has managed several projects and scientific activities, developing technological applications and methodological approaches to support networked collaborative learning. Since 2002 he teaches Network Technology, Knowledge Flow and Human Resources Development at the University of Turin. He has authored several papers and some books on the themes of Technology-Enhanced Learning. Since 1999 he is contributing editor of Educational Technology (USA).

STEVE WHEELER

Steve Wheeler has spent his entire professional career working in media and technology, predominantly in nurse education and teacher training. He is currently Senior Lecturer in Education and Information Technology in the Faculty of Education at the University of Plymouth. Steve's research interests include e-learning, Web 2.0, distance education, creativity and student support and he has published over 150 scholarly articles in these fields. He serves on the editorial boards of ten peer reviewed education and medical journals, and is the co-editor of Interactive Learning Environments. Steve has presented his research at many of the major international conferences and is a regular keynote speaker at e-learning and education events worldwide. His most recent book, Connected Minds, Emerging Cultures, was published in 2009 by Information Age Publishers, USA.

DAVID WHITTIER

David Whittier, EdD is an assistant professor at the Boston University School of Education, whose teaching and research interests include the Time Online research project, distance education research and design, and faculty development for online teaching. Professor Whittier's research projects include the Teacher as Software Designer program, winner of a 2004 CITE/JTATE Technology Leadership Award, a PT3 faculty development grant, and Cyberethics as the study of ethical behavior and identity development online, offering online development in cyberethics to a global audience of teachers. Whittier directs the graduate program in educational media and technology, the Instructional Media Center at the School of Education, and serves as an advisor on educational technology and virtual schooling to the Massachusetts State Department of Elementary and Secondary Education.

GAIL WILSON

Gail Wilson has taught in higher education and adult and vocational education institutions, and has held management roles in the public and private sectors in Australia, including higher education. She has worked in teaching and learning roles in several Australian universities, and is currently a Senior Lecturer in the Teaching and Learning Centre at Southern Cross University. Gail's doctoral research examined the use of information and communications technology (ICT) in higher education, incorporating a collective case study of six teachers, all early adopters of ICT, who used ICT to facilitate their use of blended learning approaches to their on-campus teaching. Her research also examined institutional approaches to faculty development for teaching and learning in blended and online environments.

Gail is active in the Higher Education Research and Development Society of Australasia (HERDSA) and serves on the Editorial Boards of the *Australasian Journal of Educational Technology*, and the UK-based *Research in Learning Technology* journal.

INDEX

G

H

I

J

K

L

M

N

O

P

T